MW00964696

Understanding Global Economic Change
and the Future of the Global Society

ABOUT THE AUTHORS:

José Miguel Andreu was Professor of Economics at the University of Seville, Spain. He also taught Economics at the Universities of Bilbao, Alcala de Henares and UNED-Madrid, lecturing on introduction to macroeconomics, theory of economic growth and money and banking for more than 40 years. In addition, he served as Economic Advisor to the Prime Minister of Spain from 1981-82, and from 2000-2003 he was posted to India as Head of the Commercial Office, in the Embassy of Spain, New Delhi. Along the years, Prof Andreu has published more than 150 articles and around 15 books on macroeconomics, banking and globalisation.

Rita Dulci Rahman is a sociologist and Dutch career diplomat. She has a Master in Socioeconomic Development from University of Leiden, Netherlands, and for several years was guest lecturer on "Introduction to Development Cooperation" at the same University. Along the years, she developed expertise in international relations, development cooperation, international trade, conflict resolution and in the field of global governance. In addition, she chaired or has been member in several Dutch and European governmental and societal institutions involved in world affairs and sustainable global development. She is currently posted as Ambassador to Malta.

Understanding Global Economic Change and the Future of the Global Society

JosÉ Miguel Andreu
and
Rita Dulci Rahman

ACADEMIC FOUNDATION

NEW DELHI

www.academicfoundation.com

First published in 2014
by

ACADEMIC FOUNDATION
4772-73 / 23 Bharat Ram Road, (23 Ansari Road),
Darya Ganj, New Delhi - 110 002 (India).
Phones : 23245001 / 02 / 03 / 04.
Fax : +91-11-23245005.
E-mail : books@academicfoundation.com
www.academicfoundation.com

Disclaimer:
The findings/views/opinions expressed in this book are solely those of the
authors and do not necessarily reflect the views of the publisher.

© 2014
Copyright: José Miguel Andreu and Rita Dulci Rahman.

ALL RIGHTS RESERVED.
No part of this book shall be reproduced, stored in a retrieval system,
or transmitted by any means, electronic, mechanical, photocopying,
recording, or otherwise, without the prior written permission of the
copyright holder(s) and/or the publishers.

Cataloging in Publication Data--DK
   Courtesy: D.K. Agencies (P) Ltd. <docinfo@dkagencies.com>

Andreu, José Miguel.
   Understanding global economic change and the future of the
global society / José Miguel Andreu and Rita Dulci Rahman.
      p.   cm.
   Includes bibliographical references (p.   ) and index.
   ISBN 9789332701489

   1. Globalization--Economic aspects. 2. International
economic relations. 3. World politics. 4. Globalization--Social
aspects.   I. Rahman, Rita Dulci, 1952-, joint author. II. Title.

DDC 337   23

Jacket cover designed by Raul Behr, FOCUS New Media Services,
Paramaribo, Suriname.

Typeset by Italics India, New Delhi.

Printed and bound by The Book Mint, New Delhi.
www.thebookmint.in

Contents

Note from the Authors

Writing a credible and consistent book on current and expectable economic and political changes in the world is not an easy undertaking. This is because most authors have a somewhat biased view of the world and its developments. Not only since they could be classified in different schools of economic thinking but also because they belong to different parts of the world, be these historically the dominating or the dominated ones. In addition, and often unintentionally, many qualified authors, due to fears to freely think or write 'out of the box,' tend to limit themselves within the margins of what their readers or colleagues may accept, thus remaining in the mainstream of their corresponding schools.

Besides these mainstreamers, one may also find 'sub-prime' authors, professionally attached to party politics in local, regional, national or multinational institutions that feel obliged to publish articles in important national and even global newspapers, concerning suggested 'plans for reforms' that use to be rather empty of originality and content, while never entering in detailed descriptions on pretended solutions.

Other authors, considered as 'founding fathers' of two outstanding political and economic errors of the last 20 years—the creation of a defective Euro-system, which is supporting the lengthening of the economic drama in the West, and the rushed liberalisation of global capital transfers—instead of discretely disappearing from the scene, continue 'teaching lessons' on what to do to solve the problems they collectively created.

Notwithstanding intrinsic psychological and sociological difficulties surrounding our attempt, we have tried to predict the future by observing reality in the most objective way, for which we have only used official data [World Bank (WB), International Monetary Fund (IMF) and others] and main available instruments and theories, capable of explaining with solvency the future economic and social trends.

According to WB figures of 2013, in the last 22 years (1990-2012), the joint GDP of developing countries has accelerated its progression while the joint GDP of the West has substantially lost speed. Although mentioned economic convergence of developing countries could be considered 'unpleasant' for the West, it should be red in a global democratic perspective. This means that the deduced economic trends and projections are fairer for the majority of people living in developing countries (counting with 84% of world population), although less favourable for Westerners (with just only 16% of global population).

Mentioned convergence, positive for the global society, is not the result of a deliberate development-cooperation policy of the West, but a consequence of hasty liberalisation of capital movements, carried out in the early 1990s in an asymmetric way, combined with a restrictive immobility of labour. In the last days of 2012, the IMF has finally recognised the exaggerations on the liberalisation of capital movements by Western governments.

Really, if the intention of Western governments had been to promote the catching up of the developing countries, they hardly could have done it better. But we suspect that they did not do so on purpose: they just committed huge mistakes by backing highly risky demands of some multinational corporations (MNC) interested in exploiting new markets. One has to admit that this operation was a wrong bet in favour of increasing Western GNI (gross national income), that necessary had to reduce the growth rates of the GDP and employment in the West, *via* growing imports and investment dislocation (foreign direct investment; FDI) abroad, mainly towards Asia.

Calculated or not, the initiative mainly taken in the early 1990s for fast liberalisation of the movements of capital—including FDI and short-term capital—has resulted negative for workers in the West. Conversely, the results have been positive for many workers in developing countries, as deducible from the catching up growth rates exhibited by all developing regions of the world in the period 1990-2012.

In the last decade, and in line with our findings, prestigious international institutions such as Goldman Sachs and Organisation for Economic Cooperation and Development (OECD) have published reports concluding that a major economic and political change in the world is underway, shifting the economic gravity centre of the world towards Asia. Remarkably, many Western politicians and media have preferred to ignore the conclusions of these reports. As the term of politicians in office is generally limited (4-5 years), many politicians prefer not to implement unpleasant but necessary corrections during their term, in order to favour their re-election. Consequently, they tend to present the economic reality polluted with irrational short-term optimism, clear mistakes and at times even right-out lies. This is in sharp contrast to the experience of nationals in many European countries who perceive that they are living in the 'decade of the broken dreams.'

One clear example of unfounded optimism is the exaggerated expectations in the production of oil and gas by means of using the technique of 'fracking.' As many say, this new technology will change the structure of production and trade of oil and gas, mainly favouring the US. However, no acceptable solutions have been found for the huge environmental degradation provoked by fracking. Besides, the application of this new technology, on increasing the oil and gas production, would profit the entire planet including emerging Asia.

We do also believe that many politicians undervalue the productive potential of the huge reservoir of redundant workers (in the sense of Lewis), today located in the agriculture-rural sectors of China and India (500 million), and the current fast increase of the joint productivity of factors in these two countries induced by the rapid progress of investments in physical and human capital. And this, not to mention the comparative high investment and saving rates of these two mega countries, which according to the most modern (neo-classical and endogenous) theories of economic growth, would favour them.

But evidence will finally expel wishful thinking; and when the economic catching up of emergent countries has sufficiently progressed, political change will necessarily follow, thus inducing internal and external political reshuffling. Indeed, when China overtakes the GDP of the US, and India economically approaches the US in GDP terms, while Russia, Brazil and others surpass France and Britain, the current political governance and institutions of the world—that is the multilateral institutions born after the

Second World War—will rapidly change, or otherwise degrade, bifurcate or, even worse, implode.

As the need for more effective global governance will progressively be felt by a growing majority of the global society, we do believe that the establishment of a new democratic UN and subordinated agencies will finally emerge. In our view, this will happen, not in the very long run, for instance in 100 or 200 years, but in just 2 or 3 decades (horizon 2040); particularly, because at that time Western countries—led by the US—will have neither the financial means nor the popular support (internal and external) as to police and organise the world. This lack of popular support, which was already perceivable at the end of the Vietnam War, has intensified in times of the recent Western interventions in Afghanistan and Iraq.

Consequently, in the next decades, main Western governments will have to negotiate with the leadership of the current developing world (China, India, Brazil, Russia, South Africa, etc.) to devise a new multilateral political structure whose agenda and priorities will have to be defined and supported by representatives of all nations (global society), and not just by the winners of the Second World War of the 20th century, which are today rapidly losing their relative economic power.

We have no doubt that a new democratic UN will finally be set up and clarify its objectives and agenda in terms of the provision of global public goods, the correction of global externalities, and the regulation and supervision of global economic transactions, and also for achieving a more balanced geographical and personal distribution of wealth and welfare. Moreover, only the creation of a new UN endowed with enforcement capacities, in which both veto-rights and consensus will no longer play a role in decision making, will enable to overcome current inefficient and undemocratic global governance, while protecting future generations from populist and totalitarian governments and defective control.

Finally, we have to underline that the views and recommendations presented in this book, are strictly personal and do not reflect any official line of thought of the institutions to which we belong (or belonged).

— Jose Miguel Andreu and Rita Dulci Rahman

1 | Introduction

Today we are making history, and you and I are fortunate to see this happening before our eyes and to take...part ourselves in this great drama.

Jawaharlal Nehru in *Glimpses of World History* (1930, Naini Jail, Allahabad, India).

Reflecting on the 'Global Economic Crisis' and Growing Uncertainty

There is a growing understanding in the world today that the current so-called 'global economic crisis'—that started in 2007-08 in the US—is not a global one but mainly a crisis of the West, unleashed by a kind of unbridled neo-liberal capitalism which acted on false expectations of continuous growth in a context of defective institutions and hasty deregulations. In fact in autumn of 2012, the global economy was growing at 3.3 per cent[1] while part of the West had re-entered in recession. Nevertheless, any attentive observer could also confirm that the crisis in the West [including the European Union (EU)] is progressively affecting the rest of the world, although concerning East and South-East Asia—the current engine of global economic growth—the impact of the crisis has been moderate.[2]

Indeed, the bleak situation of the economy of the West in the winter of 2012-13 had to do with a confluence of different causes. The most mentioned is the appearance in 2007-08 in the US and Europe of a financial crisis, induced by a series of excesses of certain irresponsible and greedy bankers, some of them real gamblers or malefactors. These excesses were facilitated by a 'policy of low interest rates and a passive monetary policy'

---

1. According to Table 6.1 of this book, the annual average growth rate of the total World along the period 1980-2010 was around 3 per cent.

2. In May 2012, IMF forecasted for China in 2012 GDP growth rate of over 8 per cent. In July 2012, Chinese government also confirmed a growth rate around 8 per cent for 2012. A rate of 7.5 per cent, forecasted by others at the end of 2012 could also be credible.

mainly implemented in the period 2000-2003 by main central banks of the West—as the Federal Reserve System (Fed) or the European Central Bank (ECB)—which, by intentionally ignoring the rapid evolution of asset prices, gave private bankers additional and inopportune abilities to enter in non-sustainable financial adventures. These non-sustainable operations were facilitated by the lack of sufficient banking and financial controls, following the deregulation policies initiated in times of US president Reagan.[3]

The shift of the industrial activity towards Asia—to a good extent induced by low industrial wages in Asia and the ultra-rapid deregulation of capital movements by Western governments under pressure of demands by entrepreneurs, mainly at the beginning of the 1990s[4]—also counts as one of the fundamental causes, in this case predictable at implementation,[5] of the current Western economic drama. This industrial shift—visible in the figures of foreign direct investment (FDI)[6]—has provoked a visible rupture in the trends of global trade and world production (GDP).

---

3. Since the 30s of former century in which a famous US Act was passed—the so-called Glass & Steagall Act, which separated the activities of commercial and investment banks—till the 80s, the Western banking systems did not suffer major crisis. In the 1980s, this principle of separation was attacked by neo-liberals in most Western countries for allegedly increasing competition and efficiency in banking, while initiating a generalised deregulation process (also in other economic activities) of lethal consequences in banking, an activity inducer of significant externalities over the rest of the economy.

4. Since in those days trans-frontier movements of people were severely restricted, a fast abating of barriers to the movements of capital was clearly not advisable for the West.

5. Certainly, the economic consequences of massive transfers abroad of capital were already predicted by Smith and Ricardo in the 18th and 19th centuries referring to the UK. Both of them recognised that if British industrialists and traders invested abroad and the economy was depending on imports, the firms would profit but Britain would suffer. Vide Chomsky, N. (2011) "American Decline: Causes and Consequences", *www.chomsky.info/articles*.

6. If we would analyse the annual figures of FDI in different moments and in the different economic blocks and countries, we would find that: while received FDI moved in China from $3.4 billion (bn) in 1990 to 38.3 bn in 2000 and to 185 bn in 2010, the FDI received by the US flexed down from 287 bn in 2000 to 236 bn in 2010. However, FDI of the Eurozone remained stable around 400 bn along the 2000s. Note as well that the evolution of FDI in East Asia-Pacific followed the figures of China (11 bn in 1990, 52 bn in 2000, and 231 bn US dollars in 2010). Vide World Bank (WB) in *World Development Indicators* (2012 and 2002).

Finally, one has to insist that the inefficient institutional structure of the European Monetary Union (Eurozone), lacking rational decision-making,[7] is compounding the effects of the (two) former mentioned causes. Indeed the mismanagement of the Euro-system has today become a real obstacle for the recovery of the Western economy, this meaning that if the Eurozone crisis is not solved at mid-term, the US and other Western countries will not easily recover past prosperity.

But mentioned crisis—whose first alarming manifestation was the appearance in 2008 of a banking crisis in the US, hastily extended to other western banks and economies, mainly Europeans—later experienced a significant metamorphosis. As a consequence of the public funding of banks in problems and Keynesian 'short term policies' applied after the second post-crisis meeting of the G-20 in April 2009 in London, public deficits went up and corresponding indebtedness of several important Western countries, including the US, underwent a fast increase. In this context of growing indebtedness in GDP terms, the misgivings of creditors in financial markets in relation with possible debt monetisation and subsequent inflation or, alternatively, with possible defaults of some EU members became justified.

At the end of 2011, many Western economies started a new slowdown, that although considered by some as a new fall belonging to a new economic cycle, clearly was no more than a re-fall, consequence of a shift in policy means and targets in the middle of an 'assumed' and incipient cyclical recovery. In fact, following recommendations in 2010 by main multilateral institutions, most Western countries, particularly Europeans, refocused their economic targets on reducing public deficits. As expectable, this sudden policy change lengthened the duration of the banking recovery, while the industrial shift to the East and its consequences remained practically unconsidered.

Concerning growing indebtedness, one may observe that the solution to the public debt problem of the US—with a high ratio, today over 100 per

---

7. This is due to several factors: (i) the rule of unanimity to protect sovereignty of members and (ii) the inconvenient participation of non-Eurozone members of EU-28 in the debate on policy to be adopted by the Eurozone to solve the crisis (what we name along this book 'the problem of inconsistency in the governance of the EU').

cent of its GDP[8]—was postponed in the summer of 2011, but not solved due to the systematic opposition of Republicans (then and now in majority in the House of Representatives, thus controlling the formulation of the federal budget) to let President Obama fully implement his Keynesian social, fiscal and investment policies. As a consequence, unemployment in the US continues being high,[9] while the financial threats of Republicans, limiting the amount of the US indebtedness, have become materialised in March and September, 2013.

In the Eurozone, the deficit and debt situation of some members[10] is more complicated, due to the fact that Germany is radically opposed to allow the ECB, to make loans—or to buy bonds in the secondary market—to governments of Eurozone, without previous commitments on severe deficit reductions in order to timely ensure reimbursement of their increased debts. This inflexible German position, kept alive during all 2011 and 2012, forced most indebted Eurozone countries to seriously cut public expenditure and increase taxes,[11] resulting at the end of 2012 in significant or severe GDP contractions.

As a result of political disagreement and lack of coordination in the West, due to the existence of a dichotomy of applicable policies—neoclassical *versus* keynesian—a large part of the World currently moves under uncertainty: over when the Western economic crisis will finish; on the speed of the industrial production shift towards Asia; and on how the post-crisis economic structure and political ambience in the world will be.

---

8. In 2010, total debt in GDP terms of just the Federal Government of the US was 76.1 per cent (vide WB in *World Development Indicators, 2012*: 260), and its public deficit was equivalent to 10 per cent of its GDP, after having had a surplus of 0.5 per cent in 2000.

9. Note that by the summer of 2013, the official figure of unemployed in the US was around 7.2-7.3 per cent of the active population, but probably the real rate was much higher. According to different observers, unemployment rate in the US could be around 13-15 per cent if involuntary part-timers and those who have abandoned the active population were included among the unemployed.

10. This situation of exaggerated public deficit and indebtedness in some Eurozone countries is a derivative of practising a reckless Keynesian policy, forcing at any time—including times of prosperity—increases in public expenditures and even reductions in taxes.

11. In the last months of 2011, the ECB 'bypassed' mentioned German restrictions, through lending money to Eurozone banks which enabled local banks to continue lending to their indebted governments.

Uncertainty is also felt in the West on the political role of China[12] and India in the future structure of global governance.

In the last three decades, changes in the income and wealth distribution,[13] favouring the rich within many developed and developing countries, have also increased the uncertainty of many individuals and families in most nations.

In relation to common needs and sustainability, the rapid growth of the global population—multiplied almost by three between 1945 and 2010—has played a crucial role, although hardly considered. In addition, many national communities are mystified by the diversity of official opinions on what should be done to solve other common problems affecting the global society in relation with global peace and security, global economic regulations, global environment, and the administration of the renewable and non-renewable natural resources (global externalities).

Consequently, no one knows where we are going to. Despite of counting with the UN as the major forum for multilateral analysis and representation, the global society has not seriously discussed how to progress: if to continue a rapid, indefinite and non-sustainable growth, as it has happened in the last 65 years—or alternatively, to a global progress in a more balanced way, consistent with sustainability of available resources and protection of the environment.[14] We do not know either how we will make the decision on the path to be chosen, if by infighting and economic or violent wars—as it has been done till now, or, alternatively, in a more civilised way, taking into consideration the representativeness of all the nations of the world, that is to say, of the global society.

---

12. Many interested global media and politicians are constantly suggesting that China will in future not represent any threat to the West, because in 5-7 years, China's amazing economic trajectory of the last three decades, with an average annual growth rate of its GDP of more than 10 per cent, will converge with the smaller rates of the West, an alleged convergence "based" on the experience with developments in Japan, Taiwan, etc. Note, however, that those who mention this possibility do not consider that even today (2013), 50 per cent of the Chinese population continues being rural—and mostly with zero marginal productivity—which will imply a rapid continuation of migration to cities and a protracted provision of relative cheap labour to industry and services. Note that this sectorial labour restructuring is today impossible in the most advanced Western countries, as their rural labour force is in all cases under 2-5 per cent of total population, a circumstance that by itself averts rapid growth.

13. Referred to the US, vide Stiglitz (2012).

14. An integral protection of the environment will require a new approach to capitalism, more oriented to collective solutions.

Structural Shift to Asia as the Core Long-term Problem of the West

In front of the two alternative macroeconomic policies essayed to assumedly get out from the crisis—Keynesian *versus* neoclassical—the first possibly inducing inflation at mid-long-term, and the latter possibly inducing unemployment at short-mid-term, Western governments have made different and non-coordinated decisions. Nevertheless, irrespective of the chosen policy (US Administration selecting a variation of the first one and the Eurozone a variation of the second, which has implied an inconvenient overvaluation of the Euro in the Eurozone), Western governments are also confronted with a problem whose solution is not well profiled in macroeconomic handbooks.

This is due to the fact that in times of the development of macroeconomics, most national economies were far less open than today,[15] while the massive geographical shift of the industrial activity towards Asia was not even imaginable. Certainly, this shift only began to be clearly perceived at the beginning of 2000s.[16] But note that this structural move of the industrial activity is actually a problem of microeconomic nature, that has to do much more with relative wages, working schedules and technological differences in the various regions of the planet[17] than with the aggregated demand policies that may ceteris paribus 'provisionally' generate more or less inflation, or more or less real activity and employment, all along the evolution of the potential GDP.[18]

---

15. Even more, in the 1950s the so-called policy of 'Imports Substitution' for accelerating the development of 'developing countries' became fashionable, subsequently degrading commercial interaction among countries.

16. Vide note 6 in which the temporal evolution of FDI is described.

17. In the stabilisation plans imposed by the International Monetary Fund (IMF) on countries with problems of balance of payments, macroeconomic corrections of a contractive character—as those implemented today—were complemented with modifications of the exchange rates (devaluations).

18. Many professionals, including well-recognised academic Keynesians, believe that in 2007, the GDPs of many Western economies, including that of the US, were on or under their potential GDP. We do believe that this is a serious mistake. In our view, many Western economies were in 2007 over their potential GDPs. Consequently any fast Keynesian move along the last years, targeting the 2007 GDP, would have re-inflated the cycle, but happily was not done.

Consequently, letting aside the problems of current fragility of the banking systems and exaggerated indebtedness of diverse Eurozone countries—which for years will additionally trouble economic recovery in Europe—the industrial shift towards East Asia is the most important economic problem to be dealt with in the West, since its effects will be far more lasting than the slow recovery-phase of the current financial crisis.

With their limited and non-coordinated capabilities, and trying to face the most urgent and visible problems (banking fragility and public indebtedness), Western governments have not dared to explain the entire truth of the current drama to their citizens: that a relevant part of what is produced by Western industry costs in other places of the world—mainly in East Asia—much less than in the West. Consequently, many Western jobs cannot and will not be saved at short-mid-term with 'bogus macroeconomic miracles' implemented by 'genial' ministers of finance without extra efforts of the population. We are here referring to traditional policy measures implemented in a context in which there were no structural shifts, such as rising one tax while reducing others, implementing a twist policy on public debt, rising public expenditure or reducing taxes, or even 'reducing' the public expenditure or the 'taxes paid by the rich,' etc. Note that these traditional policies, as defended either by academic Keynesians or neo-classics,[19] were approaches relatively valid in the 20th century, but insufficient for achieving the required economic adjustments in the West in next decades.

Although at times knowing the truth is unpleasant, Western governments will finally have to inform their citizens on the magnitude and scope of pending adjustments for reaching more sustainable lifestyles; otherwise the people will become disoriented when year after year governments demand new efforts without clarifying the context.

Steady growth rates of GDPs and jobs will not return to Western countries until they fully adjust their labour markets to what the West itself devised mainly along the last two decades. We are here referring to

---

19. On the Keynesian side, Stiglitz, Krugman and others have not presented well-profiled policies, free from inflationary and exchange rate risks, in a context of already over-indebted countries, and on the neoclassical one, main academicians, defenders of systematic deregulations and downsizing of the state, seem to be out of the debate since the Lehman Brothers collapse in 2008.

the almost entire freedom of outwards movements of capital,[20] which has provoked a quasi-globalisation in the traffic of goods, services and capital, that has favoured job creation in developing countries. At the same time keeping practically untouched[21] the restrictions on international movements of labour, Western governments 'tried'[22] to arrest the possibility of a real downwards adjustment of wages in the West, thus temporarily blocking an easier adjustment of their labour markets, while stopping a progressive move towards a fairer global income distribution.

Certainly, the comparative trends of the GDP and per capita GDP in the last three decades, and particularly in the last 10 years, leave little margin for error in interpretation: the US is losing part of its favourable cumulated differences in terms of GDP and per capita GDP with the most important emerging countries, particularly in relation to those of Eastern Asia, and especially to China; and Europe is relatively losing positions in GDP and (less) in per capita GDP terms in comparison to the US. In this context, unless Western real wages significantly converge with Asians, job creation will be further undermined in the long term in the West and, with even more intensity, in the Southern Eurozone countries.[23]

Further analysing this long-term jobs losses, we may affirm that if some contra-historical movements do not appear, as for instance a severe return to protectionism in the West or in the Eurozone (or in the EU),[24] the current industrial production and GDP shift towards Asia will consolidate.

---

20. Note that the mentioned freedom is not entirely bi-directional, due to the fact that many developing countries do not accept unrestricted entries of capital, while outward capital movements are mostly publicly controlled.

21. This happened with the exception of internal movements of labour within the European Union.

22. Note that Western governments only tried to sustain the real wages, but to keep untouched the real wages of the West in a much more competitive world—as that designed along the 90s—is just impossible. Inflation and/or devaluation (external or internal) will finally play their role, thus reducing Western real wages.

23. We have learned in 2011 that France has lost in the last decade, 2000-2010, around 500,000 jobs in industry and 100,000 in the last 3 years. This means that France lost 400,000 industrial jobs in the booming period of 2000-2007, which clarifies that French industrial jobs may have 'moved' towards Eastern Europe and Asia long before the beginning of the financial crisis. The same may have occurred in other Western countries. Vide *lemonde.fr* of December 28, 2011.

24. The recent initiative of the US and the EU-28, for promoting a free trade zone (FTZ) among them, could be seen as a defensive maneuver against full free trade.

At the same time, as it has already happened in the last decade 2000-2010, the joint exports of the developing countries, including the emerging ones, due to its faster growth, will in a maximum of 25 years be equivalent to those of the richest ones; and the defence expenditures of the West will also be overtaken by those of the developing countries (including China) in around 25-30 years. The economic results based on former expectations, supported by econometric projections, will be more or less alike to that presented in 2003 in the famous report of Goldman-Sachs on the BRICS, but with a faster catching up than foreseen: probably between 2040 and 2045, in the first ranks and with huge advantage on the rest of countries, will be placed, and by this order, China, US and India.[25]

Letting aside other consequences, we will here underline that the industrial shift towards Asia, promoted by Western governments, will produce several microeconomic changes in the West, very difficult to elude: (1) a significant reduction of the current wages in the West—in real terms or in exchange rate terms[26]—in relation to those of Asia; (2) an increase in the absolute and relative profits of Western firms generated abroad, transferred to the US and mainly to the Eurozone; and (3) as a consequence of former trends, a change in the personal income distribution within the West, less favourable to workers.

At macroeconomic level, modest figures of average GDP growth of around 1.8 per cent could for long be the ceiling of the potential growth of the West as an average. This will occur due to the demographic stagnation in the West, the lack of redundant man-power in rural areas, and the relative shrinking in industrial and services productivity.

---

25. Note that by these three leading countries (China, US and India), a 'European Federation,' if established, will be placed. According to our perspective, this European Federation will be a unitary state containing around 8-12 current members of the Eurozone. This federation will be created in some few years in order to overcome the current structural and institutional stalemate of the current Monetary Union. Vide Rahman and Andreu (2005).

26. Facing international trade, for a country which is a unique and independent political entity, a devaluation of its currency plays a role similar to internal reduction of wages. For a country that shares currency with others—as it happens in the case of members of the Eurozone—if it had previously paid excessive (direct or indirect) wages or subsidies to workers, a significant reduction of nominal wages and subsidies will be an almost forced derivative for recovering trade equilibrium 'within' the currency area.

Along with this trend towards a relative decline of the economy in the West, and after years of naïve waiting for an easy recovery of past prosperity, successive political crises—which in the next 2-4 years could reach its zenith—are predictable in some Western countries. Mentioned political crisis will recede when Western citizens start adjusting to the new parameters ruling the world economy in the first half of the 21st century, this is to say, when they start accepting significant reductions in their consumption patterns and life-style, to be competitive. Observe that, at the same time, the remaining 84 per cent of the global population (in developing countries) will experience significant long-term improvement in their average life standards.

Wrong Policies of Western Countries: Globalisation at Different Speeds and Hasty Liberalisation of Capital Movements

If one compares the recent and rapid liberalisation of the movements of capital in the West with the slow and asymmetric progress in trade liberalisation by the successive GATT meetings[27] starting in 1947, one has to admit the risky peculiarities observed in the development of freer capital movements.

Given its possible short-term effects on local employment, the liberalisation process of external trade has always been done by different countries of the World (GATT rounds) in a very cautious way. Even the EU member-states slowly liberalised their mutual interchange of goods and services to reach their unique market: a process that lasted nothing less than three and a half decades, from 1957 to 1992.[28] Contrary to this prudent behaviour, from the 1990s onwards, the West promoted a rapid liberalisation of the movements of capital, while the international movements of people remained prohibited in most economic regions.[29]

---

27. These General Agreements on Tariffs and Trade (GATT) became part of the World Trade Organization (WTO) in 1995.

28. This is the period between the signing of the Treaty of Rome (1957), which created the European Economic Community (EEC), and the moment in which the Treaty of the Single Act (1986) came into force (1992).

29. Another manifestation of reckless behaviour of European politicians was the creation by the EU of a highly defective monetary union.

Even more, mentioned liberalisation of international movements of capital—clearly favourable to developing countries at long term (FDI)[30]—was planned in the West to increase Western gross national income (GNI), which would only favour a happy few. However, Western strategists (IMF, etc.) did not fully consider the induced effects on the West in a context of general equilibrium, but just taking into account certain direct effects on GNI of capital dislocation. Indeed, as predicted by Smith and Ricardo in relation to the consequences of capital exports from the UK to colonies in the 18th and 19th centuries, the addition of direct and indirect effects of capital dislocation were not positive for the West (Table 6.2): the GDP share of the West significantly dropped in the last two decades (1990-2010), inducing a meaningful relative loss of jobs.

As we have analysed in other places,[31] a sudden liberalisation of long-term movements of capital at a regional scale has clear and predictable negative effects on local employment if some of these local labour markets are not flexible enough and/or migrations are limited in the region. And this is what has happened in some Eurozone countries with less flexible labour markets. To the extent that within the EU the capital movements were liberalised, but the labour markets, although formally liberalised counted with significant natural barriers (language, education, etc.), internal labour migration was marginal, while the expectable reaction (downwards) of wages to the capital export movements abroad was practically not perceivable, thus inducing undesirable unemployment within EU-capital exporting countries.

At a global scale, if long-term capital moved away from Europe—as happened with the industrial shift to Asia—unemployment in Europe would quickly grow, if wages were rigid downwards and the labour migration abroad was not possible or very difficult.[32] Alternatively, if foreign capital came into a local European market and the labour force at the receiving end was significantly scarce while immigration was (naturally or legally) limited,

---

30. Note that developing countries did not liberalise so much their capital markets, thus selecting sectors for capital imports while, in many cases, limiting capital exports.

31. Vide Andreu and Rahman (2009b).

32. Apart from other legal difficulties to migrate, this practical impossibility could have been caused by the lower wages in countries such as China and neighbours to which the capital had moved, while unemployment benefits in the EU were higher than mentioned lower wages in China or in other places.

local wages could shot up, thus choking the profits of the arrived capital, or unleashing additional inflation.

All former arguments and experiences drive us to two main conclusions: (1) liberalisation of long-term capital movements should not be fast if the different labour markets within the liberalised area were not totally flexible, because in this case a fast liberalisation could drive to the creation of significant social problems. To clarify the conclusion, one should note that fast movements of capital were mainly directed from the Eurozone towards countries with significant lower unitary costs of production, and sufficient infrastructure for exports. These movements enabled western entrepreneurs to solve their problem of competitiveness in goods at a world scale, while western governments would necessary be confronted at mid-long term with a fast increase of national unemployment[33] and forced progressive reduction of real wages. (2) The liberalisation of capital movements among countries in a monetary union should not be fast if there were not a common authority and rules in banking, financial and fiscal issues within the monetary union, a problem that has become evident in the case of the EU (f.i. with the financial problems created by a high concentration of loans from Northern in Southern European banks, and from the latter in the domestic housing sector, without enough banking supervision).

As many years ago Lipsey and Lankaster[34] described in their well-known 'Theory of Second Best' to totally liberalise an additional market (capital)—if others are not completely liberalised (labour)—does not warranty an improvement of the general welfare of citizens in the liberalised area. As a result, and taking into consideration the foreseeable consequences of a sudden liberalisation of capital moves, this policy should have been developed more cautiously in the West and not in a rushed way. Even more, taking into account that these moves[35] are normally realised through multinational banks that may put at risk the national or regional payments systems, a separation of activities of banks was vital but neither implemented nor restored before the initiation of the crisis (2007-08).

---

33. In some places—such as US, Ireland, Spain, etc.—expectable growing unemployment provoked by industrial dislocation was for years disguised by an accelerated non-sustainable growth of jobs in housing.

34. Vide Lipsey and Lankaster (1956).

35. Be these at short or at long term.

Lack of Global Governance and Global Economic Regulations

Although many recognise that we live today in a globalised world, few have accepted that we urgently need to institutionalise democratic global governance, capable of producing and enforcing, among others, global economic regulations. Instead, the current practice is one of half-hearted voluntary 'coordination', often induced by punctual political alliances in forums such as the G-20. Note that these forums cannot systematically and efficiently provide relevant global public goods for the global society—such as global economic regulations—due to the contradictory interests of participating countries.

For instance, the 'agreed' rejection of fiscal paradises[36] by G-20 has practically not materialised except for criminal prosecution by the Organisation for Economic Cooperation and Development (OECD) countries, leaving the bulk of hidden money practically intact.[37] Similarly, one may observe deep silence concerning necessary collective measures against monopolistic and speculative behaviour in certain markets (of strategic raw materials such as crude oil or even cereals), which over the past decades have caused either serious cyclical disturbances or promoted spasmodic prices fluctuations or fast inflation.

---

36. While general liberalisation of movements of capital has been made at an exaggerated and clearly inconvenient high speed, allegedly to reduce the costs of financing and production, fiscal paradises—that by themselves shelter financial institutions whose main activity is hiding money against high 'professional fees'—continue their existence. Effectively, after some quantitative arrangements with them and agreements mainly for criminal prosecution, Western governments have not forced the isolation of fiscal paradises that consequently continue being operational.

37. Contrary to what has been done by the G-20, just a partial and minimal correction, the final abolishment of fiscal paradises is very important and urgent for improving the welfare of the global society. It is absolutely inadmissible that petty fiscal paradises, including those of certain European countries 'with prestige,' continue living from the blood of the majority, particularly in times of sharp crisis. Henry (2012), in his publication *The Price of the Off-shore Revisited* suggests that the amount of capital unduly protected in fiscal paradises reaches today $25,000 billion, a quantity similar to the joint GDP of the US and Japan and equivalent to 40 per cent of the GDP of the world. According to Henry, the current annual deposits in accounts in fiscal paradises represent an amount that results in annually diverting (thus defrauding governments) all over the world for around $280 billion. On the other hand, the *Financial Times Deutschland* has recently mentioned that Singapore is substituting Swiss as a fiscal paradise for Germans, who in the first half of 2012 have redeposited in Singapore around $500,000 million.

Most remarkable is the fact that, far from steadily correcting global market failures, in less than four years, G-20 has unexpectedly changed its macroeconomic mindset in two opposite ways: moving from recommending generalised expansion of public expenditures (2009) to prescribing severe reduction in budget deficits and sovereign public indebtedness (2010) and finally to recommend in 2012 a softer adjustment of budget deficits. Mentioned moves were clearly contradictory and destabilising, and masterminded by some powerful market participants and leading conservative governments. Contrary to what has happened, in our view policies for cyclical corrections should have been implemented in a less fluctuating way under the control of an effective global government.[38]

Although the need for global governance is patent, it is remarkable that most academicians have not taken any critical position in relation with the above mentioned global economic problems. This is because most of them are grouped in academic families and attached to their mainstream principles, including nationalism, while most of them exhibit an exaggerated respect for those who are currently in charge in national, multinational and multilateral financial institutions. Certainly, mentioned academicians often dream to finalise their careers by joining these very institutions, an observation also valid for politicians. This contra-scientific behaviour of many academicians—which makes that they often turn a blind eye to economic and financial developments which contradict the accepted paradigm—was already described in 1975 by the recently deceased Feyerabend[39] as an insurmountable fear to criticise.

Effective Global Governance in Need of Convergence of the Two Current Approaches to Capitalism

Experience in the last two decades has proven that reaching agreements among important countries to solve collective-global economic problems is practically impossible, due to the extreme defence of neoclassical policy

---

38. In October 2012, the IMF—mystified by the messy evolution of the Western economy—has again partially contradicted its recommendations of 2010, now encouraging much more flexible corrections of deficit and indebtedness, thus lengthening the adjustment periods and their possible derivatives.

39. Vide Feyerabend (1975).

(reduction of public sector) by some of them, or the defence of radical Keynesian policies and public sector intervention by others.

As observable, traditional capitalism developed in the 19th century, a sort of economic structure in which national public goods and services were not considered except for governance, defence, justice and police. Needless to say that in this century global public goods were simply not recognised, while the working of main traditional capitalist institutions—private property[40] and production, combined with extreme freedom for economic initiative and contracting—drove the 19th century capitalist economies to exploitative working conditions—home and abroad—and to unfair distribution of income.

This non-sustainable labour and distribution context, well described by Dickens[41] in his writings, was a good breeding ground for new thinking: socialism (Marx and Engels). Subsequently, national movements of trade unions and labour parties led to unrest and uprisings in many industrialised countries, finally resulting (in 1917) in the establishment of a first 'Communist' experiment: the Soviet Union. However, the major failure of this experiment was the total rejection of private initiatives and markets, irrespective of whether the produced or interchanged goods were private or public.[42]

As a consequence of mentioned full resource allocation to the public sector, both in the Soviet Union and later in China, food security became a huge failure while industrial production, although growing fast, resulted highly inefficient in terms of the involved invested resources, and this while any political and academic criticism was simply crushed.

After the Second World War, and mainly in war-torn Western Europe, a general understanding that traditional exploitative capitalism of 19th century

---

40. In the 19th century, private property was concentrated in the hands of some few.

41. Vide writings of Charles Dickens. According to this author—born in Landport, Hampshire—the "new industrial age" created misery for a huge class of low-paid workers, and induced the birth of socialist theories.

42. As defined by the Economic Theory, public goods are goods that are necessarily consumed simultaneously by many citizens, as for instance governance, defence system of a country, etc., and that have to be financed with taxes because cannot be individually priced. Conversely, the use by individuals of private goods is mutually excluding (an apple, a washing machine, etc.), and consequently these goods have to be privately provided through the market, against a price.

and first decades of the 20th should not be restored in Europe gained ground. Simultaneously, Western Europe also discarded the inefficient alternative economic system, communism, by instead introducing some social-democratic policies and more humane working conditions in their societies. Note that these reforms of traditional capitalism were not implemented with the same intensity in other parts of the Western Hemisphere.[43]

After a period of booming social democracy in Western Europe (1945-1975)—which created a certain convergence of the two main economic systems as suggested by Tinbergen—two oil crises in the 1970s and a critical reduction in the speed of growth in the West produced a pendulum movement against the praxis and philosophy of social democracy. This pendulum shift was triggered by: (1) the arrival to power of conservative parties in Britain and the US (Thatcher and Reagan) who politically exploited the observable failures of the naïve Keynesianism of those days; (2) the difficulty for the Soviet Union to simultaneously finance the weaponry race with the US (Stars War) and the war in Afghanistan, all resulting in the rapid crumbling of the East Block; and (3) the booming of Asian tigers, whose 'liberalised export oriented economies'[44] were then 'sexed-up,' proclaiming them as more efficient than the European social-democratic-interventionist model. Finally, at the end of the 1980s (1989), the fall of the Berlin Wall was interpreted by neo-conservatives as the concluding victory of free capitalism over any other alternative.[45]

The new movement (conservative-neoclassical patronised by Reagan/Thatcher) prone to the fast recovery of 'basics' of traditional capitalism,

---

43. Note that in the US, in times of president Roosevelt, a New Deal policy was implemented, mainly consisting of public investments in infrastructures in order to create jobs.

44. The so-called Asian tigers were Taiwan, South Korea and Singapore, plus Hong Kong which in those days still was a British colony. Observe that these tigers were generously supported by the West in their economic development process, as they were political allies of the West for counteracting neighbouring communism. Note additionally that these 'tigers' had a certain content of fiscal paradises (Hong Kong and Singapore), or offered FTZ (Free Trade Zone) to investors, reasons why their models of growth were not entirely valid for transplantation to countries of larger sizes, not 'protected' by their Western governments.

45. Recklessly and rashly, Fukuyama and others alleged the final victory of American Capitalism and Western governing system on the rest, thus proclaiming the US as the sole hyper power on Earth, and the 'end of history.'

allegedly to improve economic efficiency, drove many Western countries to exaggerated privatisation of public services (public transport, health services, drinking water, electricity, etc.), liberalisation of markets, and deregulation of critical (financial) sectors. Note that the most absurd example of this modern liberalisation process was the introduction of private contracting in the US army for fighting in the Iraq and Afghanistan wars. Finally, in the first decade of the 21st century, neo-liberal exaggerations and uncontrolled capital movements led to international speculation on globalised activities and to a banking-financial catastrophe.

One may here underline that the new neo-liberal movement in the West (1980-2007) committed a comparable, be it reversal, mistake as it was done by the communists in the Soviet Union and the Popular Republic of China when they took power. The latter moved all activities under public control and surveillance, while conversely conservative neo-classicals tried to minimise (at any cost) public intervention and control. As far as in the economic world there exist private and public goods and externalities, and also dangerous adventurers to be controlled, these two extreme approaches essayed in the 20th century and first years of the 21st painfully proved to be wrong.

Summarising, once discarding communism, solving current global problems—specifically those of the 21st century—will require a definitive convergence of the two main economic approaches to capitalism applied in the second half of the 20th century and first decade of 2000. Otherwise, searching for consented policies on effective global governance (as attempted by G-20) will fail, and the creation of a democratic UN indispensable for applying efficient global policies will be blocked, due to disagreement on basic economic principles (private property, and freedom of enterprise and contracting of private goods on the one hand, and public control and regulation of global public goods and externalities on the other).

New Collective Needs:
The Problem of National Sovereignty

As mentioned before, in the last six and a half decades (1945-2010), the world has meaningfully changed, particularly, in relation to the acknowledgement of new needs of a collective nature, such as the provision of global public goods,[46] the correction of global externalities[47] and the reduction of the per capita income gap among nations.

Irrespective of whether it concerned environmental degradation of the planet or correction of global social failures (very high gap of per capita income among different nations), the attempts of leading countries— mainly since the 1970s—to formulate international policies via lengthy and time consuming negotiations resulting in treaties or agreements, have in the end not (or not sufficiently) solved most of global needs and problems. The reasons are clear: these treaties and agreements have always been on minima—in order to reach consensus without losing national sovereignty—and never on optima, while they neither have been inclusive, nor compulsive. The result of these failures is that the world currently progresses without sufficient control and priorities; that is to say without knowing where it goes.

The failed global governance attempts have also proven that nations, as 'purported' independent collectives, are incapable of dealing with global problems, because they are reluctant to conveniently transfer sufficient portions of their sovereignty to the global society.

As it happened in other moments of history, in which national states were created from smaller power entities to pursuit targets of a higher level, the new collective needs of a global character will necessarily force the creation of a global government, which in the 21st century will have to be supported by a democratic representation of all nations. Therefore, we believe that the current UN—progressively losing its value and becoming obsolete to solve global problems—will necessarily have to change into democratic to become efficient and fair.

However, the strong intensity of the current 'economic crisis' in the West has made that, against own interest, Western governments show

---

46. These public goods include peace and security, protection of the global environment, global economic regulation, etc., although not all of them—as for instance, global economic regulation—have been felt as such till very recently. Note that there is a case of indispensable global economic regulation, referred to fiscal paradises, that—although recently mildly globally 'regulated' by the G-20—continues being an authentical shame at a global scale.

47. Among these externalities, we could mention those related to natural resources, be these renewable (fishing, logging, etc.) or not (strategic raw materials, etc.).

little concern for the promotion of democratic global governance. Today, the objective of increasing employment and consumption back to the levels of 2007 has become the paramount aim of every Western government, although these targets may not be reachable in many places, even at mid-term. Sadly, these governments are forgetting the relevance of providing or correcting global public goods and externalities, while they are reducing their budgets for sustainable development (fight against global warming) and development cooperation (fight against poverty).

Although long-term collective economic expectations for the West are not favourable, Western governments, mainly the most important ones, have amazingly kept reluctant to hand over any additional chunk of sovereignty to a superior government, be this in the EU or in the UN, thus postponing the provision of regional or global public needs,[48] or the correction of regional or global externalities; pro-collective moves however could help to alleviate the current economic and political problems.

Note however that this postponement of sovereignty transfers cannot last for long, mainly for economic reasons.[49] This is due to the fact that, from a moment onwards, the US and allies will not be able to economically sustain their traditional roles as mediators or qualified actors in conflicts, or as seeds in the formulation of international economic and political treaties. According to our view, based on economic projections of main indicators (including the evolution of defence expenditures), three decades could be the temporal limit of the working of the current 'non-democratic' multilateral political structure that finally will necessarily change into democratic. In the same direction, although at much shorter term, a political change will occur within the EU, whose main Eurozone countries will probably be forced to federate to keep the European project afloat.

---

48. In this regard and in a recent meeting of the European Council, all EU countries, except Britain, have accepted changing the Treaty, in order to introduce new financial restrictions referred to the 'nil structural deficit,' and to a maximum of '3 per cent of the observed deficit' in GDP terms.

49. Note that the role of leading Western countries as arbiters in common economic issues has time ago started degrading. From frontal opposition to their views in global warming conferences, to the appointments of bosses of WB and IMF, traditionally distributed among US and European prominent citizens, emerging countries have started a new international political time in which traditional dominance is not any more recognised: in March 2013 the BRICS have formalised the creation of their own BRICS Development Bank, independent of the Bretton Wood institutions.

Effective Global Governance should be Democratic

In relation to political systems of governance, it is indisputable that in the last 25-30 years, national-democratic systems have gained credibility at a planet scale, and many nations—around 150-160 according to the UNDP—celebrate general elections on a fixed period basis.

Note that, despite the geographical extension of national democracy and the common believe in the West that their countries have decades ago reached the top level of democratic behaviour and governance, the reality is that no single attempt for setting up global democratic governance has ever been undertaken. But in order to democratically legitimise[50] undertaken actions on global public goods and externalities, and for solving social failures of a global character, a democratic global government is absolutely indispensable.

In connection to the different levels of democracy attained, one may classify the countries in the following manner: (1) democratic countries at national scale that behave undemocratically at global level when they act unfriendly or abusively in their relations with their neighbours,[51] or when they veto UN resolutions when these resolutions count with majority support;[52] (2) non-democratic countries at national level that however fulfill all the UN resolutions and mandates, thus behaving democratically at a global scale; (3) countries that are not democratic at any of former described levels; and (4) countries that behave democratically both at national and global levels.

Previous classification means that in current times of general perception of existence of global public goods and externalities, most of countries are just partially democratic. This conclusion is particularly applicable to the most important Western countries, being some of them clearly adverse to the democratisation of the UN, the sole institution

---

50. Currently it is often considered that if the behaviour of a nation in international affairs adjusts to a resolution of the current UN, it is legitimate. However, as the origin of the UN resolutions is based on adhesion to a charter, drafted by veto-owners in 1945, mentioned legitimacy is factual but not democratic.

51. The case f.i. of Israel and the US in certain situations, when Israel is non-condemned by resolutions of the UN due to the veto right of the US, is certainly one of global non-democratic behaviour.

52. The US, the Soviet Union and then Russia, and China have frequently used their veto rights to torpedo resolutions which counted with support of majorities, thus all behaving non-democratic at global level.

capable of solving the problems unveiled by the existence of global needs and externalities.

As known,[53] magnum political and social movements for progress—as that of democratising the UN—have traditionally moved in history under great inertia and reluctance to change that, happily, has been overtaken in last decades. Note in this regard that although the invention of agriculture took place about 400 generations ago and absolute monarchs continued dominating the political scene till just 10 generations ago, while only 6 generations ago slavery was even in its apogee, and just 4 generations ago women of incipient democracies fought for their voting rights, things have recently changed in a hyper-geometric way. Observe however that even though the establishment of democracy at national level has quickly expanded in the world in the last 25 years, democracy will still have to permeate global governance.

It is extremely important to underline that even if all the 193 countries of the UN were democratic[54] at national level, they hardly could reach consensus on solutions for collective problems, as it happens—at a lower scale—in the European Union, formed by just 28 national democratic countries. Consequently, total extension of national democracy in the world will not guarantee efficient global governance (if based on consensus), due to the high number of views and interests on any matter. Therefore, effective global governance will only be achieved with the democratisation of the current multilateral institutions (UN and multilateral agencies).

Concerning global governance, we have also to underline that till recently (2008), the provision of global public goods either has not been democratic (in relation to peace and security) or simply has been done in a very deficient way (global environment, etc.) or marginally developed (in the case of indispensable global economic regulations).[55] One may also perceive serious deficiencies or absence of global ruling in relation to the

---

53. Vide Boyce (2002:135).

54. To reach generalised national democracies does not mean that all over the world, democracies will have to be based on the current Western model that also has its imperfections, and to some extent is degrading. National democracies will have just to fulfill a minimum of rules as celebrating periodic free elections, application of the majority rule in parliamentary representation, respect to minorities, and total separation of military, religious and civil power with full supremacy of the latter.

55. Along the years up to now, only trade regulations have been developed (GATT rounds and WTO).

administration of global externalities on renewable or non-renewable natural resources, on quasi-monopolies or cartels at global scale (crude oil, etc.), or on fiscal paradises. But all this will have to change to protect mankind from its current trend towards self-destruction, as would happen in a sine die non-democratically regulated 'global capitalism.'[56]

Consequently, a new thinking for the protection of mankind will have to inform all future global actions to be undertaken. This new ideology will have to be founded on the attainment of economic and social optima, extracted from the concept of long-term efficiency, and not from 'short-term' market competition, many times overreacting and irrational. And for that, it will be necessary: (1) encouragement, keeping on, or reinforcement of the social economy of market at any level of public action and (2) development of a global democracy.

The Case of the European Union

For understanding the process of establishing an effective global governance, one could learn from the experience of the EU, as a collective of democratic countries 'trying to establish' an economic and political union. The current economic and political stalemate in the EU illustrates the impossibility, from one stage onwards, of advancing by consensus among 28 economic heterogeneous members of which some of them do not want to hand over a single inch of adittional sovereignty.

In the last two decades, the EU has become a totally dysfunctional and schizophrenic organisation—with a government of the Eurozone within another of the EU-28—in which the paramount common final goal (a political union), as 'insinuated' in the Treaty of Rome, has lost track. While for long moving simultaneously in the right direction, a bad architecture of the single currency (Treaty of Maastricht, 1992, and complementary rules) combined with opting outs of some members and improper enlargements in 2004-2007[57] has totally derailed the Union project.

---

56. One should not forget that many free markets, although self-regulating, many times overreact at short term due to psychological-irrational behaviour of players. An additional problem in non-restricted traditional capitalism is that free markets are less the rule than exception.

57. As if nothing important was happening in the EU or in the world, a new member, the 28th member, Croatia, received in January 2012 green light for EU access. Even more, two members (Romania and Lithuania) are preparing their access to the Eurozone.

Certainly, what pompously is called the 'European Union' constitutes a group of 28 countries placed at different stages in the process of integration: some members are in the stage of monetary union—the pioneers—while others are still in a customs union or in a common market regime with the pioneers. On the other hand, the EU is today a group of 28 heterogeneous countries in terms of spoken languages, geographical size, inhabitants, technological development, per capita income, cultural and social development, historical past and political ambitions.

In this context of multiple heterogeneity and mentioned 'double governance' in the Eurozone and the EU-28, the consensus or unanimity rule, applicable for decision-making in most relevant issues,[58] will not enable to progress efficiently in relation with the very serious decisions to be made. As the reader may understand, there is a clear similarity between the stagnating governance of the EU (28 countries deciding on consensus which implies the existence of 28 veto owners) and the ineffective global governance of the UN and agencies (193 countries also looking for consensus with 5 official veto owners actually deciding, plus some unofficial additional blockers).

The Problem of Transferring Sovereignty in Europe and in the UN

In a world of rapid changes and large political unions as the US, China, India, Russia, Brazil, Japan, etc.—to count with a population as that of the EU-28, of more than 500 million, but practically without collective decision-making capacities on relevant internal and external issues, will give Europe no significant advantage. Even more, the lack of collective decision-making capacities is a problem that will induce waste of economic and political opportunities, which will accelerate the current EU trend towards political irrelevance and relative economic decline.[59]

---

58. Since the Treaty of Lisbon of 2007, future decisions will be adopted by a 'double majority' of countries and population, with the exception of a list of around 70 issues— the 'fundamental ones'—that will be adopted by unanimity.

59. As we will clarify lines below, the annual average GDP growth rate of the EU, although positive, has in the last 30 years become significantly smaller (and progressively less significant) than that of the world average.

Too much actors with divergent interests, mutual distrust among them and absence of reasonable and reachable targets are circumstances that make that most of EU countries do not want to transfer any additional sovereignty to the collective. And even, when they officially allege to have done so, they have only transferred it in an apparent way, as it happened in the Lisbon Treaty, which confirmed the need of consensus[60] for decision making in relevant issues, while qualified majorities (in population and countries) and minorities for blocking were defined just for minor issues.

Certainly, when 28 member states representatives sit around a table, with the same decision power—because unanimity is required—and one of the countries has a population of 82 million (Germany) while 12 member countries have a population under 5 million, and 6 countries count only with 2 million or less, with a part of the smaller countries substantially poorer than the rest, one cannot expect meaningful advances, and that because the smaller countries will tend to rise the price of their assent.

Indisputably, to keep current individual sovereignty—while at a planet scale[61] all EU members are of small size—and to simultaneously trying to individually compete in economic and political terms with the much larger mentioned unitary states, is like to square the circle or as to make an omelette the without breaking eggs. Union engenders strength while individualism and mistrust avert to reach it. It deals about something as simple as that which paradoxically has few official defenders.

Observe that the problem of governance of the EU-28, or that of the Eurozone, is *mutatis mutandis* similar to the formerly introduced problem of effective global governance when the world has to deal with the provision or correction of global public goods or externalities. In the same way as the global society cannot solve global problems without transferring a portion of sovereignty to a democratic UN, the Eurozone will not be able of solving

---

60. In any problem of optimisation, the more restrictions are introduced, the lesser solutions will it have. Reaching decisions by consensus suppose introduction of restrictions by all players, thus forcing not only abandoning optimum solution, but also others of successive lower level.

61. Not even Germany, with its 82 million of inhabitants (more than 1% of the global population), may be considered as a sufficiently sized country as to politically compete in future with the great unitary entities quoted in the text.

its intrinsic common problems—as f.i. those of the 'Eurozone-EU-28 inconsistency' and the ill devised economic and monetary union—without transferring more sovereignty to a central government: the government of a feasible European Federation[62] that will necessarily have to be born to get out from the current quagmire.

Political Implications of Successful Economic Catching-up of Emerging Countries

Although the economic emergence of the so-called BRICS and other fast growing developing countries is something that everybody may verify in the WB, IMF and WTO statistics, a certain disregard of this phenomenon and its political consequences is perceivable in the West.

China, the apparent contender of the US, seen by many as the next global hegemonic power, has become object of smear campaigns in Western media.[63] It is understandable: in history no society has lost its primacy without presenting significant battles, which use to start with defamation campaigns. But the fast economic catching up of China, and to lesser extent that of India, is something that the citizens in the West should not ignore, since this ignorance is counterproductive because it averts adjustments to the new reality.

Economics, as other social sciences, is a soft science. This does not mean that observed trends along decades have no importance and that things may stay forever as they are. Certainly at short-mid-term, there are

---

62. We do believe that the European Federation to be probably set up along next years will be a selective one, although of a variable geometry. In our opinion, it should start with a maximum of 12 members today belonging to the Eurozone and the rest of the 28 could further embody, if they want, when fulfilling established rules for accession. Note that under the pressure of banking problems and the deficit and debt crisis in the Eurozone, and in connection with limited transfers of sovereignty, the EU is today awkwardly evolving to just a sectorial increase in integration (banking union, finance union, etc.). We are convinced that this procedure for sectorial progress is insufficient and will in the end force the birth of a federation.

63. In particular, since the beginning of the current crisis in the West (in 2007-08), one has frequently seen or listened news (appearing in media) underlining the imminent crash of the Chinese economy, due to multiple causes: its growing inflation, its fast growing wages, the collapse of its housing bubble, the growing urban pollution, the uncontrolled immigration towards cities, the uprisings of peasants whose plots have been taken over by local governments, etc.

different opinions on what should be done to solve cyclical problems, but at long term, differences in opinion—except composition of private and public sector activities—are not so acute. Everybody in the profession agrees that the investment rate[64] is crucial to accelerate the process of growth of GDP, that the role played by the evolution of technology is substantial in the growth process, that a growing level of education encourages the process, and that investment in research steps up technical progress. It is also generally agreed that countries with huge percentage of their populations attached to rural activities have ceteris paribus a higher potential growth rate—through the shift of redundant agriculture workers to the urban sectors—than other countries which made the shift some decades ago and that the increase of the exports rate in GDP terms enables to accede to superior levels of welfare; and this without taking into account that the size of countries also plays a positive role by means of increasing the economies of scale in defence, external representation, and other public activities.

Once said that, we cannot ignore that the current trends of the main economic variables and indicators are called to exert a relevant influence on the political future of the world. Certainly, we have to underline that in the last decades some relevant convergent trends among the developing and industrialised countries have become observable, and cannot be overlooked if one purports to make a realistic analysis on how political developments will evolve. These trends refer to: the industrial production of the different countries and continental regions, the evolution of their GDP, their share-shifts in international trade, and even the evolution of their shares in defence expenditure; such trends that if maintained in next decades—which in our view may happen with a high probability—will have an enormous influence in the setting up of future economic and political relations and institutions in the world.

In relation to the industrial production, we have to point out that— using the statistical data of the WB for the realisation of corresponding

---

64. Naturally, this will be true if investments are necessary for updating or improving the infrastructures of the country in order to solve foreseeable industrial or transports bottlenecks, not if expenditure in infrastructure is done in an absurd way, as for instance investing in regional airports without foreseeable demands of traffics (as it has recently been the case in Spain).

econometric projections,[65,66] the industrial production of the current countries of just emerging Asia[67] will overtake around 2050 the then joint industrial production of the today 'developed countries,' including US and Japan.

Projecting now the evolution of the joint GDPs (purchasing power parity; PPP) of high-income countries and that of the medium and low income, we have to conclude that the joint GDP of the latter will overcome the aggregated GDP of the high-income countries in some few years, from around 2020 onwards.[68] If we would now refer to the evolution of the share of these medium- and low-income countries in the total world exports of goods, we could conclude that from 2035 onwards, developing countries will jointly export more than the rich ones. To illustrate the rapid catching up in exports, one should remember that at the beginning of 2000 the high-income countries exported around 70 per cent of the total world exports.

But what is even more outstanding, due to its political implications, is that the countries of medium and low income will overcome the West also in the sensitive issue of 'defence expenditures.' This will occur around 2035. Logically, the main determinant of mentioned change is what will happen with the defence expenditures of China and the US.[69]

In relation to the case of the US—a country which today realises more than half (55%) of the military expenditure in the world—and China, its apparent competitor, we have to conclude that, working with data of the

---

65. Most of these data are published by WB (2010), or accessible in the Web entering in the World Development Indicators e-book. In the next comments we will refer to the results found by Alberto Muñoz, PhD in Statistics and Applied Economics, National University of Distance Education (UNED), Spain.

66. There are commentators that suggest that economic projections at 10, 20 or 30 years are irrelevant because in so large periods may happen singular events that could falsify the projected results. Although this could be true, we also share the view that consolidated trends in the last 2 or 3 decades also contain inertia from which it is difficult to get rid of.

67. Emerging Asia is formed by just six countries: China, India, South Korea, Taiwan, Thailand and Singapore.

68. Of course, in relation with high-income countries and low- and middle-income countries, their differences in per capita GDP terms will diminish, although remaining for long in meaningful values favouring rich countries.

69. Vide to this respect Andreu and Rahman (2010). Intervention in the UN; speech already commented. Vide also Andreu (2011).

World Bank, relative to their GDPs (in 2010 around 2.5 times higher in the US than in China), to their very different economic growth rates (along the 2000s, 6 times higher in China than in the US), and to their different shares of their defence expenditures in their total GDPs (2% in China *versus* 4.8% in the US), American military supremacy will not last more than another 20-30 years.[70]

Even more, the fast speed of progress of Chinese Defence Expenditures, based on the fast growth of its GDP[71] and not on its growing share in the GDP, will not choke Chinese taxpayers, while the attempt of lengthening the defence supremacy of the US would force this country to raise the share of its defence expenditures in GDP terms.[72] But note that in the next two-three decades, and with high probability, the US GDP will grow at limited rates of around one third the rates of China.[73]

In our view, a sustained rising of the share of the defence expenditures in the US will not be possible for long because it would force American taxpayers to do a fiscal over-effort which would result progressively unprofitable in economic and political terms. This probable lack of profitability will force the US and the West to look for multilateral systems—ultimately democratic at a global scale to be acceptable[74]—for the

---

70. The length of the additional period of American supremacy in military expenditure may slightly differ depending on the additional introduced assumptions.

71. The average GDP growth rate in the last 20 years (1990-2010) was 10.7 per cent in China and 2.7 per cent in the US. Vide WB (2010: 214).

72. The military expenditure of the US in 2010 was equivalent to 4.8 per cent in GDP terms, while that of China was 2 per cent, and the world average 2.6. In particular, the average GDP growth rate of China in the period 2000-2010 has been 10.8 per cent, while that of the US has just been 1.8 per cent, 6 times smaller. Vide WB (2012:214).

73. In relation with the current capacity of China and India for in future to grow at high speed, for instance at rates over 7-8 per cent along next three decades, we will have to necessarily refer to: (1) their technological capacities, today not far away from the western ones, particularly in the case of China; (2) their higher saving rates, placed now over 50 per cent of the GDP in the case of China, and around 35 per cent in India; and (3) the high number of exceeding or redundant active population in agriculture—jointly around 500 million in China and India—which will be transferred in next two and a half decades to urban activities, while keeping relative sufficiency in agricultural production.

74. To this respect, one should not forget that the current population of the West is around 16 per cent of the total world, and the developing world count for 84 per cent. This means that in a democratic global context the West will no longer be able to impose its views, if these are prejudicial for most human beings.

provision of the global public goods—including defence and security—for the correction of relevant global externalities, and for economically re-balancing the world.

Concluding, if the high-income countries lose preeminence in formerly mentioned economic aspects, as industrial production share, global GDP share, global export share, and particularly in defence expenditure share, the current multilateral institutional framework—that most of times has worked rather neglecting the less developed majority of the world (today 84% of the world population)—will necessarily have to be reorganised under the pressure of the latter, this time resulting in a democratic UN, politically acceptable for the global society.

Evolution of Politics and the Economies of the World: 1945-2010

Is Capitalism-Democracy the Optimum Combination for Governance and Prosperity?

Since the Second World War, the world has changed significantly. Capitalism mixed with democracy has triumphed as the better combination up to now:[1] on the one hand for achieving long-term economic prosperity—although at times generating economic cycles and painful production shifts of sectorial or geographical character—and on the other for governing societies towards equality, and against exploitation and exclusion.

However, since the French Revolution, initiated in 1789, the relation between 'traditional capitalism'—prone to the creation of severe economic unevenness—and democracy, a political system with an intrinsic trend towards economic redistribution, has always been unstable and subject to debate. This is the reason why in practice the capitalism-democracy combination has emerged with various profiles and different degrees of success.

Following several historical phases of cyclical recessions and recoveries since the beginning of the Industrial Revolution, and after the appearance during the Great Depression of the 1930s of an unknown phenomenon of sustained and massive unemployment, many believed that 'traditional' capitalism was near to bankrupt and that it would be substituted by socialism. However, capitalism was partially rescued in those days by

---

1. It is very common to hear that democracy is the 'less bad' political system. The same could be said about capitalism in its more human version, the social economy of market; it has its failures but, doubtlessly, is the 'less bad' of the various economic systems, including free capitalism.

a rudimentary Keynesianism,[2] while other forms of social intervention (welfare state) would produce years later a more social version of capitalism.

In the 1930s and 1940s, years of academic uncertainty in relation with the stability of the combination 'traditional capitalism-democracy,' the conservative economist Schumpeter[3] explored not only the uncertain survival of traditional capitalism in a democratic context, but also the feasibility of some forms of public sector interventions combined with a functional economic system, that time after would be named 'social economy of market' or 'mix economy of market.'

Against what many conservatives have suggested in last decades (1980-2012), and contrary to certain appearances, capitalism in a social democratic context seems destined to finally triumph in future, *versus* the two alternatives that ruled the world in the 20th century and early 2000. First, against real socialism which after some decades of inefficient development, crumbled, leading to the dismantling of the Soviet Union in 1989,[4] and second, against unbridled neo-liberal capitalism, as practised between 1980 and 2008, leading to a major crisis in Western economic history.[5] Note that the current economic crisis, mainly visible in the West,[6] has also proven the weakness and non-sustainability of global capitalism in absence of social-democratic global governance and control.

In parallel with the progress of commercial and financial globalisation, the world has in the last 3-4 decades become aware of new needs of a global

---

2. This applied Keynesian policy, mainly deducible from the General Theory (1936) of John Maynard Keynes, was very simple and far away from that applicable in the 21st century, with much more opened and sophisticated economies, and with a widespread desire for monetary stability and against inflation.

3. In his famous book titled *Capitalism, Socialism and Democracy* (1942).

4. The case of China is different: until this moment the economic-political combination in this country has been 'state-capitalism' with a political system of 'unique party', formally non-democratic, although in a slow process towards democracy.

5. Let us remember that existence of capitalism in its primitive and 'traditional version'—a capitalism also unbridled, like the recent 'neo-liberal one' (1973-2008)—was precisely at the backdrop of the evolution of the great crisis in the 1930s. Note that these two main crises of capitalism—that initiated in the US in 1929 and that started in 2008—emerged for similar reasons: overproduction and speculation.

6. As we have already mentioned, although many observers talk about a 'global crisis', the reality is that the World was growing at the end of 2012, at a rate of 3.3 per cent, a figure a little under that of 3.9 per cent corresponding to the maximum global GDP growth rate of history, in times of the golden age of capitalism, 1950-1973.

or collective nature, many of them not felt before: the provision of global public goods, the correction of global externalities and international monopolies, and the correction of the high per capita income gap among nations.

Apart from globalisation and appearance of new 'collective needs,' not sufficiently provided or corrected by the global society—circumstances that have seriously modified the Schumpeterian analysis on capitalism and democracy—we have to underline that in the last 65 years (1945-2010), besides the registered population explosion which has multiplied the inhabitants of the planet almost by three, the world has significantly changed in many other aspects: (1) sociologically (family life, women emancipation); (2) technologically [information and communications technology (ICT) revolution]; (3) politically (decolonisation, collapse of the Soviet Union, apparent consolidation of the US as hegemonic power, obsolescence of the UN, etc.); and (4) environmentally and economically (climate change, depletion of natural resources, rapid structural change favouring some developing countries as China and India, problems in the West related with the slow economic adjustment to the new situation, etc.).

Focusing on politics, we have to underline that along the last decades, democracy has become the sole reference for the governance of nations. Extrapolating this 'national' democratisation trend to the global sphere, we have suggested[7] that only the setting up of a global democracy (a new democratic UN) will endow with democratic legitimacy the necessary political actions to be undertaken for solving the common problems of the global society.[8]

Note as well that the concept of global democracy and the way of its implementation has practically remained absent in the multilateral political debate (although not in the academia). This has mainly occurred because the current UN—an embryo of the global democracy that will necessarily emerge in the first half of the 21st century—was initially conceived as a non-democratic organisation, in which the five permanent members of the UN

---

7. Vide Andreu and Rahman (2009b).

8. Along this book, when we mention 'global society,' we are referring to the collective, today of 7 billion people (100% of mankind), to be represented democratically in a new UN, and not to the so-called 'international community,' an expression used by Western media and politicians, which in general refers to the current most powerful Western countries (the US, Britain, France, the EU, etc.).

Security Council, the 'Victors of the Second World War,' gave themselves a veto-privilege on all discussed multilateral issues. As the veto-rights group (three plus two[9]) defended two radical different conceptions of the world, attempts of 'non-aligned' groups along the past 65 years to change the non-democratic *status quo* of the UN, systematically failed.

Facing the new global problems—which demand global solutions based on democratic global governance—we consider that overlooking them, or denying their existence, will only result in economic and political impasse, or even in violence. We do also believe that a re-legitimisation of 'traditional capitalism,' which hardly admits the existence of global problems while rejecting most collective solutions, should be discarded, because such a re-legitimisation would be a political time bomb, even for consolidated democracies in the West, due to expectable mounting inequality and environmental unsustainability.

Sources of Non-tenability of the Current Global Capitalism-National Democracy Combination

We do believe that current combination of 'global capitalism with national democracy' is not tenable for several reasons: (1) capitalism has progressively gained ground across the world, becoming global, but lacking the necessary (global) democratic control to legitimately oversee and rule global economic activities, and this while mentioned 'free' capitalism has induced progressive degradation of the personal income distribution[10] within many Western and developing nations, thus not guarantying at long term social stability and democracy even at national level; (2) current capitalism, many a times with a dangerous trend towards excessive market orientation, treating labour almost as a commodity, is putting at risk in many places the psychological or physical health of (overstressed) individuals, and the

---

9. Till the 1970s, the fiction of Taiwan representing Continental China gave to this group a composition of four plus one.

10. The International Monetary Fund (IMF), in its semiannual *World Economic Outlook* (2007) examined how former globalisation (1982-2002) had affected the personal income distribution in the developed world. From this report, one may clearly deduce that Western workers lost income share around 0.2 per cent a year, which means a loss of around 4 per cent in the considered 20 years. Vide the *Economist*, April 7, p.72.

basic foundations of societies: family life, socialisation and solidarity;[11] (3) progressive degrading of global environment and depletion of some essential non-renewable resources is threatening the tenability of a capitalistic world that has made 'growth-mania and maximum consumption', the pattern for measuring economic success, be it collective or individual; (4) inexistence of democracy in global governance makes the legitimate and efficient provision of global public goods, as desired by the global society, impossible, thus putting in the hands of a self-defined aristocracy of nations—at times manipulated by the multinational corporations (MNC)—the definition and the provision (or not) of these global public goods;[12] and (5) human security, as integrally understood, has globally degraded in the last three decades and become patent in a world in which abject poverty remains, domestic personal income distribution often degrades, and political rights of minorities are neither respected nor enforced, while many greedy financiers or unscrupulous adventurers are in charge of global entities without passing political filters.

We conceive democracy as an integral political system for, among other things, providing public goods and correcting externalities and monopolies with legitimacy (at local, national, regional and global levels). But observe that nowadays the most democratic (developed) countries of the world are just in the middle of the way, since they do not consider—because it is not convenient for them—the need of democratic provision of global public goods, and this while others have just recently started the road towards national democracy. Both the former and the latter will have to make significant efforts to reach a more tenable world. This means that the leading Western countries will have to hand over their current non-

---

11. In a context of deep specialisation, absence of *de facto* working hours limitations, unconditioned geographic flexibility (full mobility), and insufficient day-care centres when both parents are working, may be conducive—through national or international competition among labourers—to non-tenable family life, reason why governments should treat leisure and supportive structures for families as 'special wants' to be provided and developed.

12. The current (non-democratic) definition of global aims (e.g. [for instance] peace administration issues) enables leading Western countries to use double standards. In some cases, they define as priority targets for their political action, non-democratic countries of strategic relevance for them. In other cases, similar non-democratic countries, but with a friendly behaviour towards the West, are declared as 'nominally' integrated in the general democratisation process of the world. Iraq was a good example of the first case, and Pakistan and Saudi Arabia are examples of the second one.

democratic global power in the multilateral institutions, in favour of a global governing body which, endowed with democratic legitimacy, will finally work in benefit of all.

Although today only some few openly defend the rights of the majority of the world population by means of creation of a new democratic UN, the explicit protests are already in the air: (1) the G-8 has become diluted in the G-20, although without delivering, and (2) more recently, emerging BRICS first called for top positions at IMF and World Bank (WB), and thereafter announced the establishment of a BRICS (Brazil, Russia, India, China and South Africa) Development Bank. All these are signs that bifurcation of the existing multilateral institutions will finally occur unless the West recognise the right of the entire global society to participate in democratic global governance.

Physical Limits and Inefficient Institutional Structure Hinders Sustainability of Global Capitalism

The conditions for sustainability of the current capitalist-democracy combination are complex and multifaceted. From our perspective, there are at least two groups of variables that may make sustainability of current capitalism possible or not. The first refers to the physical ones: the natural resources involved in the economic development of nations. This process of development—mainly founded in growing industrial activities, much of them are high consumers of energy and water—should in future be reorganised with extreme respect to the environment and available natural resources. Otherwise, the future of mankind will be problematic and surrounded by catastrophic events induced by global warming and climate change.

Note however that the existence of physical limits to growth is not the sole condition for sustainability of current global capitalism. There are also additional conditions belonging to the sphere of politics (developed by multilateral institutions) that have (or will have) significant influence on the administration of mentioned physical limits.

It is our view that current political and economic multilateral institutions—acting as the legal rulers of current global capitalism—will not efficiently work in future, due to their lack of adaptation to the needs and expectations of the global society.

Observe additionally that the international economic structure (production and trade) in the second half of the 20th century is rapidly changing. This is mainly due to the ICT revolution and the fast embodiment of the two Asian giants (China and India) and neighbouring South-East and South Asian countries in the international division of labour. As a result, in next decades industrial production will be mainly located in East, South-East and South Asia, as well as a big chunk of out-sourceable services.

In this new economic context, current international distribution of power will not survive because it will become inconsistent with the new economic realities. Consequently, the power structure in multilateral institutions will have to adjust to the new economic realities for favouring the sustainability of global capitalism.

Sustainability of Global Capitalism Requires Fairer Personal Income Distribution

In the context of the trade-off 'efficiency-equity'—key aspect for sustainability of capitalism—and to illustrate the case, we will firstly recall the domestic anxieties which appeared in European countries in the period 1870-1914. Let us remember that in those days, the behaviour of absolute monarchies and 'liberal' states concerning 'human rights,' and wages and working conditions of workers—which directly affected the personal distribution of income—was one of non-consideration; or even repression when workers, commanded by trade unions, protested or demonstrated.[13]

The derivatives of the principle of action and reaction between trade unions and left opposition on the one hand, and absolute monarchies or conservative governments on the other were manifold in the political battles for taking or defending power, or simply in negotiations on working conditions. In the aftermath of the First World War and Russian Revolution—and based on the growing fear felt by industrial owners concerning spreading and consolidation of the socialist movement—fascism,

---

13. In the name of freedom of contracting, also applicable to labour markets—as if labour was a simple commodity—these negative practices (repression) were also patronised by nascent liberal states.

corporate movements and other purported 'third ways' appeared. Note that some of these 'third way' movements developed in a context in which the role of the states was rightist, totalitarian and geographically expansionist.

After two human and material catastrophes (First and Second World Wars), Western European governments learned the lessons of history and, from 1945 onwards, started building (or enlarging) the so-called 'welfare state.' Previous economic exploitation of masses by firms and frequent human rights violations by the political machinery of absolute monarchies or traditional quasi-democracies were no longer acceptable patterns of behaviour. The social costs had been huge and could not continue after the Second World War. With the establishment (or enlargement) of the welfare state, societies became more fair and stable, particularly in Western Europe.

Regrettably, 'lack of memory' of European governments (and others) made that some decades later (from 1980 onwards) a new version of traditional capitalism re-appeared, negatively affecting Europe again. In fact, despite the positive effects of the construction of the welfare state[14] on internal peace, security and prosperity, the last three decades (1980-2010) witnessed a significant reversal of former trends. Note that this reversal materialised in a general degradation of personal income distribution and social protection in the West, and in a piecemeal slimming of middle classes in western societies.

As we have explained in other places,[15] sustainability of democracy at national level will depend ceteris paribus on the evolution of the personal income distribution and on establishing or maintaining extended middle classes, and less on reducing the number of poor under the so-called 'poverty line' as it is today defended in many international forums.[16] Indeed, there is no doubt that any economic globalisation has to increase the

---

14. We have to admit that, in the development of the welfare systems and labour rights in some EU member-states, there were some exaggerations that had to be corrected or downsized.

15. Vide Andreu and Rahman (2009b).

16. In many international meetings, the acceleration of globalisation in the period 1990-2007, was 'praised' as an economic movement that had achieved significant reduction of the percentage of poor under the so-called poverty line. But in fact, and against expectations, between 1990 and 2010, the reduction of poverty, as currently defined, has been mild in absolute terms.

economic efficiency of the vessel Earth and its global GDP.[17] But national democratic governance (and the global one in future) will not be sustainable if the resulting distribution of gains were not fair enough.

In fact, regressive movements in the national distribution of personal incomes have been (or are) again observable in many countries, developed and developing, particularly since the initiation of the last impulse to globalisation in 1990: the liberalisation of capital movements. Mentioned regressive distribution has become even more serious in the West after the start of the 2007-08 financial crises. Nevertheless, the long-term movement towards economic divergence among the large regions of the world seems to have stopped or reversed in the last two decades (in terms of average per capita income). This is mainly due to the rapid economic expansion of emerging countries (China, India, Brazil, etc.) and the relative weakening of the West in the period 1990-2010.

The Current Debate on Social Democracy

A General Perspective on the Future of Social Democracy

Indeed, social democracy is a political doctrine, allegedly situated between communism and capitalism that paradoxically (although temporary) has become rather empty of practical content in the West after the last step towards globalisation: the liberalisation of capital movements. To the extent that social democracy was born in the coordinates of modern 'national' capitalistic-democratic states, it inherited 'nationalism' as a restriction, thus just trying to better redistribute income among national citizens. Indeed, all this worked acceptably well for several decades after the Second World War, precisely when capital movements were very limited among nations and trade was not so extended (globally) as it is today.

---

17. As advanced by J.F. Nash—Nobel Prize winner in Economics—in his article of 1950 "The Bargaining Problem" (*Econometrica*), the central issue is not to know if a particular bargaining solution is better for all participants than not bargaining at all— which is something sure—but if different possible bargaining actions contain fairer solutions for the collective than others, thus being more convenient. This message could be today translated into global economics saying that a certain way of additional globalisation—as that implemented under the Washington Consensus—would have always been better than no additional globalisation at all, but at the same time, it could have been relatively unfair and inconvenient in comparison with other (till now non-implemented) ways of globalisation.

The problem of the social-democratic movement today is that it cannot go against 'national' capitalists—for improving the lot of workers—because capital may rapidly be sent abroad which would destroy national jobs. On the other hand, social democracy cannot go either against global competitiveness among nations—by promoting the reintroduction of protectionism—because in that case it would prejudice the poorest people of developing countries, by repressing the creation of jobs in these nations, as it was the case during the long colonial and neo-colonial periods. Even more, this undesirable protectionism in the West would certainly provoke retaliation of developing countries and, consequently, would destroy additional domestic jobs in the West: those devoted to production directed to developing countries (today around 30% of the total western exports).

So, once the economic framework has changed to a global scale, social democracy should adjust, for surviving, to this new global playground. Among the adjustments, social democrats should promote larger political unities—be this by federations of states, by enlarging regional cooperation, or by pushing for the creation of democratic global governance—in order to introduce a superior control on the working of markets. Otherwise, the maintenance of the current scenario of geographical fragmentation of political power combined with liberalised capital movements will induce the indefinite continuation of sovereignty of markets, some of them monopolistic and at times over-speculative, and the degradation of the income distribution. During the transition, and to the extent that today there are emerging developing countries with much smaller real wages and social protection than those of the West, social-democrats should impulse increase of wages and social protection in developing countries, while in the West social democrats should support the progressive moderation of wages for achieving significant jobs growth, global economic convergence and a more sustainable life style in the world.

Certainly, the globalisation of the movements of capital or wealth, although initially suggested and lobbied by the Western private industrial sector to avoid national industrial disputes with trade unions and to place capital where profit expectations were the highest, was mainly implemented by moderate parties in office in Western countries. But paradoxically, this capital liberalisation has not and will not favour its political promoters because whenever they are in power they will also inherit the lateral effects of having followed the interests of the domestic industrial sector: dislocation of jobs, mainly favouring Asia, and prejudicing the West, particularly Europe. Even more, when political opposition reachs power following democratic alternation—as it has already occurred in the past—they will not be capable of modifying mentioned lateral effects of capital liberalisation: a trend that in the end has favoured the richer few, because the political power of the incumbents (old and new) will be just national, and very conditioned by international competitiveness.

As a result of former considerations, and taking into account that the distributive solution of unbridle capitalism is not politically sustainable, we do believe that in two or three decades, the creation of larger political unities for improving democratic global governance—f.i. a European Federation and/ or a new democratic UN—will be the political answer for democratically limiting the current sovereignty of markets (mainly dominated by multinational corporations, MNC) at global scale.

Certainly, next two-three decades will be interesting times for academic global analysts, but adverse for Western workers and nations that will economically walk some step backwards to just partially compensate the exaggerated and unfair economic advance the West took in colonial times.

After the arrival to larger political units, and in particular to global governance, social democracy, when in future it obtains majority representation, will recover the great influence it had in Western Europe till 1980s, thus favouring workers again, although this time not only favouring 'national' workers—which at times played against the interest of non-European workers—but also the rest of workers of all over the world. And this will occur because social democracy—the natural administrator of the mix economy of market—is the only solid doctrine for managing public goods, or for correcting externalities, and also for fighting against monopolies in some markets of private goods.

Note that if this process towards global democracy finally became a reality, conservative doctrines on non-intervention in the economy will become rather obsolete, and political discussions in the democratic UN parliament and corresponding agency (GERA)[18] will mainly range, according to circumstances, around the degree of intervention or control deployed.

---

18. The future's new UN should count with a Global Economic Regulations Agency (GERA) as one of its more relevant agencies.

Watching again with perspective and acumen to what has happened in the formulation of policies in the last century, we should clearly admit that the margin for practicing policies for either economically defending exclusively the individuals (traditional capitalism) or the collective (communism) has become progressively narrower. Certainly, since the beginning of the 20th century till the fall of the Berlin Wall, there were two very different ways of understanding economics which were politically positioned as mortal enemies.

Errors of first communists in Russia and China made them to socialise any production, although these were private goods, as f.i. food. This was a tremendous mistake—which at the end of the day produced deadly famines—similar to that committed by traditional or neo-liberal capitalists, who declaredly preferred to produce almost all by the private sector, although it dealt about public goods and externalities, as f.i. defence, public transport, public health, etc., and with minimal control. But regrettably, total freedom of production initiatives by private sector—and without significant controls—as desired by neo-liberal capitalists, has for instance resulted in catastrophic bank failures in the 1930s and last 2000s, or in allowing agriculture production moving in favour of liquid fuels instead of attending the basic feeding needs (cereals) of the global society.

Along the 1980s of the 20th century, and mainly after the bankruptcy of the Soviet Union, it became clear that the socialist-communist economic system had to be discarded and filed, as it had been done in China. So, in the early 1990s, the world had shortened the space open to economic options by half in comparison to the available options at the beginning of the century. This meant that from 1990s onwards, politics could only oscillate from social democracy to neo-liberalism. However, the liberalisation of the movements of capital initiated in the 1990s, which confronted geographical economic freedom with absence of global governance, seemed to condemn social democracy to disappear, due to the apparent lack of margin for maneuvering among the two remaining ideologies. This lack of margin has 'forced' social democrats, when they took power in the West, to concentrate their actions in minor 'progressive' social policies such as gay marriage, review of history, etc., while in economic policy they adjusted to neo-classical or neo-liberal economic approach.

Nevertheless, the current economic crisis (started in 2007-08) has finally put the focus on global governance and on global economic regulation. But in this regard, there is today an almost total consensus that global economic regulations cannot be provided by individual nations but only by the involved collective, the global society in particular, when this global society will be represented in a democratically reorganised UN.

Consequently, we do believe that the space for political discussion has again become re-compressed and re-centered. From the idea of supremacy of private sector, defended by traditional capitalism or by recent neo-liberalism (1973-2008), public sector is regaining and has to regain importance, particularly in future. Of course socialism-communism will not return, as will not return extreme economic liberalism, because both extremes misuse a great part of the economic potential of nations.

Therefore, the Marxist dream of the final arrival to a global communist society, and the recent ideas of American 'neo-cons' according to which from the collapse of the Soviet Union onwards, the history would have finished on the other extreme of the political range both seem to us wrong. Evolution of demography and sustainability of the planet, existence of new global needs and externalities, and globalisation of the markets will force public global intervention and control, giving again space to social democracy, although this time to work at a global level. And to its own surprise, neo-liberalism will lose significant space and will be in need of re-centring itself, facilitating more public sector intervention.

On Microeconomics of the Welfare State to be Managed by Social Democrats

Letting aside the big lines of the future political developments in the world, with social democracy (in its different centred versions)[19] as the unique political solution for achieving social stability,[20] and entering now

---

19. We do believe that in future, current or moderate rightist parties will move to the centre of the political spectrum, thus politically competing with current social democracy that, in some cases, will have to shift also towards the right. This means that in those days all political parties will be re-centred, and will behave more or less as social democrats.

20. As a result of re-centred political competition, public sectors sizes will range between 35 per cent and 45 per cent of corresponding GDPs. Correspondingly, the space for private sector activities will be the rest till 100 per cent.

into the political debate between current neo-liberals and social democrats, we have to underline that, as a direct consequence of the financial crisis starting in 2007-08, every political group is blaming others for what has recently happened.

Going back some decades, we have to remember that after the Second World War, Western Europe started building up or enlarging a system of social security, in order to avoid the social unrest that had finally brought communism and socialism to power in some countries. After 1945, the understanding in Western Europe was that former 'non-social security system' which did not protect the people against misfortune— unemployment, disease and lack of care for the old—should not continue. In parallel, communist parties were forbidden in certain European countries.

Note that in the last 50 years, a majority of Western Europeans has continuously and democratically supported higher and progressive taxes for financing state-run social security. However in the same period, a rich minority kept defending that individuals should protect themselves against misfortune by contracting insurances with private companies.

From mid-1950s onwards, it was generally accepted that basic education should also be financed by the state in order to provide equal opportunities for all, and to avoid any waste of available human capital. But once again, those who positioned against state-run social security also preferred private financing of education, alleging that it was unfair that some few, the rich, would have to pay—through taxation—for the education of all, while lacking control over political orientation in teaching materials and content.

Even more, one has to recognise that this pro-and-con debate on social services is related not only to the distribution of the financial burden, *via* taxes or prices, to finance their provision, but also to the efficiency (or inefficiency) of the provided services.

Indeed, although taxes may generate injustices, the system of prices applied to goods and services containing huge positive externalities (such as education) is totally counterproductive for creating fair and (long term) efficient societies. In general, and reflecting on social services, a full prices system of financing will be unjust because most of citizens, on being placed under the average per capita income,[21] will not take enough insurances against misfortune, and talking on education, parents will not allocate enough investment in their children's studies.

As a result, by applying a system of full prices to social services and education, most citizens, but also the nation as a whole, would lose opportunities. To this respect, we should not forget that expected infra-demand of social services and education by poor at full prices has a lot to do with the initial economic situation of the different agents, those who have assets or those who have not, and not so much with the personal efforts deployed by the poor that many times are more intense than those of rich. Consequently—and conversely to what fashionable neo-liberals proclaim— rich are not necessarily 'the makers' as the poor are not necessarily 'the takers.'

Even more, a system of full prices for financing social services will also be counterproductive from another perspective: it will create an economic unbalanced society without extended middle classes, in which the income will be concentrated in the hands of a minority. This will result in a politically unstable society more prone to social unrest.

Rich neo-liberals also defend their position of rejecting paying taxes (or minimising them) for financing social services, by alleging that the collective provision of the social services has always been inefficient, and therefore mentioned services could have been provided better and cheaper by private firms. Even more, they allege that the contained subsidy in certain social services—as the 'unemployment insurance'—is a machine of generating slackers that do not want to work. They also criticise the public health system as a bottomless well of inefficient expenditure, totally unbalanced with the 'revenue taken from workers and entrepreneurs.' The neo-liberals also criticise the public pensions systems because they consider as unfair that people who do not want to save enough for paying its own insurance still receive a public complement. As they insist, the state should not enter in this financing because it produces a big burden that has to be paid with taxes, which destroys jobs and reduces the growth capacity of the economy.

---

21. The density function of the distribution of income in societies is not a normal-Gauss one, but another where the median is nearer the origin than the average. This implies that much more than 50 per cent of the population has a per capita income under the average income of society.

Finally, there is another argument—very strong according to neo-liberals—coming from the competitive conditions of the new globalised world, that suggests that to compete with the new emerging countries that have no, or low, social security, the so-called social expenditures in rich countries should not be financed *via* taxes because this would increase the internal costs of production of national firms, thus placing the domestic industry in a position of under-competitiveness.[22]

Once exposed former arguments, mainly those of neo-liberals, we have to clarify our position in the debate, which is placed between the positions of neo-liberals and extreme trade-unionists. We do believe that the welfare state, as far as it has been developed, has accumulated some inefficiencies and deadweights, which should urgently be corrected in a reasonable way. Consequently, we are not in favour of stubbornly holding on to all the 'social rights' of citizens as historically achieved, as these rights may have become non-sustainable or even could have been defined in an irrational way. We do not share either the stubbornness of neoliberals who continue defending extreme market positioning, even after the economic disaster caused by an international deregulation of capital movements (in the 1990s), and by national deregulation and privatisation carried out in the 1980s-1990s, in a globalised world without global governance.

Analysing item by item, and suggesting some solutions, we could start with alleged abuses of the unemployment insurance. We have to emphasise that in some European countries, this insurance has been an object of significant abuses, in particular by those who receive the subsidy while they are working black. Clearly these abuses, which contain an illegal deviation of public funds, should be qualified in the penal code of these countries. In relation to abuses referring to rejection of job opportunities in another firm, industry, sector or region, by unemployed people while they receive the unemployment subsidy, we do believe that they should also be economically penalised with subsidy reductions, or even with exclusion.

Entering into the finance of the health service, we have to say that corresponding administration should clearly define the cost per medical action and surgical intervention and complementary treatment, and reckon

---

22. As we will prove in lines below, competitiveness does not exclusively depend on hourly wages. It also depends on the per hour worked productivity, on the number of annually worked hours and on the exchange rate.

the contributions of every one (directly, or indirectly through the firm in which he or she works) to the financing of the health system. All this would increase transparency, while it would enable everyone to know their own position as creditor-debtor of the system in front of those of the rest of associated.

On the other hand, it should be underlined that some surgical interventions or treatments to some patients could be socially considered as very expensive as to be publicly financed. In this regard, we have to clearly state that without lengthening the number of years worked by active citizens and/or without raising specific contributions or taxes taken from them, the fiscal and health systems will not be able to support the indefinite lengthening of the average life of citizens, and their growingly expensive heath care.

The same could be said on public pensions and unemployment. Indeed, the current system of pensions based on distribution—with a majority paying while working, and a minority receiving pensions at the old age— only may sustain if the proportion of those who pay do not significantly move downwards per comparison to those who receive pensions. As agreed in many Northern European countries, if population ages, the retirement age has to be retarded, being this as the Law of Gravity. At the same time, those who should work cannot be for long in the dole because this financially prejudices the entire system of protection, including pensions and the health system.

Consequently, in a context of global competitiveness, things cannot be approached as black and white by any of the involved parties: trade unions in their protest should not go against the economic fundamentals of the system, while governments and private entrepreneurs should not treat labour as a commodity.

Finally, we support the public financing of education (partial or total) till a certain age or level. This means that everybody should count with the support of the public financing, but neither unconditionally nor indefinitely. Those who fail in their studies should be excluded from the system of educational subsidies.

In brief, our position is an intermediate one between the increase of provided welfare services irrespective of their costs and the economic situation of the country, and the minimal or nil social protection demanded by neo-liberals. Finally, we do believe that the assumption by neo-liberals that global competitiveness will force the drastic reduction of social expenditures is to some extent an imaginary problem. Western Europe has the greatest productivity per worked hour in the world. But competitiveness has to do not only with mentioned hourly productivity but also with the total retribution per worked hour, the number of the yearly worked hours and the ruling exchange rate. Note that in any case, total or hourly retributions can be paid to the workers either through the social security system in subsidies—financed partially by workers (payroll taxes)—or privately as a net after-tax wage (per hour or per year).

So, in a context of global competition, by electing a certain system of social protection with its corresponding subsidies, local society will be making a choice on the net paid wage.[23] Consequently, political actors who without significant increases in the productivity per hour, or in moments of economic crisis, simultaneously try to maintain the number of worked hours or to reduce them, and to maintain or increase monthly after-tax retributions while rejecting expenditure-cuts in education, public health or pensions, are just dangerous dreamers and bad administrators, who want to fully pass the burden of the crisis to others, be these national capitalists— that today may move their capital elsewhere—or to their own children by means of increasing the deficit and the public debt.

In relation to competitiveness, it is true that protectionism is always there as a temptation, but retaliation of developing countries is today more than a simple threat. The West could not continue exporting the same quantities if—under pretexts—it reduces its imports from developing countries as China, India and other neighbouring nations, by rising customs duties or other trade barriers. This is again something which goes against any rationale. At the end, we have to go back to the initial arguments exposed in the introduction of this book: times have changed, and the recent ones—those of the period 1980-2007 of high consumption but of progressively degraded production in the West—probably will not return in

---

23. This annual net paid wage will be: a fraction (to leave a part for retribution of capital) of the average hourly productivity of labour expressed in monetary units—the latter depending of the price of output—multiplied by the number of hours annually worked, less annual contributions to the social protection system (health, pensions and unemployment).

many years, or simply they will not return any more, because the West is losing its former economic 'dominance.'

As we have mentioned in former item, social democracy and its economic policies are not dead in the West, but are provisionally non-operative due to unbalances between existing national governance, and global trade and capital movements. In the near future, the main role of social democracy in the West should be to fight against market fundamentalism, but without exaggeration in defending former positions acquired by western workers. Extreme defence of former wages and 'social rights'—not adapted to the new economic realities—could condemn Western economies to a fast decline in relative terms. Indeed, a soft landing into the new realities of the first half of the 21st century could be the main contribution of current social democracy to the stabilisation of Western economies.

Social Democracy and the Big Trade-offs in the New Societies

Having catalogued the problems of sustainability of capitalism and democracy, outlined the multi-foundations of uncertainty in the current world, and analysed some causes of dissatisfaction, we will now approach some of them in detail, trying at the same time to establish certain aims consistent with global economics and social sustainability. To this respect, we will begin with what we define as the current manifold crisis in the Western philosophy of life that social democracy should try to solve.

In our opinion, the multifaceted life crisis, starting in the late 1970s and today permeating most layers of the political and economic world,[24] has to do with several disputable aspects related to human life that paradoxically few people dare to criticise. Perhaps the quasi-absence of this debate derives from the acceptance of some 'sociological trends,'[25] soaked in deep individualism and purported limitless freedom, that shapes 'modernity' as understood in North America and Europe.

---

24. Note that this 'life crisis' has a different form and content among the Muslim population in the world. They, with an amount of 2.1 billion people, although in general fighting to leave poverty and become richer, consider themselves as different from the people of the Western World.

25. This way of living is massively supported by publicity in suffocating Western media, prone to the ongoing change towards individual consumerism.

In this regard, we consider that long-term generalisation of some of the current western habits—f.i. private individual transport—may likely be conducive to an impasse in the development of capitalism in the 21st century, due to congestion of cities, exhaustion of certain resources, or arrival to a radical climate change.[26]

Observe that individual transportation, often with several cars per nuclear family, implies a stage of individualism that, besides its environmental costs, has also huge private costs: need for individuals to work more hours—to finance the cars and complementary style of life—in harsher competition with others, and just to occasionally feel freer, faster and undisturbed, which only happen in valley hours, when most citizens do not use their vehicles.[27]

Note additionally that the current individual life style of Westerners—of which possession of individual cars and houses in suburbs are just some of the most visible traits—is now being imposed by publicity to the rest of the global society without considering its sustainability.

In reaction to this panorama, some disputable features of our behaviour as human beings—in opposition to their respective alternatives—will be analysed in lines below. In particular we will discuss the cases of: (1) efficiency *versus* equity; (2) income *versus* leisure; (3) consumerism *versus* environmental protection; and 4) uniformity *versus* diversity in culture, religion and political organisation. From these discussions, we will deduce the aims that social democracy or political centre should promote in future.

Efficiency and Equity

In relation with the first dichotomy efficiency *versus* equity, today pervasively inclined in favour of (short-term) efficiency as defended by neo-liberals, we should here remember that the ideal construction of the first rational economic model based on economic freedom—Smithian

---

26. For a rather pessimistic analysis on what could happen in future in relation to Earth Warming and annual economic costs of doing nothing—up to 20 per cent of the global GDP over the end of this and next centuries—vide Stern (2006),

27. In 2050, generalised individual motor transport at affordable costs will not be probable on a daily basis in big cities. Besides, in a world of 8.9-9.0 billion people, in which at least 60 per cent will be urban, the congestive character of the individual transport will make it impossible, with the possible exception of bikes.

economics—practically coincided in time with the French Revolution, prone to political freedom[28] and also to equal opportunities.

All along the last two centuries, both ideas of economic and political freedom and equality—respectively conducive to efficient production and interchange, and equal opportunities—have been at the core of political discussions, political reshaping of states, and even internal uprisings or interstates armed conflicts.

Note that, to the extent that market freedom and political liberty could not (and cannot) be effectively exercised without a minimum background of economic resources in the hands of individuals, some redistribution of the economic assets or income was (or is) necessary for the sustainability of democracy, when democracy surges in a context of high concentration of wealth.

Observe that if the new owners—or the new bourgeoisie—were scant,[29] and in parallel did not exist an extended middle class, the new economic system, although more efficient in economic terms than the former one, would be incapable of delivering a minimum of equity, thus inducing social instability and unstable democracy.[30]

Concurrently with the evolution of the liberal states, it is also interesting to observe that in the first third of the 20th century, as well as in the last one—periods mainly dominated by 'economic liberalism' in its different approaches—Darwinism was transplanted to the theories of social life in opposition to the ideals of equality and brotherhood. Darwinism, transplanted to economics, is nowadays falsely presented by market extremists under the rationale that any solidarity usually results in economic disincentives for the poor, thus becoming detrimental for the speed of progression of the collective.

---

28. Note that the concept of 'political liberties' has historically been one without monotonous progression in franchising and other civil rights, and at times even with periods of regression or breaking up. Needless to insist that after a maximum participation of the population in the constituent Assembly and further in the convention along the French Revolution, Napoleon took over in 1799, thus certifying than the French Society was not mature in 1789 for constructing a 'sustainable' democracy.

29. And consequently, ownership of production assets was also concentrated in some few hands.

30. This phenomenon of political instability following a democratic revolution, without a convenient distribution of assets, was clearly perceivable after the initial stages of the French Revolution. Vide Saboul (1972).

But unfortunately for current Westerners, forgetting the poor—under the pretext of creation of disincentives—in a context of fully informed societies, is an irrational behaviour because a stubborn and long-lasting neglect of the others will be conducive to negative spill-over effects in terms of security and prosperity for all.

In this regard, one should not overlook that the alleged short-term negative effects on efficiency of many pro-equity actions have many a time been more than offset by the mid-long-term induced advantages, advantages that have normally resulted from the significant improvement of the socio-economic 'climate' in which the economy and private businesses had to operate.

In this respect, one should not forget that in the conventional neoclassical microeconomics, the production functions—in principle defined as technical relations among factors of production and output—have also to include the organisation of the productive activity. Logically, this organisation will have to necessarily adjust to the dominant ideas about what is desired by society in connection with industrial relations,[31] thus imposing restrictions on the use of labour by firms.

Although these restrictions are limitations to the free contracting of labour, few people—except economic fundamentalists who wrongly think in pure short-term economic efficiency[32]—would support the abolishment of them. In this respect, it is easily deducible that such an abolishment would be counterproductive because, besides the negative effects at long term on society (reduction of leisure time which makes family life difficult, etc.), it would induce significant labour or political disruptions, based on its perceived unfairness.

We do believe that the ideas about what are fair industrial relations have exerted a very positive effect on the concept of long-term productivity

---

31. As for instance, working schedules, shifts, security, holidays, leaves of absence, geographical mobility, etc.

32. Instead of suggesting to help the poorest countries to initiate the building up of welfare systems to align their social security with that of Western Europe, thus deactivating social complains of the poor majority, Western economic fundamentalists try to degrade the current social protection system in the West for 'recovering competitiveness' against the poorest economies.

of labour.[33] Certainly, this is a concept much more comprehensive than the cold short-term productivity of labour, the latter resulting from mere technical relations among factors and production, and often from the abuse of workers in schedules and working rhythm.

It is not difficult to transplant these microeconomic ideas to the joint macroeconomic field, that is to say to the evolution of the joint productivity of factors and global prosperity. Accordingly, what sometimes appears to be non-productive expenditures, in the context of firms, use many a times to result in a long-term profitable action for all parties.[34]

Concluding, moderate long-term measures taken to reduce unacceptable differences in the living standards of citizens (via public expenditure in education, health, pensions, etc., and progressive taxation) or for the setting up of balanced rules to ease industrial disputes, should be considered as positive, and not against the efficiency of the productive system.

Consequently, we do firmly believe that what we could call, in a simplified way, the European model of social protection,[35] far from disappearing at a world scale, will be finally accepted—of course after indispensable corrections—and adopted in the long term by most countries in the world, with the support of big political unities of new creation, and the future democratic UN. This will necessarily occur because voluntary components of any private self-protection system never will work at general scale, thus resulting in undesired under-protection of the less prudent or poorer individuals,[36] who always are significant in number.

---

33. Although internal 'economic freedom' in the West probably reached its zenith in the period 1870-1914, although not for all—let us remember the bleak economic situation of metropolitan workers and those of colonies—the average annual growth rate of the labour productivity was not at all the highest of the last two centuries.

34. Vide Elson (1998: 51).

35. One could discuss if there is just one European model of social protection, or if there are several ones. Certainly, in Europe we find different models of social protection: (1) the Centre-European model (France and others) characterised for providing generous unemployment benefits and pensions, while somewhat limiting by law the capacity of firms to fire workers; (2) the Nordic countries model (including Netherlands), which is more prone to poverty reduction and dole compensation, while more easily authorises firms to fire workers; and (3) the Mediterranean one, basically inclined to keep the people working irrespective of the current labour needs of the firms, while giving petty dole compensation. Vide the Economist (2005) "Choice your Poison" October 1st.

36. Note that any operation of self-insurance carried out by individuals could neither be of general scope nor profit from the "law of large numbers" and optimal distribution of risks.

Working Time and Leisure

In relation with the trade-off between working time and leisure, we have to underline that there are prosperous and industrialised countries whose labourers have in the last quarter of the 20th century progressively reduced the number of their annual worked hours[37]—basically in Continental Europe (France, Germany, Netherlands)—while others (f.i. the US and the UK) have surprisingly increased the length of their average working time.

This phenomenon in the US and the UK, of progressively increased worked hours when per capita income rises, could theoretically mean that in these countries either leisure was or is not a normal good,[38] which is illogical, or the substitution effect of less leisure for more income was or is of a very large magnitude, thus making people prone to work much more, even when real wages per hour (before or after taxes) just slightly increase.

But far from mentioned hypothesis, the real cause of the extended worked hours in mentioned countries may have been rather different. Available data enable to affirm that in the US, the observed increase in the average worked hours per worker is consistent with a reduction of the median wage per worker—which could have forced most workers to work more hours for the same monthly income—while the average wage per hour would have increased.[39]

Although not easy to understand, we could say that, till recently, the citizens of some Western countries—as f.i. in the US and the UK, and

---

37. Indeed, the reduction of the weekly worked hours per person has been one of the most important targets of trade unions along the last hundred years, a target successfully achieved by them in the West. Nevertheless, observing the data, one may deduce that in the last quarter of the 20th century an up-turn of the annual worked hours per worker has been registered in some countries, particularly in the US and Britain. Specifically, between 1973 and 1998, the number of per capita worked hours in Continental Western Europe decreased 12.2 per cent, while those of the US increased to 12.9 per cent. Vide Maddison (2001: 132).

38. In microeconomics, a normal good is defined as that whose demand grows when individual real income rises.

39. This is due to the shift of the internal distribution of income among wage and salary (non-capitalists) earners. Indeed, in the US as in other Western societies—and in the last two-three decades—top executives of firms, actors, singers, top sport-men or women (all of them placed in the inefficient 'markets of winners') have seen their income risen in a very disproportionate way with respect to normal workers, thus probably forcing an upward move of the average wage, consistent with a decrease of the wage of median labourers.

also others—brainwashed by media, have acquired a very individualistic approach focused on short-term 'consumerism.' This means that they, to continue with their current overconsumption in a context of decreasing median wage per hour, would have simultaneously decided to work more hours[40] and save less. Consequently, they penalise themselves in the short and long term *via* miss-consideration of own leisure (at short term) and own necessary future consumption.

This negative attitude of citizens could also be caused by the under-valuation of one of the primary objectives of community life, which is to enjoy friendship, social interaction and family life. At the end of the day, their target has become an endless race to consume more than others, in detriment of their current leisure and future economic security.

More understandable than the case of overstressed labourers in rich countries is the case of workers in some developing countries. These labourers, in many cases without the support of a social protection net, performing trade unions and/or fair labour legislation, work more hours just to earn a minimum living, against an unfavourable framework of superabundant manpower, and a relatively scant demand of labourers, due to agriculture, agro-industry (food processing) and services protectionism in the West.

Consequently, it is expectable in these developing countries that, when their demography becomes less pressing, their per capita GDP becomes high enough and their societies become more democratic, the number of annual worked hours per worker will diminish, thus initiating (also) in this domain a convergence process with richer societies.

Note that the competitiveness of the different countries in the global context has to do with different variables and not exclusively with the number of the annual worked hours. Indeed, the competitiveness of a country will also increase when the labour productivity per worked hour grows in comparative terms, when the annual gross salary including social security burdens (measured in internal currency) becomes smaller in

---

40. This idea was defended by candidate Sarkozy to the Presidency of the French Republic in the elections of 2007. The slogan defended by Sarkozy was: "Work more to earn more", certainly an idea to encourage overconsumption, while forgetting environmental protection and leisure time as something positive from a human perspective.

comparative terms, or when *ceteris paribus* the national currency devalues or depreciates.[41]

Consequently, looking to main Asian countries, and considering the cheapness of labour and the huge number of the annually worked hours per person in them, a reduction of leisure time in Europe—as for long demanded by EU conservative politicians—to offset the low cost of Asian labour, seems simply an irrational positioning, given the enormous gap existent today in terms of both hourly wages (much higher in the EU) and annually worked hours (much higher in Asia). In conclusion, even a hypothetical use of the most available hours per EU-worker would not enable to bridge the competitiveness gap, although it would increase the profit rate of the EU firms. So, for the time being and in the context of a social-democratic programme, there is no need to increase working hours at short-midterm in Europe, but to moderate wages.

Overconsumption and Indebtedness

Many western citizens have acquired the habit to either overuse banking credit or working additional hours to increase their consumption. Exaggerated borrowing and, at times, additional income enabled them till 2007-08 to immediately increase consumption of goods and services, while neglecting their own future, due to reckless accumulation of debts, difficult to pay when high unemployment finally reappeared.

Indeed, growing indebtedness and low (or very low) familiar saving rates, as displayed before 2007-08 by many Western countries in their national accounts,[42] were clear indicators of the 'consumerism and short-termism' of the Western society combined with growth rates significantly under the world average.

Observe that the recent massive and obsessive consumption process in the West—a phenomenon which has also (partially) affected the rest of the

---

41. Note that the management (or controlled floating) of the national (or the EU) currency in terms of the international ones provides to national competitiveness—complemented with other measures—a total flexibility in terms of adjustment capacity.

42. This model of overconsumption in demerit of saving and investment, and financed with progressively higher private indebtedness—partially coming from abroad—is today known as the model of highly leverage growth, a model which became fashionable in the West in the last decades.

world—has induced a huge waste of natural resources, many of them non-renewable, and corresponding accumulation of at times dangerous residuals. Overconsumption and to some extent parallel overproduction has also been accompanied by increased emissions of greenhouse gases (carbon dioxide; CO_2)—thus accelerating climate change[43]—or by significant degradation of soil and water and sea resources, all in detriment of the environment and nature that our descendants will inherit. As part of the problem of overproduction and overconsumption, food processing including the use of sugar, preservation chemicals and fast food has resulted in epidemic obesity in the world and consequently in a rise in health costs, of course not paid by the food processing industry.

Letting aside overconsumption of Western citizens—around one billion people—we have to additionally consider that the billion of the poorest of the world[44] also tend to overuse natural resources. But in opposition to what happens in the West, depletion practised by the poor is due to their pressing survival needs, mainly deriving from extreme poverty and high fertility rates. Note that these pressing needs force poor[45] in LDC[46] to overuse the natural resources at their disposal, progressively destroying the forest to meet their food and fuel needs, thus inducing deforestation,[47] soil degradation and sometimes desertification. All this does not mean that a significant percentage of urban-people in developing countries is not affected by the new obesity pandemic provoked by industrialised fast food.

---

43. The case of the US is a clear example of former proposition. The level of metric tonnes of per capita emissions of CO_2 of the US at the dawn of the current 21st century (2008) was more than double than Europe, 3.4 times higher than China, 12 times higher than India, etc. Vide World Bank (2012: 172). Note that although developing countries issue a small level of per capita CO_2 emissions, they generate practically all the non-industrial greenhouse gases (burning fuel-wood, vegetation to clear plots, etc.).

44. Approximately one billion people in the World live with less than one US dollar a day per person.

45. In South Asia, more than 70 per cent of people live in rural areas, and in sub-Sahara Africa more than 60 per cent. Additionally, around an estimated 72 per cent of the poor of the world live in rural areas, and its absolute number continues growing. Vide World Bank (2012: 140).

46. The acronym LDC refers to the so called 44 'least developed countries', according to the terminology of the WB. Along this book, LDCs are often included in the more general expression 'developing countries.'

47. Deforestation combined with heavy rains may at times induce land sliding, thus destroying assets (shelters or factories) and taking human lives.

Indeed, Western academicians and governments should reconsider the role of the internal consumption in their models of economic growth. The traditional models of economic growth have always put the emphasis on the development of physical and human investments (private and public), which after creating more GDP would induce additional consumption. But in the West, and in the last three decades, the sequencing has rather been the opposit (first increase consumption in order to increase GDP), thus directly favouring private industry, while at the same time public investment was postponed in many relevant countries due to the prevalent economic philosophy in the period: neo-liberalism and reduction of the public sector. But when in the decade 2000-2010, the consumption of cheap imported goods massively started coming from Asia, and competition started playing against Western industrial production, in many countries of the West, investments—partially financed through foreign indebtedness—were massively and wrongly redirected to housing or international speculation, while continuing with overdone levels of consumption.

To this respect, we have to affirm that social democrats should in future intervene in the reformulation of the model of growth, clearly biased towards consumption and towards the degrading of the environment. Of course, such a reformulation would need a mayoritarian political power of the social democracy, this time at a global scale in the new democratic UN.

Homogenisation in Consumption and Social Behaviour

We will now refer to another trait of the recent globalisation process that social democracy should modulate: the strong trend towards homogenisation in consumption, sociopolitical behaviour and habits. This trend has become widespread due to the fact that Westerners, from the colonial days onwards, have tried to impose their culture and behaviour on others. With the ICT revolution and the access to live information in the most remote places of the planet, former trend has accelerated, thus 'persuading' developing countries to step up certain economic or political changes to reach 'modernity.'[48]

---

48. Note that this forced 'modernity', although wrapped in different pretexts, hides the desire of widening markets for Western goods and manufactures.

These recommended changes that could be understandable in the field of economics[49]—provided that the changes were selectively, progressively and cautiously implemented—are much more disputable in other (political and social) domains.

In relation to social domains, differentiated attitudes in developing countries[50] concerning roles of families in society, social habits, and even some human rights[51] use to be considered in the West as unbearable backwardness. This 'unacceptable delay'—to certain extent caused by former colonial powers, which in general refused to develop serious education systems—combined with superiority feelings, makes that the West presses for urgent political change in some developing countries, and this while forgetting that, achieving and sustaining these changes may take several decades, as happened in the past in the process of modernisation of Western countries.

Mentioned lack of historical perspective and equity becomes even more asymmetric when the West tries to hastily and forcibly impose Western political (democratic) systems[52] on certain developing countries, particularly in (undemocratic) non-friendly countries considered as relevant from geographic or strategic perspectives (resources).

Apart from being historically superficial, such forced political and cultural changes have also proven to be 'non-intelligent.'[53] In the

---

49. Particularly, in relation to the liberalisation of trade and opening to financial interchange.

50. Note that these differentiated moral attitudes come from recommendations of different religions, or by the absence or mix of other sources of moral principles.

51. Many a time condemnations coming from the West, about violation of human rights in certain places, are focussed on individual rights with exclusion of more collective socioeconomic rights. These condemnations, although often reasonable, cannot hide the fact that, in the middle of a great indifference, Western countries systematically neglect (financially) the poor, depriving them of a decent life, access to literacy, numeric knowledge, etc., thus violating basic human rights to be educated and remaining healthy, as defined in the ruling Charter of the UN.

52. In relation to the long history for arrival to a (partial and defective) democracy in the US (in connection with the intense political pressure exerted by North America for rapid change towards democracy in other countries), vide Willentz (2005).

53. Indeed, the aggression strategy developed by Western allies from September 11th, 2001, onwards and the support to the 'Arab spring' has facilitated in many countries the accession of near-salafist parties to power (Iraq, Palestine, Tunisia, Libya, Egypt), and has brought more legal-political influence of Islamic parties in other places (Lebanon, Turkey), and this while political consolidation of sustainable democracy in Iraq and Afghanistan continues being far from completion.

current case of the Muslim-Arab countries of the Middle-East and North Africa, the pressure applied on them by the West in the last decades to force democratisation of their political systems may have resulted counterproductive. Undeniably, if the socioeconomic background of these countries was not mature for achieving (at short-mid term) sustainable (western styled secular) democracies, forced institutional changes towards democracy, far from being effective to the purported ends, could cause the arrival of durable theocratic political regimes.

Consequently, it is our view that today it is more necessary than ever to continue with indirect support to democratisation processes in the Muslim-Arab World, but mainly by means of contributing more significantly to the development of their human capital,[54] in particular referred to access to education and professional promotion of women.

Economic Profiles and Trends in the World in the Period 1950-2010

After explaining the qualitative changes registered in the world in the last 60 years, and in order to reliably project economic perspectives for the coming decades in the sub-continental regions of the world, it will be necessary to first know the economic evolution of these regions in the period 1950-2010. In this regard, we will mainly base our analysis on the figures presented in 2001 by Prof. Maddison,[55] figures that will be complemented and updated by official figures of the WB (2012), referring to 2010. For comparative purposes, we will also refer to the Maddison figures of the period 1870-1914, the so-called period of the traditional 'liberal order.'[56]

---

54. There is a fatal tendency in the West to support "political modernisation programmes" only run by local "Westernised" non-governmental organisation (NGOs) which, logically, are incapable of influencing mainstream popular education. Often, and contrary to expectations, these NGOs, after supporting political change, are sidelined by non-democratic parties.

55. Vide Maddison (2001). We will also consider, as a complement, additional figures relative to the economic evolution of countries and regions in the period 2000-2010, taken from the WB (2012).

56. This 'liberal order' refers to the economic system 'enjoyed' at that time by a minority group of Western countries. This order, far from being liberal in all senses and directions, was mainly patronised by Britain, and developed in consistency with the restricted trade rules of 'colonialism.' Vide Rahman and Andreu (2006).

To analyse the period 1950-2010, we have divided it in two sub-periods: (1) the period of generalised and growing prosperity, 1950-1973, frequently called the 'golden age of capitalism,'[57] and (2) the 'neo-liberal period' which, extended from 1973 to 1998 and further (at least up to 2007), has meant a certain updating of the ancient 'liberal order' (1870-1914). The rest of years till 2012 correspond to what we have defined as the so-called 'Financial Crisis,' period that has been explained in Chapter 1.

Note that the analysis will be done in aggregated terms. Although this approach could hide interesting details concerning certain prominent countries, it will not contradict the general trends of the different regions of the world.

Trends of the World Economy in the Period 1950-2010

It is well acknowledged that in the second half of the 20th century (1950-1998), the world economy obtained—excluding environmental degradation and depletion of resources—its best ever results. According to Maddison,[58] the global GDP grew at an average growth rate of 3.9 per cent per annum[59] compared to a growth rate of 1.6 per cent per annum in the long period 1820-1950. Another indicator of buoyancy of the second half of the 20th century is the average of the per capita growth rate per annum, which in that period was 2.1 per cent against 0.9 per cent between 1820 and 1950. This means that in the second half of the 20th century the global per capita GDP grew at a rhythm that allowed doubling the global standards of living every 35 years, as compared to the time frame of 80 years that was necessary for per capita income doubling during the period 1820-1950.

The former aggregated figure of 3.9 per cent of the GDP annual growth rate for the period 1950-1998 is the weighted average of that of the 'golden

---

57. Observe that this 'golden age', was basically 'golden' for Japan and Western Europe, whose per capita incomes grew very fast.

58. Vide Maddison (2001). Note that the periods selected by Maddison are arbitrary and consequently arguable. However, we will not enter into discussions on this issue, because any other arbitrary selection would not significantly modify the results.

59. For pure comparative purposes, we have to insist that at mid-2012, the world GDP was growing at a rate near 3.3 per cent, certainly not a rate of 'global crisis' as one may often hear in the West.

age of capitalism' (4.91%) and that of the period of 'neo-liberalism' (3.01%).[60]
Note additionally that in the 'golden age' the per capita GDP grew at a rate
of almost 3 per cent per annum, the greatest ever in history (conversely, this
rate grew only 1.33% in the period 1973-1998 and 1.5% in the first decade
of 2000).

Entering now into details of the regional GDP growth in the 'golden
age,' we will mention that the average growth rate of Japan was remarkable
(9.29%). Against what one could have imagined, the European Immigration
Countries (a group of countries containing the US, Canada, Australia and
New Zealand, hereafter referred to as EIC group) experienced in this 'golden
age' the lowest GDP growth rate (4.03%) of all considered regions,[61] even
below Africa (4.45%), Western Europe (4.81%), USSR and Satellites (4.84%),
Asia excluding Japan (5.18%) and Latin America (5.33%).

Regarding the first part of the neo-liberal period (1973-1998),[62] in which
global GDP growth rate per annum was 3.01 per cent, that is to say around
three-fifth of that of the 'golden age,' we should underline the economic
failure of Eastern Europe, with an average annual rate which turned negative
(-0.56%), from former 4.84 per cent. Also Japan decelerated its previous
spectacular rhythm of growth, progressively converging to the average growth
rate of the world.[63] Note additionally that while Western Europe had annually
grown in the Golden Age almost one percentage point above the EIC group,
the situation reversed in the so-called neo-liberal period, with the EIC
growing almost one percentage point more than Western Europe.

Significantly above the world average, the Asian (ex-Japan) countries
not only maintained their annual growth rate of the 'golden age', but also
surpassed it (5.46%), reaching a figure almost double the world average.

---

60. In the period 2000-2012, the GDP of the world grew at an annual average rate of 2.6
    per cent, while low- and middle-income countries annually grew at an average of 6.3
    per cent. Vide WB (2013).

61. These regions are: Japan, Western Europe, EIC group, Soviet Union and Satellites,
    Asia (ex-Japan), Africa and Latino America-Caribbean. As we will see, the regions
    used by the WB are slightly different.

62. For practical reasons, we have divided the entire neo-liberal period 1973-2007 in two
    parts: 1973-1998 following the analysis of Madisson and 1998-2007 to include the
    rest of economic developments up to the financial crisis in the West.

63. In the period 2000-2010, Japan grew at an average rate of 0.7 per cent, a rate even
    under that of the Eurozone (1.1%).

No doubt, this period 1973-1998 of general deceleration in global growth was the period of the economic resurgence of Asia, commanded by a vanguard group of seven fast growing countries.[64] Even more, this economic resurgence of Asia further accelerated in the first decade of 2000.[65]

To continue with our aggregated analysis, we will now focus on the evolution of demography in the periods 1950-1973—the so-called 'golden age'—and 1973-1998, the neo-liberal period. As we can see in Table 2.1, the growth rate of the world population in the period 1950-1973 was 1.92 per cent per annum, which roughly meant a population doubling every 37 years. This stage was the so-called period of the 'population explosion' at a world scale, due to advances in (and spreading of) medical services.

Entering into details, we will add that in the 'golden age' the average annual population growth rate peaked in Latin America (2.73%), followed by Africa (2.33%) and Asia ex-Japan (2.19%). In the same period, the demographic behaviour of Europe landmarked a trough (0.70%), while the population in Japan grew at 1.15 per cent, the USSR and Satellites evolved at 1.31 per cent and the EIC group grew at an annual average rate of 1.55 per cent.

Contrary to what had happened in the period 1950-1973, the average population growth rate of the world lost momentum in the first neo-liberal period (1973-1998), moving from 1.92 per cent to 1.66 per cent per annum, a downwards trend that continues today at a rate of 1.2 per cent.[66] Most of regions reduced their population growth rate in this period with the exception of sub-Sahara Africa that reached an average figure of 2.73 per cent per annum, a rate that hardly flexing—reaching 2.5 per cent in the 2000s and expected 2.4 per cent in the 2010s—is capable of roughly doubling the demography of sub-Sahara Africa every 26 years. In the period 1973-1998, Latin America reduced its annual population growth rate to

---

64. Note that the extraordinary growth rate in Asia (ex-Japan) during the neo-liberal period was due to the growth rates of seven countries of fast growth: the so-called Asian Tigers—Hong-Kong, Singapore, South-Korea and Taiwan—plus Malaysia, Thailand and of course, China (India could also have been included since 1980).

65. The average GDP growth rate of East Asia-Pacific region in the period 2000-2010 was 9.3 per cent, while the annual average of South Asia was 7.2 per cent.

66. The deceleration of the global growth rate of demography resulted confirmed in the period 2000-2010: its average annual population growth rate moved down to 1.2 per cent and expectations for the decade 2010-2020 are 1 per cent.

around 2 per cent, a little bit over that of Asia (ex-Japan) 1.86 per cent. And, amazingly, Europe halved its previous low growth rate, from 0.7 per cent to 0.32 per cent, while the USSR and Satellites experienced a sharp fall of their population growth rate from 1.31 per cent to 0.54 per cent.

Table 2.1

GDP, Population and Per Capita GDP, 1950-2010
(Average Annual Growth Rates)

	GDP (% Real Terms)			Population			Per Capita GDP (%)		
	1950-1973	1973-1998	2000-2010	1950-1973	1973-1998	1990-2010	1950-1973	1973-1998	2000-2010
West. Europe	4.81	2.11	1.3	0.70	0.32	0.5	4.08	1.78	0.8
EIC Group*	4-03	2.98		1.55	1.02		2.44	1.94	
Japan	9.29	2.97	0.9	1.15	0.61	0.0	8.05	2.32	0.9
Asia (ex-Jap)**	5.18	5.46		2.19	1.86		2.92	3.54	
Latin America	5.33	3.02	3.8	2.73	2.01	1.2	2.52	0.99	2.6
Sov.Un. and Sat.	4.84	-0.56	5.4	1.31	0.54	0.2	3.49	-1.10	5.2
Africa	4.45	2.74	5.0	2.33	2.73	2.5	2.07	0.01	2.5
World	4.91	3.01	2.7	1.92	1.66	1.2	2.93	1.33	1.5

Note: *The EIC Group countries includes US, Canada, Australia and N. Zealand; **the group of Asia ex-Japan includes China, Hong Kong, Malaysia, Singapore, South Korea, Taiwan and Thailand, plus eight additional Asian countries with significant growth rates (Bangladesh, Burma, India, Indonesia, Nepal, Pakistan, Philippines and Sri Lanka).

Source: Maddison (2001: 126). The more recent figures (2000-2010) have been taken from WB (2012).

A simple look at these figures enables to identify the most problematic regions in the world. During the 'neoliberal age', the case of the very high population growth rate in sub-Sahara Africa, the poorest region of the World in terms of development and welfare, was tragic because it increased at a time in which the rapid growth of the 'golden age' was over. This high growth rate of the population—which continues today at 2.4 per cent—constitutes an enormous hindrance at short mid-term for the per capita income increase in the region.

It would be also convenient to remember that in the second half of the 20th century, the population growth rate of Western Europe never surpassed the figure of 0.77 per cent, being the average growth rate in the period 1950-1998 around 0.50 per cent. This small figure made easier the achievement of higher internal savings in Western Europe, private and public, which served to successfully finance during decades its development process and growing welfare state. Note also that the sharp fall in the population growth rate in Russia in the period 1973-1998, extended till 2010 and further continues being a cause of deep concern in this country, because its negative population growth (-0.2%) limits the Russian possibilities for quicker catching up in GDP terms, potentially coming from the exploitation of strategic raw materials (mainly oil and gas).

As a consequence of the differentiated annual evolution of global GDP and global population in the two mentioned periods of the second half of the 20th century, the global per capita GDP also grew at different rates. In the 'golden age' the average per capita growth rate per annum in the world was 2.93 per cent, while in the first neo-liberal period, former rate more than halved, reaching a figure of 1.33 per cent. Nonetheless, this figure—despite the initiation of the crisis in 2007-08—has mildly recovered in the period 2000-2010 reaching 1.5 per cent, mainly as a consequence of the reduction of the annual world population growth rate (from 1.7 to 1.3%) and the faster annual growth rate of developing countries (6.2 *versus* 1.8% of rich countries).

In the 'golden age' period, 1950-1973, the annual growth rate of the per capita GDP of Japan was the highest in the world (8.05%). Even in this period of maximum prosperity, the per capita GDP of sub-Sahara Africa grew annually at the lowest rhythm, 2.07 per cent. The EIC group and Latin America registered per capita GDP growth rate of around 2.5 per cent per annum, while the per capita GDP in the Soviet Union and Satellites grew annually at 3.49 per cent. Observe that in this period—the period of the European reconstruction—the citizens of Western Europe experienced a significant increase in their per capita GDP growth rate per annum, almost doubling the rates of the EIC Group.[67]

---

67. The enormous effort of European citizens for the reconstruction of war-torn Europe, initially facilitated by the Marshall Plan, made this rapid per capita GDP growth rate possible. Japan experienced a similar process. Both Europe and Japan profited from the economic battle of the US against communism in the early years of the Cold War period (1947-1991). Main European countries also profited from the end of independence wars in their former colonies.

Table 2.2

*Evolution of the Per Capita GDP in Prominent Stages of Capitalism
(Weighted Average of Annual Growth Rates in Different Periods)*

	1870-1913 Class.Lib.	1950-73 Gold. Age	1973-98 1st N-Lib.	2000-2010 2nd N-Lib
Western Europe	1.32	4.08	1.78	1.3
EIC group	1.81	2.44	1.94	(..)
Japan	1.48	8.05	2.34	0.9
Asia (ex-Jap.)	0.38	2.92	3.54	(..)
Latin America	1.79	2.52	0.99	2.6
Africa	0.64	2.07	0.01	2.5
World	1.30	2.93	1.33	1.5

Source: Same as Table 2.1.

However, in the 'first neo-liberal period' (1973-98), the growth rate of the per capita GDP experienced a generalised downfall except in Asia (ex-Japan). This Asian (ex Japan) region moved from an annual per capita GDP growth rate of 2.92 per cent in the 'golden age' to a 3.54 per cent in the first neo-liberal period. On the contrary, in Eastern Europe this period was a clear catastrophe, not only in terms of economic performance, which significantly reduced the standard of living of their citizens, with a negative per capita GDP growth rate per annum of -1.10 per cent, but also in political functioning. Note that in the middle of the period, the communist economic model of the region bankrupted. This bankruptcy was followed by a period of high political and financial instability provoked by the sociopolitical dismantling of the Soviet Union under Russian president Jeltsin (as advised by IMF).[68] The economic and political instability ended with the arrival of Vladimir Putin to the presidency of the Russian Federation in 1999.

The per capita GDP of sub-Sahara Africa did not grow at all in the first neo-liberal period (1973-1998), just reaching 0.01 per cent per annum—later recovering to 2.5 per cent in 2000-2010—while Latin America grew only at an annual rhythm of 0.99 per cent (also recovering to 2.6% in 2000-2010). Note that in the period 1973-1998, the loss of steam in Western Europe was also significant, experiencing an annual growth rate of per capita GDP (1.78%) which only surpassed those of Latin America

---

68. For an evaluation of the wrong economic dismantling of the Soviet Union led by IMF, vide Stiglitz (2001).

and Eastern Europe. In the period 2000-2010, the per capita GDP of the Eurozone just grew at 0.8 per cent, proving the absolute loss of steam of the EU, whose governing institutions simply did not deliver.

Shift of the Economic Gravity Centre of the World towards Asia

The main and the more durable problem that many rich nations of the world are facing today is the fast geographical restructuring at global level that is taking place in the economic field. Indeed, for the first time since the Industrial Revolution, a human mass of around 37 per cent of the total world population (China and India) moved from a position of being out of the international division of labour—till 1978 in the case of China and till 1991 in the case of India—to a process of progressive integration, and this in a very short period of time.

Since reaching significant embodiment in international trade and financing took China around two decades, this country did not become an obvious challenger in international matters till the end of the 20th century. Now then, in the last 10-15 years, and particularly after its entrance in the World Trade Organisation (WTO) in 2001, China has gained momentum in international trade and is today the first single world exporter, while also overwhelming the West with its rapidly growing GDP and involvement in investments and trade in Africa and Latin America.[69] Note that, despite reiterated inaccurate statements of some Western authorities, in the last 10 years fast exports growth of China went hand in hand with around 30 per cent revaluation of the yuan.[70]

The case of India is currently less worrying for the West than that of China. This is due to the fact that India initiated its embodiment in the international division of labour in 1991, more than a decade later than China, and even in a very hesitant way. This delayed economic opening of India has made that this country is currently playing an economic role[71]

---

69. In the last decade (2000-2010), the annual increase of the Chinese world exports share has been around 0.5 per cent, which has enabled this country overtaking the US and German exports at the end of the decade.

70. Vide XE history of last 10 years of China yuan-US dollar exchange rates.

71. In relative terms, India is more inclined to the production and export of services than China (vide WB, 2012: 234). Note that the value added of services in India was in 2010 equivalent to 55 per cent of the Indian GDP.

similar to that played by China in the last 1990s, although relatively more tilted to the exports of services.

As we will explain later, the real GDP growth rate of these two countries along the last 30 years (1980-2010) has been around 10.5 per cent in the case of China, and around 6.5 per cent in the case of India. This difference of around 4 per cent favouring China, plus a more rapid population growth in India, has made China has today, 2012, with a per capita income of 5,680 US dollars,[72] more than triple of that of India, being 1,530;[73] and this while in 1978—the moment of the initiation of Economic Reforms in China, in times of president Den Xiao-Pin—the per capita GDPs of China and India were alike.

Many Western observers of the current Chinese and Indian economic progress wonder on the possibilities of these two countries to continue with their current high rhythms of growth and for how long. Some of these viewers, exaggerating the political and economic difficulties that both countries will have to necessarily face in next years, provide 'pessimistic' prognosis, suggesting that their current high growth rates will wear out in some few years.

Nevertheless serious analysts (Goldman-Sachs) concluded in 2003[74] that these two countries will finish the first half of the 21st century with GDPs (in absolute terms) alike to that of the US, although of course in 2050, the citizens of China and India will be—particularly in the case of India—much less affluent than the US citizens.

Additionally, the phenomenon of the very high growth rates of the regional exports in East and South-East Asia, and in South Asia, in comparison to the world export figures in the last decade 2000-2010, and in

---

72. For comparative purposes, we will mention the per capita income (gross national income; GNI) of the world in 2012 (10,012 US dollars), the Eurozone (37,935) and the US (50,120). Note that former mentioned figures are not elaborated in purchasing power parity (PPP) terms, but in terms of exchange rates. If elaborating them in PPP terms, figures would have reached values of 9,060 for China, 3,840 for India, 37,653 for the Eurozone and 50,610 for the US. Vide WB (2013).

73. If mentioned figures were measured in PPP terms, the per capita GNI of China would be more than double than that of India. Vide WB (2013).

74. The period of catching up of these two countries, China and India, in absolute GDP terms, seems today to be shorter than predicted in 2003, the moment of the publication by Goldman Sachs.

comparison to those of the US and Europe, confirm former positive opinion on the economic future of China and India.

All point out—including the much higher rates in domestic investment and savings—that these two countries will continue keeping a more than significant comparative advantage in industrial (China) and services (India) wages. This has placed the US and the EU in a very difficult position to compete with manufactures and services coming from China and India. Indeed, given the huge differences in real wages between China and India and the West, and growingly similar used technology—initially supplied to China and India by Western dislocating firms—increasing competitiveness by Western industrial firms cannot be just a matter of increasing the annual growth rate of the labour productivity per hour—always a small percentage— or the annual growth rate of the productivity per person by means of raising the number of annually worked hours. In fact, for adequately converging, a significant and sustained downwards correction of the Western real wages will be necessary[75] in front of the enormous tidal wave of new cheap labourers who have entered or will enter in next decades–*via* international trade—in the global division of labour.

Unfortunately for the West, its current economic problem of lack or insufficiency in jobs creation will not finish in 5 years' time, or in next decade (2023), as some have suggested thinking that China and India will rapidly follow a convergence process with the West in unitary costs (salary costs/productivity of labour). On the contrary, it is our view that taking into account their huge reserve of active but redundant population, currently attached to agricultural activities—with a joint volume of around 500 million workers—and after considering the annual absorption capacity of workers by the industrial and services sectors of these two countries, the

---

75. There are recent studies made by the Organisation for Economic Cooperation and Development (OECD) and other institutions that advance mild negative forecasts for the future evolution of the median real wages in the EU in the next 10 years. Although a reduction of just 1 per cent per year is mentioned in these studies, we do believe that in the next 10 years the correction will be much more significant. Note that for reckoning the effective reduction of the real wages in the US and the EU, it would be relevant to count with realistic estimations of the 'rates of inflation,' and not with the current consumer price index (CPI), that cannot accurately measure the evolution of the general level of prices.

internal process of labour-shift towards industry and services activities may *ceteris paribus* last up to two and a half decades.[76]

Bearing in mind mentioned magnitudes, we do believe that if conditions of international trade keep on,[77] this new and unprecedented structural change will for long induce a rapid growth of employment in the industrial and services sectors in China, India and neighbouring countries, and at mid long-term, probably a stagnation or even decrease of the employment figures in the US and the EU.[78] This will force Western countries to focus on an economic soft landing that may last one or two decades, that is to say till the moment in which the industrial shift towards Asia finishes.

Administrating this 'post-crisis' restructuring period in an appropriated way will make the difference among good and bad Western democratic governments and citizens. As far as Western economic low-growth rhythm continues, it will have a huge influence in politics: few governments in power will regain elections. In this unfavourable context, achieving a 'soft landing' to acquire sociopolitical stability could become the acid test on the sustainability of Western democracies. Only Western governments capable of clarifying the future scenario of the economy to their citizens, and of warrantying social peace during the transition, will achieve this soft landing.

Indeed, to enable the soft landing and to avoid further disruption in Western economies, negotiations with China and India for timely smoothing the negative impact of Asian exports on Western economies will be necessary. In exchange, the West will have to give China and India far

---

76. Recently, officials of the Government of China, trying as usual of presenting a low profile to the rest of the world, are predicting a future period of rapid growth in China no longer than two decades, and with GDP growth rates of around 8-8.5 per cent. But we should remember that in the last 10 years, Chinese economic prognosis made by own officials have always resulted 'pessimistic': reality has always surpassed official projections.

77. We are mainly referring to current levels of tariff and non-tariff protections on imports, while keeping exchange rates coming from the natural evolution of the markets.

78. Several times the British magazine *The Economist* has pointed out that the current process of industrial production shift towards Asia will finally be a boon for the US and the EU, which will see how their employment rates in the services sector over-offset the current losses of jobs in the industrial one. However, we do believe that when saying this, *The Economist* is thinking in the historical shifting process observed domestically among the productive sectors of the leading developed countries, but not in the international and massive breaking up of the current economic and trade structure, induced by the mentioned 37 per cent of the world population (working at very low wages per worked hour), that recently embodied the international division of labour.

more influence in current multilateral institutions, more in accordance with their populations and GDP. Any other solution, be this a commercial war, or even aggressions direct or indirect under pretexts, should be discarded because it would be a destructive experience for the whole planet.

Technical, Economic and Political Changes in the Period 1950-2010

The four and a half decades that the Cold War (1947-1991) lasted witnessed not only localised violent conflicts but also an unprecedented economic expansion practically extended to the entire world. In addition, the Cold War period implied a significant change in the philosophy of life of Western citizens that progressively spread out to other less developed regions. During the period, a generalised progression in human rights definition and implementation was also visualised.

Reconstruction of Europe, decolonisation of Asia and Africa, socialist experiments in Russia and China, democratisation process in Latin America, plus changes in technology, and better macroeconomic knowledge made faster GDP growth easier almost everywhere. Technology, by drastically reducing the private unitary costs[79] of transport, made national and international trade easier and changed individual travelling (by car or plane) into a common thing. Trade among a growing number of General Agreements on Tariffs and Trade (GATT) members experienced significant progress,[80] while in the late 1960s and early 1970s some concerns on the environment and exhaustible resources emerged.[81]

Nonetheless, these environmental problems—particularly those of global incidence—initially were not object of significant official action.[82] Only the sharp hikes in oil prices, successively occurring as derivatives

---

79. If we additionally include the 'social costs' of transports, mentioned reduction of costs would have been less spectacular.

80. For a briefing on the evolution and evaluation of GATT-WTO, vide Rahman and Andreu (2004:81).

81. Analysis on environment and resources depletion became visible mainly since the Report to the Club of Rome titled 'Limits to Growth' [realised in 1972 by Meadows and Meadows and a team of the Massachusetts Institute of Technology (MIT)].

82. If serious action had been implemented some decades ago, the current (2012) severity of the perceivable climate change could have been avoided.

of the Yon Kippur war (1973) and the Iranian Islamic Revolution (1979), drew attention to the scarcity of natural resources. More recently, the embodiment of China and India into the international division of labour and their corresponding growing demands of raw materials, plus growing evidence on current climate change, have finally placed the environmental degradation as one of the most relevant global problems to be solved in future.

Note that along the years of the Cold War, problems of underdevelopment and difficult conditions of life of billions of human beings—although somewhat considered by rich countries—were clearly underfunded and many times treated under geopolitical considerations.

Let us remember that from mid-1970s onwards, and as a result of sustained economic failures in the Soviet Union, its economy started degrading and the Russians had finally to file the Soviet-socialist model. This gave way in the West to the 'moral' reinforcement of an extreme version of the so-called 'neo-classical' economic model, according to which most internal and external markets should be hastily liberalised and freed of public controls, and many useful public activities transferred to the private sector. Note that this approach not only promoted a significant reduction of the size of the public sector in rich countries, but also proclaiming in a exaggerated way that the growth of the developing countries should be a matter of freer trade and foreign direct investment (FDI) than of official development assistance (ODA) and development policies, an approach also officially adopted by the so-called Washington Consensus.[83]

In the 1980s and 1990s, these extreme neo-classical or neo-liberal ideas progressively gained ground and became mainstream economics, the so called 'unique economic model for global prosperity', which included the tragic deregulation of the banking activity in the West and the liberalisation

83. What John Williamson, of the Institute of International Economics in Washington, DC, named as the 'Washington Consensus,' describes the conditions considered as necessary for a poor country to get itself on a path of 'steady growth.' The main conditions of this consensus were: no inflation; sound fiscal policies; broader tax bases and more moderate marginal rates; free internal markets and liberalisation of the external ones including the exchange rate; export orientation of the economies, public expenditure more tilted to investment in infrastructure, health and education; and fight against poverty. Although one cannot deny the importance of the above-mentioned main conditions for growth, one should not overlook the fact that freer trade and FDI may bypass LCDs, the latter being in need of ODA for taking-off.

(uncontrolled and unlimited in the West) of the movements of capital, two bad profiled initiatives that ended up in the current Western economic drama.

From the crumbling of the Soviet Union onwards, the democratisation movement at national level gathered momentum, particularly in most of the ancient Soviet Union-Satellites. Observe that this democratisation occurred in parallel with mentioned new version of the neo-classical model (unbridled capitalism), mainly applied to microeconomics (reduction of public sector size, and liberalisation of international trade, finance and domestic labour markets). Inconsistently with the choosen economic (neoclassical) model, most Western governments (including conservative ones) continued applying cheap money policies[84] and reductions of taxes, thus increasing deficits while at the same time narrowing the margin for future anti-cyclical action by the public sector.

With the disintegration of the Soviet Union in 1991, the world apparently became uni-polar in economic and political terms. This was a new situation seemingly favourable for Western leadership but negative from the perspective of the necessary development of democratic global governance, the sole system capable of providing the global needs with legitimacy and efficiency, as desired by the global society.

In those days, many people still thought that the US could act as the sole leader and arbiter in all economic and political matters and conflicts. Irrespective of the non-desirability of this unipolar approach—remember that optimum in economics and politics may only be approached when power is distributed and negotiations are necessary—apparent US hegemony was just a transitory mirage, as it has recently been proven in the aftermath of the Afghanistan and Iraq invasions,[85] and also by the fast decelerating GDP growth figures of the US in the last decade (2000-2011).

---

84. Discredit of Keynesianism was to a great extent induced by reckless Keynesian politicians who, progressively indebting their countries to the extreme (instead of resorting to unpopular additional taxation), forced the resumption of the inflation in the late 1960s and early 1970s. These increases of prices, later multiplied by the first oil crisis of the 1970s, were initially accommodated by central banks.

85. Although the US has enormous and high-tech weaponry piles, the human factor of its army is clearly insufficient and overstretched for its purported role of policeman of the world; this is a job that could have not been done without the cooperation of the rest of the Western international community. Indeed, mentioned overstretching has become patent in the fight against 'international terrorism', when invading some predefined 'rogue states' (cases of Afghanistan and Iraq).

In the decade of the 1990s, some observers thought that the former huge military expenditures, carried out by the main contenders in times of the Cold War, particularly by the US,[86] would be diverted towards more human endeavours, as f.i. towards a significant increase in development funding. On the contrary, but in consistency with the lack of political competition following the disappearance of the Soviet Union, the 1990s witnessed a decline in ODA in real terms and in GDP terms of donors, while the West also reduced its military expenditures in GDP terms.

However, in the first years of the 21st century, the US (and others) increased their military efforts in GDP terms, mainly as a consequence of their declared war against 'international terrorism.'[87]

Consequences of Implemented Globalisation: Changes in Global Income Distribution and ODA

The working of the neo-classical model, with its free trade, its flexibility in prices of goods and services and its free mobility of all factors—labour included—'should' in theory and in the long run automatically equalise the per capita GDP of different countries and regions of the world.[88] As a result, any initial difference in prices of factors, wages and interest rates should

---

86. In 1998, the Brookings Institution published the most comprehensive independent estimate on the US military spending in the previous 60 years. According to its figures, the US had spent along mentioned period more then $18 trillion, of which nearly a third in nuclear weapons. Military expenditure was by far the largest simple expenditure of the Federal Government for the previous 60 years; by comparison, the nation had spent in this period $8 trillion in social security. Money spent in nuclear weapons alone far exceeded the combined total spending in education, law enforcement, agriculture, natural resources, environment, sciences, space and technology, job training, employment and regional development. Vide Parker (2006). According to figures of 2010 of the World Bank, the annual US military expenditure amounts today to 4.8 per cent of its GDP, this representing 55 per cent of the total military expenditure of the World; really, a more than exaggerated figure to 'defend' a population (that of the US) smaller than 5 per cent of the total population of the world.

87. As devised, this war against terrorism—with frontal attacks against formal states— was not easy to be won, as we mentioned many years ago in our book *Responsible Global Governance* (2004: 19). Although with a certain delay, the British Prime Minister also confirmed our views. Vide Eaglesman (2006: 4).

88. The degree of convergence of per capita GDP would be seriously conditioned, among other things, by the initial distribution of the available assets (land, capital, etc.) among the different countries, and among the different groups of citizens in every country.

in time become smaller, thus generating a progressive convergence in the standard of living of all citizens in the world. Provided that these equal (or not very different) standards of living were accepted by societies, mentioned process of unconditional economic convergence[89] should induce political and social stability at global scale, thus hugely degrading the economic significance of nationalism.

However, the real economic world has until now hardly adjusted to mentioned neo-classical ideas. In this regard, one should not forget that some natural barriers to trade and movements of factors exist, thus averting or delaying convergence. One of these barriers refers to the so-called transactional costs. In this case, the larger the invested resources in settling contracts are, the lesser will be the profits coming from interchange. As a consequence, an increase in the facilitation of contracting will favour the mobility of goods, services and factors, with gains for all players.

Another natural barrier to trade is the existence of transport and communication costs. These costs introduce an additional limitation in the working of the principle of the comparative advantage, thus negatively affecting those countries that are far from the gravity centre of the world trade, or relatively disconnected.

Consistently, the cheaper and the quicker are the modes of communication and transport,[90] the more perceivable will be the comparative advantage of the different countries, and all the more international trade will be promoted, thus increasing the total gains coming from trade.

Although natural barriers to trade and movements of factors, including labour, have always existed, it is clear that the unitary transactional,

---

89. There are at least three possible scenarios for the evolution of living standards throughout the world: unconditional convergence, conditional convergence or no convergence at all. Following Abel and Bernanke, "by unconditional convergence we mean that the poor countries will eventually catch up the rich countries so that individual living standards around the world become more or less the same... (In this regard, we have to say that) the neoclassical model predicts unconditional convergence (only) under certain special conditions" (2001: 28).

90. Costs of transports dramatically fell in the 19th century when railways and steam boats became common. In the 20th century the development of transports by road, and the introduction of containers, also additionally reduced the costs of transports in a relevant way. The reduction of the information costs along the second half of the 20th century (ICT revolution) has also been spectacular.

transport and communications costs have experienced a monotonous decrease along the last 150 years, and amazingly in the last 25 years with the ITC revolution, and this while in the last half a century, artificial barriers to trade have progressively, although asymmetrically, been abated in successive GATT-WTO negotiations.

Logically, if this joint progressive abatement of natural and artificial barriers had worked properly, including obstacles to labour movements, it would have made the functioning of the neo-classical corollaries in the international field easier and facilitated the working of unconditional convergence.

Evolution of Global Income Distribution and Economic Convergence

However, as measured by Maddison (Table 2.3)—based on per capita income disparity analysis among continental regions—with the exception of the 'golden age of capitalism' (period 1950-1973), real convergence has not moved according to expectations resulting from the pure neo-classical model. Firstly, in the period 1870-1913, also called the 'age of traditional liberalism,' the disparity of the per capita GDP in the world[91] far from declining almost doubled, thus widening the gap between the most prosperous group of countries (EIC group) and the poorest one (sub-Sahara Africa). This disparity became even much greater between 1913 and 1950, increasing threefold as compared to that of 1870.

In the 'golden age' period (1950-1973), when paradoxically public intervention in Western countries was more intense than before—mainly for reconstructing Europe—Keynesian policies were applied for reduction of the unemployment rates, and the welfare state was intensively promoted mainly in Europe, the world economy experienced its quickest growth rate,[92] while the degree of regional/continental disparities of per capita GDP downgraded

---

91. This disparity is measured by the quotient of the per capita GDP of the richest region of the world and that of the poorest one.

92. In the early 2000s, global GDP growth rates were also significant, although due to the fact that the applied model was one tilted towards unbridled markets, the working of the economy, prone to speculation and overheating, finally provoked a severe financial crisis which accelerated the already unpleasant economic trends unfavourable to the West.

from 15:1 to 13:1.[93] Conversely, years later, in the first stage of the 'neo-liberal era' (1973-1998) which contains a significant part of the recent period of additional impulse towards 'globalisation', the global disparity of per capita GDPs mounted—according to Maddison—to a figure of 19:1.

Now then, contrary to deductions based on former figures and methodology of Maddison and according to 2012 figures of the WB, disparity has significantly dwindled in the last two decades (1990-2010), due to the fast growth of Asia and the rest of low- and middle-income countries. Certainly, following the WB figures, in the last 20 years (1990-2010), the growth rate of the developing world—the low- and middle-income countries—has shot up, particularly in 2000-2010, thus introducing an average factor of convergence among regions at global level [f.i. the annual average growth rate in sub-Saharan Africa in 2000-2010, the poorest region of the world, was significantly higher (5.0%) than the average of high-income countries (1.8%)]. This however does not warranty that convergence has occurred[94] in all individual countries of every developing region, or within countries.

This relative prosperity of emerging and developing countries in the last two decades does not mean either that the neo-classical model has worked in a satisfactory way. And this because the aggregated macro results—favourable to developing regions—have been due to a twisted liberalisation of some markets (pro-capital) while forgetting others (labour).[95] Within nations, be developed or developing, neo-liberal capitalism—as implemented

---

93. After gaining independence, relative increase of public expenditure in infrastructures and setting up of public industries were strategies adopted by many developing countries. These initiatives, jointly with a generalised implementation of 'import substitution policies'—directed to encourage domestic private industrialisation—provisionally pushed activity up in many developing countries.

94. In relation with mentioned aggregated convergence and its defective contents, we could refer to a report of the United Nations Conference on Trade and Development (UNCTAD) (2006), quoted in Le Monde (2006). In this report it was said: "the 50 poorest countries of the world will not develop if they do not create—or if others do not help to create—production and employment capacities." Indeed, the strong growth (5.9%) experienced by LDC in 2004, after decades of semi-stagnation, has been based on exports of raw materials and increased agricultural production; a growth that has not created employment. Vide Le Monde (2006: 9).

95. Apart from other economic costs and delayed adjustment, we have to mention that, at a global level, forbidding the international movements of people has partially resulted in a growing (criminal) problem of trafficking in human beings. Note that along the borders of the West, millions of people are trapped and adrift while many people daily lose their lives on trying to enter the West, just for gaining an assumed better life.

in the period 1980-2007—has mainly produced increased unevenness, which has reversed former trend (1950-1973) favourable to social mobility. Note that social immobility is economically very inefficient because of its huge waste of human capital, due to exclusion from competition to many players positioned in lower strata of society.

This leads to the conclusion that, although we should not get rid of the neo-classical economic model for masterminding certain policies, we should remove the huge dysfunction and inefficiencies of current interpretation of neo-classicism—extremely biased against public sector actions and prone to marginalising the poor—while introducing a sustainable welfare state, as a more rational and comprehensive approach to capitalism, giving priority for supporting economic convergence among nations and supporting growing social mobility within all countries.

Table 2.3

Per Capita GDP and Interregional Differences, 1870-1998

(US dollars of 1990)

	1870	1913	1950	1973	1998
Western Europe	1,974	3,473	4,594	11,543	17,921
EIC group	2,431	5,257	9,288	16,172	26,146
Japan	737	1,387	1,926	1,439	20,413
Asia (ex-Japan)	543	640	635	1,231	2,936
Latin America	698	1,511	2,554	4,531	5,795
Sov.Un. and Sat.	919	1,501	2,601	5,729	4,354
Africa	444	585	852	1,365	1,368
World	867	1,510	2,114	4,104	5,709
Disparity	5:1	9:1	15:1	13:1	19:1

Source: Maddison (2001).

Finally, if the recent (1990-2010) aggregated trend towards 'per capita income convergence' continues (favourable to poor countries), former trend towards increasing disparity (favourable to the rich) deducible from Maddison figures (1973-1998) would have changed its direction, thus reducing the intensity of the problem of disparity. This does not mean that in the current world of full and live information, the huge amount of marginalised people should just wait for better days to come. It is our view that in the current context of high economic unevenness and slow or moderate correction, political situation will not be sustainable in the mid-long run, and the urgent and necessary setting up of democratic global governance will continue being unavoidable, for reaching (physical and political) sustainability in the world.

In brief, globally evaluating the 'convergence process', as it has occurred in the last two decades, we have to underline that, if international movements of people are not free, those of capital are asymmetric, exports of agricultural products from developing countries have not free access in the West, and poorer countries of the world have larger growth rates of population than the richer ones, unconditional convergence will not be reached, although in the last two decades the problem has resulted partially attenuated.

The West and its Relation to Developing Countries: Trade and ODA

For decades (from 1950 till today), Western countries, including the European ones, have not been capable of organising a decent financial plan to solve in a reasonable period of time (2 or 3 decades) the economic problems—including the building up of an incipient social security—of the poorest developing countries, mostly former colonies.

Even more, for four decades—1950-1990—Western countries did not significantly open the agriculture and services markets in which developing countries had a comparative advantage. In the mentioned period, only the manufacturing sectors of developed countries were open to imports, but at that time, developing countries were not competitive in these sectors. However this lack of competitiveness of industry in developing countries started changing when in the 1990s the capital movements were liberalised, which enabled a progressive industrial shift to Asia and Eastern Europe. The combination of low local salaries with transferred Western technology gave a new impulse to the industrial production and exports in Asia (mainly in China, Korea, Taiwan, Indonesia, Malaysia, etc.) and also in Eastern Europe.

As the Asian industrial expansion moved forward, its need for raw materials, mainly coming from Latin America, Russia and Africa, also stimulated growth in the latter countries and regions. To facilitate the import of raw materials from LDCs, China, Korea, Taiwan, Turkey, and other countries started a policy of development financing (official foreign aid), materialised in modern infrastructure and human development.

Along the last two decades, exports of emergent Asia were directed not only to the West but also to neighbouring Asian countries, and progressively to other continents. As a result of former phenomena, one has to recognise that in the last two decades, developing and emerging countries have performed (and also in exports) much better than the high-income countries in GDP terms. Precisely, this combination of the special performance of Asia and the progressive lack of competitiveness of the West is what has produced a new trend towards economic convergence among the big regions of the world.

Although this is a positive development, totally unexpected in the 1980s and growingly focused on South-South cooperation, one should insist that the observed convergence is based on 'aggregated' differentiated performance in GDP and exports of sub-continental regions. In other words, although in emerging countries middle classes have appeared or gained ground, the accelerated growth experienced in the last two decades have also left behind poor individual countries (LDC) and/or pockets of poverty in many of the new developing regions.

Entering now in comments on ODA, we have to say that, for decades the US has used its scant proportional aid (0.15-0.20% in GDP terms) mainly for supporting geopolitics.[96] Europe, more prone to financially support LDC, from the 1980s onwards also renounced to make a sufficient financial effort for the promotion of growth in LDC. In the 1990s, the West being more confident in trade and FDI than in foreign aid (ODA) started a reduction in their budgets for financial cooperation while, at the same time, polluting the figures of ODA with military expenditures and payments for reconstruction of former satellites of the Soviet Union, and later by paying the bills for bringing democracy by armed interventions in Afghanistan and Iraq. This unenthusiastic 'new development cooperation policy' of the West gave the opportunity to a new group of donors, not belonging to OECD (China, Taiwan, Korea, Malaysia, Saudi Arabia, Qatar, etc.) to enter in the game with traditional means and ends, which significantly favoured the

---

96. In this period, the US was the leading 'donor' in absolute terms, although very modest in GDP terms. Note additionally that the US donations were mainly geopolitical and just incidentally conected with poverty alleviation. Perhaps all this happened because the US, despite having implemented the Marshall Plan after the Second World War, did not trust 'international public transfers' of funds to poor countries, as an effective way for enhancing development and avoiding future international political problems.

access of the mentioned 'new group of donors' to strategic natural resources in LDC.

However, despite the growing share of foreign aid of the new breed of donors (today almost 30% of global ODA), their influence in the existing multilateral ODA institutions continues being insignificant. This is a typical defect of the Bretton Woods institutions, which continue refusing to accept the consequences of the recent economic mutations in GDP and trade growth rates, thus artificially disconnecting the current rapid change of the economic weight of nations with their participation in multilateral policy and decision making and this with independence of the structure of population, in which the West is in severe minority (16% of the total).

No wonder that the mainstream policy of the WB and IMF continues synchronising with the so-called Washington Consensus policy. Even more, it has become visible that in the structure of its main annual reports, new developments have not been informed, and others—unfavourable for rich countries—have been omitted, disguised or blurred. This once again brings us to the conclusion that the UN has to be democratised, as well as the Bretton Woods Institutions and other UN agencies.

Trade of Goods and Services and the Movements of Capital during the Period 1950-2010

The above-mentioned higher but geographically diverse GDP growth rates at a world scale in the period 1950-2010 were mainly due to three important developments: first the reconstruction (up to the 1960s) of war-torn European countries and Japan; second, the increase of public investment (up to the 1970s) in many new independent countries; and third, from 1980s onwards, the significant upwards impulses of GDP registered in East, South-East and South Asia. These higher GDP growth rates were also founded on the registered advances in the productivity of labour, induced by the application of more productive capital goods to human efforts. As a complement, mutual commercial and financial relations among the different regions of the world experienced—through GATT and WTO—a sharp increase, thus giving an additional impulse to the process.

Specifically, the growth rate of trade in raw materials by far surpassed that of the GDP, and as an average, the quotient between total exports and

GDP at a world scale moved from 5.5 per cent in 1950 to 17.2 per cent in 1998 and to 24.3 per cent in 2010. Founded in new technologies, transport and communications also experienced an accelerated development, which enabled cheaper transports and fast spread of knowledge and information concerning markets, thus increasing the opportunities for interchange.

The international flows of capital also increased significantly, particularly in the last two decades. Although the bulk of these flows were concentrated in the developed world, capital also flowed to developing countries of Asia, Latin America and (less to) Africa. As a consequence, the gross value of accumulated foreign capital in developing countries increased from 4 per cent of their GDP in 1950 to 21.7 per cent in 1998,[97] and possibly up to 30-35 per cent in 2007.

Apart from successive multilateral negotiations within the GATT, progressive liberalisation of international movements of capital, which accelerated in the past 1990s, triggered a process of de-segmentation of former narrow financial markets of nations. Although in principle mentioned accelaration could have improved the efficiency of the international use of capital, ultimately—due to the lack of official controls by a global authority—it has resulted in exaggerated quantities, mainly those with origin in the West, while in some cases indulging in pure speculative behaviour, totally detached from the needs of the real economy.

Note also, and this has to be underlined, that the long-term flows of private funds from the developed world to the developing countries (basically FDI) were mainly directed towards a limited group, namely to those endowed with enough human and non-human capital (strategic raw materials, infrastructure, educated population, etc.) in order to generate non-risky and short-term capital gains.

Alternatively, in the first decades of the Cold War, and for political reasons, some developing countries (South Korea, Taiwan, etc.) received significant amounts of public foreign funds (ODA), mainly in order to strengthen walls between the communist world and the West. Many other developing countries that were not selected for any of the former (economic or political) reasons were left to their own financial possibilities, which

---

97. These are figures of Maddison (2001).

meant leaving their growth rates far from those of catching up, that is to say, to their own survival.

In recent decades, China has been the most successful and remarkable developing country in initiating ultra-rapid convergence. In 1978, it started a sustained process of economic reforms and development, being the latter mainly pushed by very high domestic investment rates, basically financed through domestic savings, but also by the Chinese diaspora and other foreign investors. Note that although in the last decade (2000s) this country has additionally received FDI, reaching figures up to 3.5-4.5 per cent in GDP terms, these capital receptions have often become more relevant by their annexed technologies than by the relative importance of the figures themselves.

In the first decade of the 2000s, the Chinese mode of development became exceedingly tilted to exports, a trend that, even before 2008 (beginning of the economic crisis in the West) should have started focusing much more on internal demand, mainly in consumption (public and private). This change in aggregate demand, although already ongoing, is resulting slower than convenient, thus moderating the growth rate of the country. The distribution of personal income in China will also have to be corrected from the excesses accumulated in the last decades.[98] Note that both mentioned targets could simultaneously be fulfilled through the rapid development of a full-fletched social security system in China.

New Direction of the International Trade of Goods

Continuing with our analysis of the main economic trends in the different regions of the world, we will now consider the recent evolution (2001-2011) of the international trade of goods. But before realising this analysis, we will refer to the regional structure of the international trade of goods in 2010. All these data will enable us to have a better knowledge on trends and potentials of the involved countries and regions at mid-long term.

According to recent figures provided by the WB (in 2013), at the end of 2011, the structure of the commerce of goods had the following profiles:

---

98. Note that in China, the Gini index is higher (42.5)—reflecting more unevenness—than that of the US (40.8), vide WB (2012). This high degree in the current concentration of income in China is something that would not have made Mao Tze Tung very happy.

(1) the exports value of the high-income countries was 67 per cent of the total exports of goods and (2) the exports value of the low- and middle-income countries, that is to say the rest of the world, only reached 33 per cent of mentioned total exports, although with a rapid trend to improve its share. To this unbalanced profile, one could add other meaningful features: (3) the volume of the total exports of Asia (excluding Japan) were of the tune of 54 per cent of total exports of the developing world and (4) the total exports of China represented in 2010 around 62 per cent of total exports of Asia (excluding Japan), that is to say 10.6 per cent of the world, thus overcoming the export figures of Japan (5.1%), the US (8.6%) and Germany (around 9%).

Note additionally that, from mentioned estimated share of 33 per cent of the total exports of goods realised in 2011 by the low- and middle-income countries (with an increase of 8.1% points in the last 9 years), 21.2 per cent were exports directed towards high-income countries, while the developing countries only mutually exported 11.8 per cent, which means around one-third of their total exports.

Now then, although mentioned mutual magnitude is small, this does not imply that this magnitude cannot grow, or that it cannot grow very quickly. On the contrary, looking to trends, it seems likely that this figure will experience a fast growth rate in future,[99] the same than the share in total exports of developing countries (mutual trade plus trade directed to the industrialised world). In consistency with former statements, the share of high-income countries in total world exports seems to contain a clear trend towards fast decrease.

To be specific, all along the last 10 years (2001-2011), high-income countries have generated growing total exports at an (average) nominal rate per annum of 9.7 per cent, a figure below the world average that was 11.6 per cent. If this disparity of growing rates continues up to 2020, the share in merchandise trade of high income countries could reach approximately 57-58 per cent from current 67 per cent.

---

99. The traditional habit of developing countries—coming from times of colonialism—of exporting commodities to the developed ones, that then after are re-exported to other developing ones, is something based either in lack of convenient transport logistics or in deficient organisation within MNC. Even more this habit tends to introduce certain distortion in the interpretation of the registered figures.

Conversely, along the last 10 years (2001-2011), the exports of goods of low- and middle-income countries have moved forward in an accelerated way. Their total exports have progressed at an average growth rate of 16.4 per cent, a figure well above the world average (11.6%). If these trends and disparities result confirmed in next years, the total exports share of the low- and middle-income countries could reach in 2020 a level of the tune of around 42-43 per cent of total exports, from recent 33 per cent.

Letting aside the industrialised countries and dividing the 'developing world' in six geographical areas,[100] we may conclude that in the period 2001-2011, all developing regions registered annual (nominal) average growth rates of their total exports of goods well above the annual average growth rate (11.6%) of the world. Focusing now on the exports of low- and middle-income countries to those of high income, we have to underline that these exports grew between a minimum annual rate of 9.6 per cent in Latin America-Caribbean region and a maximum of 16.8 per cent in South Asia.[101] Concerning now growing of exports to low and middle income countries, while the West exported at an annual rate of 14.5 per cent, all developing regions performed at higher rates (22.2%), with East Asia Pacific region reaching a maximum of 25.1 per cent.

A relevant detail of the commercial figures in the first decade of 2000s (2001-2011) is that referred to the average intra-regional export growth rates per annum in the different regions of the world. In this regard, only the 'high-income economies' have experienced mutual intra-trade growth rates[102] below the total world average (7.6% *versus* 11.6%).

Conversely, the intra-regional trade was more than extraordinary in two developing regions of the world that share borders: East Asia-Pacific and South Asia. Particularly outstanding was the intra-regional growth of trade in the East Asia-Pacific region, which grew at an average annual rate more than two times the world average (21.3% *versus* 11.6%), and this while the

---

100. These regions are: Eastern Asia and Pacific, Eastern Europe and Central Asia, Latin-America-Caribbean, Middle East-North Africa, South Asia and sub-Sahara Africa.

101. Observe that the annual growth rate of these macro-regions uses to experience certain volatility as a result of the fluctuations of prices of raw materials, particularly oil, contained in their exports.

102. This intra-trade growth rate refers to the mutual trade of the high-income countries, mainly the US, EU and Japan.

intra-regional growth of commerce of goods per annum in South Asia was also much higher than the world average (18.5 *versus* 11.6%). These high growth rates of mutual trade in the last 10 years are clear indicators of the present and future trade performance of these two regions, commanded by China and India.[103]

Even more, if we consider the mutual import-export relations of these two super-dynamic neighbouring regions, we find something extraordinary. (1) That East Asia-Pacific has exported to South Asia in the period 2001-2011 at annual growing rhythms of 28.7%, while (2) South Asia has exported goods to East Asia-Pacific at an annual growth rate of 25.4 per cent. These figures—jointly with those 'intra-regional' as mentioned above—have generated along the first decade of the 21st century (2001-2011) annual gowth rate of exports within the common perimeter of these two regions, of the tune of 20-25 per cent, which in any case means more than doubling the growth rate of total world exports, 11.6 per cent.

If we turn again to the so-called 'high-income countries' we may deduce some additional clarifying profiles, although this time rather dark. First of all, we have to mention the fact that the US and Japan have exhibited, along the first decade of 2000, growth rates of their total exports (of goods) well below the world average. According to the WB, the total exports of goods of the US and Japan along the period 2001-2011 to other developed countries grew respectively at annual rates of 6.2 per cent and 4.1 per cent, well under the world average (11.6%), and this while total exports of goods of the EU to developed countries grew at an annual rate of 10.9 per cent (also, although mildly, under the world average). The behaviour of the exports of the high-income countries to developing countries has been better, but then again in most cases, under the world average. While high-income countries exported to developing countries at a growing annual rate of 14.5 per cent (Japan grew at 13.2% and the US at 10.9%), all developing regions experienced growth rates of their exports to other developing regions much more important (China at 30.3% and India at 23.6%).

As deducible from mentioned data, we do believe that Asia (excluding Japan) has entered in comparative terms in a self-sustained process of

---

103. The exports of China to the rest of its region grew along the period, at an annual rate of 26.0 per cent and those of India to its region at 19.1 per cent.

exports at high (or very high) rates of growth. The causes of this rapid gain in exports share of Asia[104] are diverse. Firstly, East Asia-Pacific and South Asia—that is to say emergent Asia—are gaining quota in internal markets of almost all 'high-income countries' due to their high competitiveness, based on the comparative low industrial and services wages. And this despite the low GDP growth rates of western countries in comparative terms— particularly in developed Europe and Japan—which have induced limited growth rates of their total imports all along the 1990s[105] and the first decade of 2000.

Note for instance that, while EU countries showed total annual import growth rates of 10.2 per cent along the period 1999-2009, the import growth rates of the EU coming from East Asia-Pacific, Eastern Europe and Central Asia, and South Asia were respectively of 18.9, 19.8 and 14.5 per cent. These growth rates of imports coming from mentioned developing regions—well above those of the average EU imports—explain themselves the difficulties for the creation, or simply for the maintenance, of industrial employment in the EU.

Almost the same could be said with respect to the US, which registered along the period 1999-2009 average annual growth rates of 6.4 per cent in total imports, while its imports from East Asia-Pacific and South Asia respectively grew at 15.2 and 8.6 per cent.

Although former export growth rates, always very favourable to developing countries, project by themselves a clear trend of fast convergence and support predictions of rapid shift in the current geographical distribution of production and international trade, there is a second argument perhaps more detrimental for the economic future of Western countries: as we have already mentioned, Asia (excluding Japan) counts as

---

104. Although after the beginning of the crisis in 2007-08, growth rates of exports of goods of China and other Asian countries have reduced its former higher values, they continue being important. Consequently, exports of Asia may continue growing in relative terms, as compared with total world exports of goods.

105 Average annual growth rates of total imports of the US and Japan along the last 10 years (1999-2009) were respectively 8.3 and 6.4 per cent, while growth rates of the total exports of US and Japan in the period were far under the world average. Note that these figures of imports and exports also display clear unbalances, which is an indicator of the lack of competitiveness of the economies of the US and Japan along the analysed period (1999-2009).

a whole with an enormous potential for rapid growth during decades, given the low level of its development and the huge absolute (and relative) figures of people attached to agriculture with nil or very low marginal productivity, particularly in China and India, the two giant countries of the continent.[106]

Summarising, the two main factors supporting mentioned automatic trend to increase the international trade share of these two Asian regions are: (1) the low capacity of competition in the US, Japan and the EU, which is inducing rapid growing exports from Asia to mentioned industrialised countries or territories, and (2) the huge and expectedly long lasting GDP growth rates of these two Asian regions, which will continue inducing rapid growth of mutual imports-exports in these two neighbouring macro-regions. Of course, these high rates of growth of exports and GDP of Asia will in future reduce their intensity, but for long they will be comparatively high.

Note additionally that forecasted higher GDP growth rates of the two involved regions, led by China and India, will *ceteris paribus* induce significant higher growth rates of their total imports. Notwithstanding that, given the current trend of the intra-regional trade growth of the two mentioned regions, their mutual growing commercial cooperation and the lower competitiveness of the West[107] in these two regions, Western countries will have serious difficulties to keep in future their current exports share in the Asian markets, this playing in benefit of mutual Asian imports-exports.

Note finally that, conversely to what is remarked by some Western economists, the expected high GDP growth rate of the Asian regions and their rapid growth in mutual trade in the first half of the 21st century will not significantly profit the West. Consequently, to the extent that the Westerners do not adjust (mainly through reductions of their real wages and unitary costs) to this new situation, a new factor of economic conflict and political non-sustainability (increased unemployment) could emerge in consolidated democracies.

---

106. To this respect vide Rahman and Andreu (2006).

107 In particular, we have underlined that while the US exports to East Asia and Pacific, and South Asia grew in the period 1999-2009 at annual rates of 12.0 and 20.3 per cent respectively, the total growth rate of imports of these two Asian regions were higher, respectively 17.3 and 21.2 per cent. Logically these figures point out to a fall—although slow—in the exports share of the US in mentioned Asian regions.

Global Democracy Indispensable for Managing Sustainability

We have described above the recent evolution of the world economy and its trends. Specifically we have paid attention to three main developments that affect international economy and politics: (1) the rapid shift towards Asia of the economic gravity centre of the world; (2) the global economic convergence in the last two decades 1990-2010, this time favourable to developing countries, although combined with a progressive concentration of personal income and growing disparity in many countries (including developed and developing countries); and (3) the absence of freedom of labour-migration, mainly due to the different stages of accumulation of human and non-human capital, and the incomplete commercial interchange among rich and poor countries. Note that if the stages of accumulation were the same and the commercial interchanges were totally free and complete, labour migration would annually be insignificant and, consequently, not forbidden.

Against this backdrop, and in a full and live informed world, frustrating commercial negotiations in the context of the WTO,[108] lack of internal opportunities for individual progress due to insufficient private and public investment (including lack of sufficient ODA), and simultaneous and pervasive non-acceptance of legal migration, except for highly qualified professionals, have shattered hope of many poor citizens in most developing countries. Indeed, without human capital (education) and productive land, with wobbly financial and health systems, and with bad infrastructures which hinder exports, poor citizens in many developing countries have found just one way for escaping their destiny[109]: illegal migration.

As an alternative to frustrating underdevelopment, high economic gap (in per capita income terms) and induced illegal migrations, we suggested

---

108. Frustrating negotiations refer to the denied access of poor countries to certain agricultural and services markets in the rich world. Note that against the rationale of the market economy, which defends the principle of 'comparative advantage,' the developed-industrialised countries have for long rejected the access of developing countries to certain local (agrarian and agro-industrial) markets, and this to protect own (Western) workers and entrepreneurs in these sectors from external competition.

109. Certainly, the destiny of the poor is not "written in the stars"—as Shakespeare could have suggested—but by parliaments and governments of powerful countries, (apparently) in their own interest.

some years ago[110] the convenience of implementing a win-win solution founded simultaneously on the opening up to trade in agricultural goods[111] and services by the West, and a the significant increase and reorganisation of the ODA fully administrated through the UN Institution for Cooperation (UNICO) by a new democratic UN.

But unfortunately, one cannot expect too much from the individual solidarity of rich countries: they do not want either to increase the ODA up to the necessary level for generalised taking-off of poorest LDC, or to give them access to western agricultural and services markets, or simply to accept them as immigrants. Indeed, rich countries—although formerly making propaganda on their contribution in foreign aid to the poorest countries (LDC), mainly for internal political consumption—are today silently halving their contributions to development financing while accentuating their restrictive immigration policies.

Nevertheless, we do believe that in a global, live and full informed context, ignoring all the above-mentioned three ways out from poverty will not be successful. The consequences of the accumulated historical problems of 'uneven development,' that rich countries do not want, or cannot individually solve,[112] will have to be re-arranged by a new multilateral institution with full powers on financing and provision of global public goods and on the intermediate economic targets (financial

---

110. Vide Rahman and Andreu (2004). Note that our suggestion of increasing the annual ODA up to a level equivalent to the 1 per cent of the global GDP—over at least one generation—to place most poor LDC in their way to sustained growth is not new. It was first proposed, in a different way but with identical capacity in relative financial terms, around four decades ago by Jan Tinbergen, the first Nobel Prize winner in Economics. We recall that in Responsible Global Governance we proposed the creation of UNICO—an agency of the new democratic UN, for reorganising and administrating multilateral ODA—and that this agency should be financed by basically using all over the world a recharge on the Inheritance Taxation, which—although at times not recognised—is always a windfall for heirs.

111. In particular, the tariff barriers for imports of processed food in developed countries are unreasonably high.

112. Note that Western countries behave as free riders in relation to the financing of the required faster development of LDC (really an intermediate target for deactivating violence and achieving peace and human security, the main final global public good).

cooperation) indispensable to reach mentioned public goods.[113] Note that this rearrangement will also favour the human security in richer countries.

As we will suggest below, our proposal of setting up a new democratic UN will automatically imply the creation of new UN-Agencies: UNICO, Global Economic Regulations Agency (GERA) and a World Environment Organisation (WEO), and the re-embodiment or the reshuffling of other existing multilateral institutions (WTO, IMF, etc.).

Finally, and referring to the Bretton Woods institutions, it is not sustainable that, in the 21st century, entities that have to deliver global public goods (as global economic and monetary stability), with significant spillover effects on all nations, are commanded by a selective group of countries that, as the wealthiest founders of the institutions in 1944, received voting quotas in proportion to their initial capital contributions. But note that in the past 68 years, the Bretton Woods institutions have hugely increased their turnover and operations, mainly by resorting to international financial markets, while the voting quotas—favouring founders—have remained practically frozen. Consequently, with their relative small initial and complementary contributions, the pioneers continue controlling decision-making of the IMF and WB, even though emerging countries have repeatedly requested (without success) more votes in exchange for voluntary increased contributions. No wonder that BRIC countries in a recent meeting agreed on the creation of a parallel BRIC development bank.

This freezing of the voting structure of the Bretton Wood Institutions is similarly wrong to what occurred in history when in European countries some of the richest citizens administered the central banks of their nations,[114] because they were the main initial economic contributors (owners). This special position of private owners gave them the opportunity

---

113. Mentioned multilateral institution—a democratic UN—would also cooperate, through a specialised agency, for the correction of global externalities, mainly in relation to sustainable provision of natural resources.

114. The reader should remember that in the 19th century and part of the 20th, most of the embryos of central banks in Europe were private (banks). Arrival to national democracy, or simply growth and rationalisation of these entities, changed them into public and purportedly neutral institutions.

to profit from the creation and emission of bank notes, and this while mentioned rich citizens had only marginally contributed in absolute terms, in comparison to the volume of funds managed by the central banks.

3 | Decline in the West

Consequences of the Industrial Shift towards Asia and Unbridled Capitalism

After economically growing at rates significantly lower than those of Asia (ex-Japan) in the period 1973-2007, the West is currently (2008-2013) progressing at rhythms even much smaller than before. This comparative loss of speed of the West is occurring not only due to the harsher impact of the current business cycle in the more industrialised Western countries, provoked by financial excesses, but also following the liberalisation of capital transfers and Western industrial dislocation towards Asia.

Entering into details, we will discuss the effects of Western industrial dislocation towards Asia, and the fast economic and exports growth of this continent, mainly with reference to China and (less to) India. We will also focus on the recent economic adversities that have overwhelmed Western countries, due to their own magnum financial mistakes and the slow and arguable implemented corrections. These financial mistakes on the one hand originated from the pro-cyclical administration of the monetary supply by the Federal Reserve System (Fed) and European Central Bank (ECB) and on the other by the catastrophic concentration of credit or funding (directly or indirectly) either in economic sectors (housing, banking abroad, etc.) or in foreign sovereign debt. To make things worse, all this happened against the background of a seriously defective Euro-system, in which the ECB administrates the single currency of the Eurozone, in absence of a common controller of Eurozone public finances, and a banking union for the supervision of Eurozone banking.

Note that the Eurozone is an economic and monetary area whose eventual failure—or slow political reshuffling—may produce long lasting economic lethargy mainly in the West, but it may also significantly affect developing and emergent countries. Certainly, the Eurozone and the

European Union (EU)-28, due to its current defective organisation and the required 'unanimity rule' among EU members for solving relevant common problems, have today become an almost unsolvable conundrum. However, this problem, being mainly political, could in our view be solved in some few years, via setting up of a selective federation with a limited agenda. Alternatively, putting in common the public finance administration of all (or of the most important) member countries of the Eurozone, and creating a common system for banking control, would be just a pretended solution because the current problems of governance of the EU and the Eurozone (mainly unanimity) would be transferred—practically intact—to the new institutions.

After the financial catastrophe induced on the one hand by the lack of control of the international movements of capital,[1] and on the other by the temporal abandonment of prudent rules on monetary growth, as well as prudent rules on banking administration introduced in 1933 (first by the Glass & Steagall Act in the US and later spread to the rest of the West), the indecisiveness of the Eurozone members in solving domestic and collective issues is blocking the available ways out from the current economic drama in the West. Note in this regard, the gross domestic product (GDP) of the Eurozone ranks high at a world scale with 19.2 per cent of the world GDP, thus playing a significant role in the evolution of the global economy including economic downturns.

This indecisiveness combined with the ill designed statutes of the ECB is creating a huge negative externality for the rest of EU-28 and the world as a whole. Indeed the Eurozone has an enormous responsibility. Consequently its defective single currency system has to be corrected as soon as possible, because if sustained, it could also affect democracy in Europe, due to systematic failing of successive elected governments.

Nevertheless, we have to emphasise and underline that, even if the EU single currency organisation were severely restructured and the current

---

1. These controls have not been exercised in the West since the early 1990s, time in which those movements started working in a multiplied way due to the lack of a world authority on these matters. Certainly, this is an authority that in our view will have to be created under the umbrella of a democratic UN, as we have proposed in several places. Note that in the last days of 2012, the International Monetary Fund (IMF), against decades of traditional inflexible pro-market rule, has suggested the eventual convenience of establishing controls on speculative capital movements.

cyclical Western problems solved—and all this may take several years—the long-term problems of adjusting the Western economies to the industrial shift towards Asia will not have ended.

The Birth of the Two Asian Giants

To understand the current trend of the industrial shift to Asia, we need to briefly depict the evolution of the main Asian emergent countries in the second half of the 20th century and first decade of the 21st century.

At the edge of 1950, the two largest countries of Asia[2]—China and India—entered or re-entered into the international political scene. After the creation of a Popular Republic in 1949 as a consequence of the victory of the communist revolutionaries over the Nationalists[3] who flew to Taiwan, Continental China experienced a radical political change towards socialism.

Since then, and during the entire Maoist age (1949-1978),[4] the exerted control of the Chinese authorities was much more intense than that exercised in times of the last Emperor and the Kuomintang (KMT). Strict economic and political controls and instructions coming from the Communist Party of China (CPC) reached all the layers of the Republic, including public firms, labour world, agricultural activity and even familiar life (family planning).

After the progressive elimination at all levels of private property rights, the Chinese economy became a copycat of the Soviet model, although more tilted to agriculture and rural areas. Subsequent to a shameful century of

---

2. We are here excluding the Central Asian territories of the Russian Federation.

3. When the empire collapsed in 1911, one nationalist party, named Kuomintang (KMT) succeeded the last Emperor in the governance of the new 'Republic of China.' After the death of the first President of the Republic in 1916, Mr. Yuan Shikai, a civil war started. Years later, after the creation in 1921 of the CCP, and the rupture of Chiang-Kai-Chek (KMT) with the communists in 1927, the latter—after the so-called Long March—gained the control of the North of the country. When in 1937 the Japanese started occupying China, both armies (nationalist and communist) fought against the common enemy, but when the Japanese withdrew in 1945, the civil war re-started lasting till 1949, year in which the nationalists (KMT) finally escaped to Taiwan.

4. Although Mao Tze Dong died in 1976, the political change, mainly tilted towards economic reforms, and headed by the then Prime Minister Den Xiao Pin, did not start till 1978.

partial occupation and surrendering[5] to foreign powers, and in order to fully defend own sovereignty, the new Chinese regime decided to economically castle the country, cutting off most links with the rest of the world economy. This decision was made in parallel with the commercial embargo imposed by the US and allies against the People's Republic of China, due to its intervention in the Korea war (1950-1953).

Mentioned commercial embargo lasted up to the 1970s.[6] In this decade, after the death of Chairman Mao and although preserving the communist essentials—mainly a socialist unique party system and the public property of land and urban soil—a new style of economic policy more in accordance to mainstream (Western) economics was initiated in China. As a result, a new age of progressive economic liberalisation and opening to trade and foreign capital imports was born.

Almost simultaneously (in 1947), led by the main promoters of the nation (Gandhi and Nehru), neighbouring India gained its independence from Britain,[7] while suffering a traumatic Partition with the segregation of Pakistan.[8] This Partition would condition the entire life of the two new

---

5. Let us remember that China was defeated by the UK in the First Opium War of 1839-1942, which resulted in the cession of Hong-Kong (Treaty of Nanking). This approach was followed by other treaties subsequent to the war of 1894-95 against Japan—a war fought for the sovereignty of Korea—which drove to the cession of Chinese territories to Russia, and the creation of a number of foreign enclaves along the Chinese coast in favour of Germany, Britain and France. These foreign enclaves, handed over to Western governments as war compensations, generated a great 'national humiliation' in China. Note that the first Opium War was launched by the UK to support British traders in its sales of opium to China, 'legally grown' in other sides of the Empire and exported to China, where the drug produced massive victims. When imports and consumption of opium were officially forbidden in China to fight against drug traders, the British attacked and ravaged the Chinese Coast, and forced the Treaty of Nanking (1842).

6. Note that some countries (officially or unofficially) lifted the embargo just at the end of the Korea War. Observe additionally that after the visit of the US President Nixon to China in 1971, the previous fiction whereby the Chinese nation was represented in all international institutions (including the UN) by the regime (of the KMT) installed in Taiwan was progressively overturned.

7. In June 1947, the UK Parliament established a process for the Independence of India that should have lasted around one year. But due to the sudden and growing violence unleashed between Hindus and Muslims, the British decided a rushed abandonment of the colony. As a consequence, the Indian authorities proclaimed the Independence of India on 15th August, 1947.

8. Pakistan was then divided in two provinces, Western Pakistan (current Pakistan) and Eastern Pakistan. In 1971, after an independence war against Western Pakistan, former Eastern Pakistan—today Bangladesh—was born.

states till our days, with the persistence of the Kashmir conflict and the recurrent communal Muslim-Hindu violence[9] in India.

Democratic from the very beginning and much more decentralised than China in economic decision-making, the Republic of India also opted for a planned economy, mainly for the development of a heavy industry, till then almost inexistent due to the restrictive colonial-industrial policy of the British. And India did it in a framework of autarky concerning its external relations. Note that in the mid late-1950s, the Import Substitution (IS) policy for the promotion of domestic industries—behind high custom barriers—gained ground in the developing world as a strategy for quickly attaining higher levels of per capita income. In fact, India not only adopted this IS strategy as own but overdid it, becoming one of the most protective and autarkic states of the then 'free' world.

In the internal economy, most of the Indian 'formal' economic activities[10] had to be authorised[11] and submitted to different powers, those of the federal government and states, many a times under control of different political parties. This trait, a derivative of the constitutional distribution of power,[12] based on the federal organisation of India, has often proven to be dysfunctional and little prone to economic change,[13] in particular when the

---

9. The last of these serious wrangling happened in Gujarat, in 2002, when around 2,000 Muslims were killed by Hindus, as revenge on Muslims, who allegedly had carried out a former attempt against a train of pilgrim-Hindus that came from the sacred city of Ayhodya. The pogrom in Gujarat against Muslims was carried out along several days while the local police—depending on local authorities (Bharatiya Janta Party; BJP)—apparently remained indifferent.

10. These formal economic activities give today employment to around 10 per cent of the Indian labour force. Note that if the Indian labour force was 472 million in 2010—figures of the World Bank (WB) (2012)—mentioned 10 per cent would only represent 47 million labourers working in the formal labour market. Most of the rest, around 425 million people, are every day confronted with their own economic destiny. Indeed, in current India, any economist may analyse *in situ* the 'advantages' and microeconomic 'peculiarities' of the neo-classical model.

11. This system of authorisation inherited from the British, was for long called the 'Raj license-permit' system.

12. In the Indian Constitution, different lists of exclusive competencies of the union and the states, and a list of 'concurrent' competencies, are accurately defined.

13. Note that India is a federal republic of 28 states plus several union territories, which are constantly and in succession calling polls to their citizens. As a result, the country as a whole is almost in permanent electoral campaign. This is a feature that, combined with the existence of many regional parties looking for coalitions in the states and/or in the centre, hampers and delays necessary consensus on relevant federal matters for economic progress. Certainly, the Indian slow decision-making case is rather similar to current one of the EU.

union government of India, seeking the unity of the internal market, tried to introduce more rationality in indirect taxation.[14]

Economic Trajectory of China and India in the Last 60 Years

Economic Underperformance of China and India during the Period 1950-1980

Letting aside the economic stagnation (in terms of per capita income) of China and India in the first half of the 20th century,[15] we have to say that for different reasons the first three decades of the political life of these two new states was not easy, while their economic performance was poor and significantly below own expectations, and this although China achieved a significant development of its industry while incurring in deep capital costs.

Concerning the average evolution of their absolute real GDP, China and India clearly underperformed in mentioned period in comparison to total Asia (ex-Japan). Specifically, while Asia (ex-Japan) grew in the period 1950-1973—the so called 'golden age of capitalism'—at an annual rate of around 5 per cent, China grew at 4.4 per cent[16] and India at an average around 3.5 per cent, the for long called 'Indian growth rate.'[17] If the real GDP of China and India underperformed, and the rates of growth of their population moved around the average of Asia (ex-Japan), which was 2.2 per cent (2.0% in China and a little higher figure in India), the per capita GDPs of these countries had necessarily to underperform.

---

14. In particular, the process of introduction of the Value Added Tax (VAT) in substitution of the Sales Tax, administered by states took too much time. After several attempts, its introduction in 2005 finally generated a quasi-single market across India.

15. The per capita income of these two countries practically did not grow in the first half of 20th century. This stagnation was caused in one of them (China) by the internal turmoil provoked by foreign incursions in its territory—lastly by the Japanese invasion—and by the constant unrest and destruction of assets and lives provoked by civil wars, the last of which finally drove communists to power in Mainland China and in the other (India) by the continuation of the exploiting strategy deployed for centuries by the British. The Indian per capita growth rate in the period 1900-1948 has been estimated by Sivasubramanian (1998), who found a figure almost nil. Vide Reddy (2000).

16. That figure of 4.4 per cent of average annual growth of China for the period 1952-1978 has been taken from Maddison (1998: 73).

17. This 'Indian growth rate' (3.5%), consistent with a contemporary per capita growth rate of around 1.3-1.5 per cent, is a well-known original expression by Prof. Krishna.

Note that while the world as a whole experienced, as an average, its maximum historical annual economic growth rate in per capita terms (2.9%),[18] China and India also underperformed. Specifically, in the analysed period 1950-1973, the per capita GDP grew in China at an average annual rate of 2.3 per cent, while in India corresponding average rate was around 1.3-1.5 per cent. Note that, letting aside the spectacular growth rates of Japan, and those of South Korea, Hong-Kong, Singapore and Taiwan— countries whose per capita GDP annually grew in these decades above 5 per cent—China and India also underperformed in per capita income growth rates in comparison to Thailand (3.6%), Malaysia (2.9%), Sri-Lanka (2.5%) and other Asian countries.

Mentioned underperformance of these two countries in the period 1950-1973 was due to several factors: (1) the internal economic instability generated in China by the experiments on land reform successively carried out, the illogic's of its forced industrialisation at time of the Great Leap Forward (1958-1963), and the political infighting unleashed in the 1960s and 1970s in the days of the so-called 'Cultural Revolution'; (2) the external political problems of India with neighboring China and Pakistan, conducive to one lost war with China and successive wars against Pakistan, plus permanent tensions and confrontations in Kashmir; (3) the somewhat voluntary economic isolation of these two countries, although for different reasons, from the international division of labour; and (4) the selected model for internal economic progress (radical socialism in China and extreme interventionism in India).

Brilliant Behaviour in Last 30 Years (1980-2010) and Current Economic Positions of China and India

The economic behaviour of China and India in the last two decades of the 20th century and first of the 21st has been very different in comparison to their respective economic performance in the period 1950-1978(1980), particularly in the first mentioned country. Certainly, after 1978 the economic policy radically changed in China: the principle of 'supremacy' of the 'collective agriculture production' was abandoned, small-sized industrial and services activities were liberalised in a phased way (performing from then onwards better than public-state firms), and the economy progressively

---

18. Vide Maddison (2001: 129).

opened to external interchanges of goods and services, and to foreign direct investments (FDI).

This new economic orientation of the Chinese economy, born in 1978, was followed neither by the Soviet Union, whose economy was degrading in those days, nor by India which, instead of embracing in the 1980s a new style of economic policy 'outward oriented,' just limited itself to some inward oriented 'corrections,' giving more chance to the national corporate private sector in industrial development,[19] while accelerating public expenditure.[20] This combination of policies in India generated in the 1980s, along higher average annual GDP growth rates (5.7%), untenable inflation and public and external deficits. Finally, in 1991, to amend its extremely difficult situation concerning available foreign-currency reserves, India had no other remedy than to start its first period of significant reforms.

As a consequence of the undertaken pro-market reforms, initiated 13 years earlier in China (1978) than in India (1991), both countries began a new stage in their economic history. Needless to say, that while the performance of India in the last three decades has been good, although less intense and more fluctuating than the Chinese, the registered new economic trend of China has simply been spectacular.

Specifically in the period 1978-2010, China, helped by a downwards trend in the growth rate of its demography[21]—which moved from an annual growth rate of 2.0 per cent in the period 1952-1978 to 0.8 per cent in the period 1990-2010[22] (and 0.6 per cent in the interval 2000-2010)—experienced an amazing annual growth rate of 8.5-9 per cent in its per capita GDP. In the meantime, India only marked a 'more modest' figure around 4.5-5 per cent in its annual per capita income rise, a comparatively

---

19. This lack of external opening in India was a 'protective' gesture towards the internal business society, after the former nationalisation by Indira Gandhi of main banks in India in 1969. After losing elections in 1977 and recovering power in 1980, Indira tried to present to the country a new image, which moved from Indian-Nerhuvian socialism to a more visible protection of national private corporations.

20. A common argument used to explain the rapid but unsustainable GDP growth rate of India in the 1980s, mainly based on public deficit expending, was clearly expressed by Ahluwalia (2002) and also by Srinivasan and Tendulkar (2003).

21. In China, from 1972 onwards the 'indirect' official pressure on families for reducing the family size was more than significant.

22. To this respect, vide corresponding figures of Maddison (1998: 66) and those of WB (2012).

compressed rate partially coming from the maintenance of a high population growth rate, of around 1.8 per cent[23] as an average in the last 30 years.

Talking about total performance, measured by the progress of the GDPs of China and India, one may deduce that in the above-considered period of three decades, the Chinese GDP grew annually at around 10.5 per cent, while that of India was around 6.6 per cent. Note however that while the labour productivity in China grew around 6 per cent in the period 1978-1995, the 'total factors productivity' (TFP) only grew at 2.5-3.5 per cent in that period,[24] which means that in the initial years of economic progress, the productivity growth of the invested capital was low. Nevertheless, the variables that may have affected more significantly the registered fast speed of growth in China are: the significant and controlled transfers of labour from agriculture to industry and services and, simultaneously, from state-owned public firms to the local public and private ones; the increase in the average level of education; and the rising share of labour force on total population, particularly induced by the embodiment of women to the labour market. Note that the average level of education and the embodiment of women to the labour market had already been encouraged in the Maoist period, giving growth advantage to China in relation to India.

The combination of their huge and growing populations; the compression or reduction of population growth, first in China and later in India; their (low) initial (in 1978-1980) per capita GDP;[25] and the two average figures of around 10.5 per cent and 6.6 per cent of GDP annual growth rates registered by China and India in the last 30 years have nowadays (2011) placed these two economies respectively in the second and third place in the GDP-PPP (purchasing power parity) world ranking (note that Indian GDP surpassed that of Japan in 2011).

Note however that the current (2011) disparities in terms of per capita GDP between China and India—to a great extent due to the earlier

---

23. According to recent forecasts, the annual population growth rate of India for the period 2010-2020 will be 1.2 per cent. Vide WB (2012: 43).

24. For entering into details on different measures of the TFP, and for different periods, vide Riedel et al. (2007: 21).

25. In the year 2012, the per capita GNI (gross national income) of China in PPP terms was around $9,060, while that of India was 3,840. Note that the per capita GNI (PPP) of the US—often taken as a base for international comparisons—reached in 2012 a figure of $50,610.

investment in human capital in China, the earlier implementation of economic reforms in China, its faster industrialisation, and its prior population compression—could significantly be bridged in future. In particular if the growth rate of the Indian population moves downwards (as it is currently happening), and if basic education is finally and effectively generalised in India, and its so-called 'second generation' economic reforms reach a finishing point.

In fact higher domestic and external savings[26] in India have in the last years enabled the achievement of greater domestic investment rates in physical (and human) resources, thus making the reduction of the current disparities between China and India possible. Note that currently the level of the potential GDP growth rate in India seems to have jumped from former 6 per cent in the 1980s and 1990s, to a figure of 7-7.5 per cent.[27]

China and India: Two Countries with Great Economic Expectations

Although we cannot ignore the average low personal income position of the Chinese and Indian citizens, who only count nowadays (2012) with limited per capita GNI[28]—$5,680 in China and $1,530 in India, both in terms of exchange rate—and related shortage in the provision of many private and public goods and services, one should not undervalue the capacities for economic progress of these two giants.

Concerning predictions on the future of these two countries, one has to move in two tiers: the economic and the political one. Specifically, the foundations of any economic prediction about the future of China and India have to rely on the theory of economic development, applicable to those developing countries that experience rapid structural changes,[29] and on the

---

26. Since 2006, a more significant volume of foreign capital has finally started arriving to India, with figures representing around 1.5 per cent in terms of the Indian GDP (FDI in 2010 was 1.4 per cent in GDP terms). Vide WB (2012).

27. Current GDP growth rate in India reached, in some years of the first 2000 decade, figures around 9 per cent.

28. These figures, corresponding to per capita GNI, measured at exchange rates, have been taken from World Bank (2013).

29. These theories are mainly based on the model of Arthur Lewis for rapid industrialisation and on the opportunities coming from backwardness, originally from Gerschenkron. Vide Todaro (2003).

conventional theory of economic growth.[30] Mentioned integral economic approach, with the help of econometric exercises, may show a trend of China to quickly gain in world shares, being these in GDP, industrial production, international trade (exports or imports) or in military expenditures. In this pure economic context, the exercise published in 2003 by Goldman Sachs[31] —whose conclusions today keep their plausibility, although in the context of a less extended period—is very illustrative.[32]

According to the conclusions of mentioned economic study, as early as 2009, a small group of four countries (China and India, plus Russia and Brazil, the so-called BRIC countries) would have reached an absolute growth of their joint production (in US$ terms) greater than that of the six more advanced countries altogether (the US, France, Germany, Italy, Japan and the UK). This meant that in 2009 the group of four would become the engine of economic growth of the world. In fact these projections, reinforced by the economic-financial crisis starting in 2007-08 in the West, changed into reality more or less in time.

As suggested by mentioned study, this catching up process of the BRICS commanded by China and India would *sine die* continue, which *ceteris paribus* would generate in 2050 a non-imagined picture in relation to the economic potentials of the analysed countries. China, the US and India, and by this order, would then be economically and politically the more powerful countries of the world. Behind them, but far away in the economic train, and consequently in the political one, would be Japan, Brazil and Russia. Finally in the last wagon, and by this order, we would find the UK, Germany, France and Italy.[33]

---

30. The modern theory of economic growth is mainly based on the neo-classical growth model and on the model of endogenous growth.

31. Vide Wilson and Purushothaman (2003).

32. Note that the authors of the Goldman Sachs exercise extrapolated the registered economic trends of China and India year by year, from 2003 up to 2050, doing the same with all the current most important countries.

33. Note that long before 2050, some of mentioned Eurozone countries plus other current EU partners may have embodied into one EU-Federation. In our opinion, it is expectable that with the attainment of a voluntary federation, this federated economy will reach significant economies of scale, reap economies of integration up to 2 per cent of its joint GDP, and significantly gather momentum. Logically, this political move will partially contradict the results of the Goldman Sachs study, and will economically (and politically) contribute to the rebalancing of the world.

Note that in economic terms, at the end of the first half of the 21st century (2050), of the six more advanced countries leading the world at the end of the golden age of capitalism (1973) (the US, France, Germany, Italy, Japan and the UK), only two, decelerating US and (today) quasi-stagnated Japan, will have remained from those who formed the old club of rich countries. Observe that only an EU (selective) Federation—if finally implemented, as proposed by us since 2002—could economically and politically rebalance the world leadership by taking third or fourth position in the ranking behind China and the US, and perhaps India.

In our view, the trend of recent economic history may mark an evolution for catching up in future not far away from the mentioned one, and mainly in the cases of China and India. These are two countries with pressing populations, mainly in the latter, with huge reserves of labour force currently stuck to agricultural activities and with nil marginal productivity—jointly around 500 million people, with a great margin for technical improvement in their physical and human capital, and with a huge capacity for generating internal savings, particularly in the case of China.[34]

Conversely to the shorter-lived success of Japan[35] in the second half of the 20th century, China and India—at the beginning of the 21st century—seem to be far away from typical positions of relative diminishing returns, suffered by Japan just three-four decades after its economic 'take off.' Indeed, China and India started their new development processes in 1978 (1980) at significant lower levels in per capita GDP terms than many of their Asian competitors, and with a delay of two-three decades. However, their current huge potentials in terms of geography, raw materials, and demography, their capacity for transferring labour from their rural areas to the industrial and service sectors, accompanied by competitive levels of education of their populations, and technological progress to some extent introduced by Western firms through their industrial dislocation towards Asia, may

---

34. Although till recently the gross savings of China in GDP terms ranged from 37-43 per cent, today (2011) this figure has jumped to 53 per cent. In 2011, the gross savings of India in GDP terms reached 31 per cent. Vide WB (2013).

35. A common argument at times heard in Western countries is that the current rapid economic progress of China may finish in some few years, as it occurred with Japan in the 1990s. Unfortunately for the defenders of this view, the arguments for supporting that scenario are not strong enough; indeed, these arguments are clearly against recent economic trends and solvent economic theory.

additionally last two and a half decades. This means that the rapid growth of China and India may protract till 2035-2040.

The Amazing Case of India

Previous comments on the brilliant long-term future (2050) of the Indian economy, placing this country side by side with China and the US, may come as a surprise for all those who, reflecting on criticism of foreign traders or investors in India, are pessimistic about future capabilities of the Indian economy.

Although acknowledging that in the last decades the way of doing business in India has not been easy, it is likely that along the next 10 years (up to 2023), many of the current problems of India will be overcome, or at least softened. We are here referring to the achievement of a real unity of market,[36] the simplification of the exasperatingly slow judicial machinery[37] —one of the slowest of the world according to some indicators—the establishment of limitations to avert wild industrial (trade-union) actions, and the reduction of complexities in mutual relations among the different Indian Administrations (federal and states), and this without forgetting the well-extended corruption in these administrations and private sector.

These corrections—together with that of the currently complicated electoral schedule, constant promoter of uncertainty[38]—are urgent and would suppose a very favourable change in the legal framework of India.

36. Till the early 2000s, Westerners have often complained about the lack of market unity in India (different indirect taxes in different states, different rates, multiple and discriminated taxation, etc.). Note however that while this unity of markets (goods and services) was sometimes bitterly demanded by the Western representations in Delhi, this unity of markets (financial ones) is today still far from being accomplished within the EU (in which there are different corporate and income taxes, different withholding capital taxes, etc.).

37. As it is well known, the slow judicial machinery of India enables that 'assumed' criminals become Members of Parliament (MPs) in successive parliaments. One decade ago, former President of India Mr. Narayanan in his last months in office (2002) made a call to political parties to not include 'assumed' criminals in the electoral lists. Unfortunately, the remains of this habit continue alive in Indian politics.

38. Observe that this uncertainty, due to constant elections at state level in India, is similar to that of the EU-28. Following the rule of 'unanimity' in decision-making, practised in the EU for relevant matters (Treaty of Lisbon, 2007), as well as in India for some federal issues, economic advance is difficult and time consuming in both the cases. The added problem of the EU is that, differently to India, the EU-28 is not a federation, but a treaty.

Finally, given the ongoing increase in domestic savings and investments, it is expectable that along the next decade, the problems of infrastructures, energy production and distribution, and education and health deficiencies of India will be corrected to a large extent, while its fast population growth rate will be substantially reduced. Indeed, these changes will steadily accelerate the rhythm of progress of the Indian economy.

The Industrial Shift to Asia and its Economic and Political Impact on the West

The rapid industrial shift towards Asia is mainly an industrial shift towards China, a country that has grown at fast speed (as an average around 10.5%) in the last 3 decades, and with a perspective of growing at a more moderate-high speed in the next 2-3 decades (7.5-8.5%). Note that China, jointly with India and other countries of East, South-East and South Asia, forms a block whose markets are expanding in such a high velocity that, besides high domestic saving rates used for financing domestic investments, they tend to siphon additional financial capital from the West.

The capital moves from the West to emergent Asia may have a double end: first to set up industrial factories behind borders for better competing in internal fast growing Asian markets and second, to gain competitive advantage (due to lower wages and unitary costs) in the production of manufactures to be sold in the West with larger margins (higher prices) and higher profits, or in developing countries with smaller margins (at lower prices) and profits.

The second aim, widely commented by media in the West, is consequently more known by non-professionals than the first one. And certainly more scaring, because when Western firms shift their industrial production to China (alone or with Chinese partners), they automatically destroy jobs in the West and create jobs in China. In addition to job losses, the displaced capital also increases Chinese (and other Asian) exports to the West, encouraged by the lower export prices. As expected, mentioned industrial dislocation is also progressively degrading the financial situation of many Western firms that did not dislocate, thus changing them into uncompetitive.

The comparative advantage of China in industrial goods has recently placed China as the main world exporter and contributed to the rapid accumulation of foreign currency reserves, making China today (2011) the main owner of US dollars and euros in the World (with total foreign reserves equivalent to around $3,254 billion).[39]

Observe additionally that the profits obtained by displaced Western firms,[40] irrespective of whether they produce for the Chinese or Western markets,[41] after being transferred to homeland, increase *ceteris paribus* the GNI of the home country but not its employment.[42]

Note that Western investments in Asia to produce for internal Asian markets or for re-exporting to the West also increase the retribution of Western capital and this while Western real wages—due to job losses induced by the shifting to the East to produce for Western countries—tend to decrease, thus concentrating Western income in favour of capital and the rich.

Concerning the future of Asia, and focusing on China's growth capacity, we have to emphasise that although its growth capacity continues being high—as we have commented in our last two books on China[43]—it will shrink in coming years, but not at the speed desired by some important Western leaders. Indeed, from the average growth rate of 10.5 per cent registered in the last 30 years, we already projected in 2006 that China's annual average GDP growth rate will fall to 7.5-8.5 per cent in next two decades (2013-2033).

Letting aside current minor Asian problem of GDP deceleration, mainly coming from the crisis in the West—particularly from EU nations with a

---

39. Vide WB (2013).

40. Normally, when Western firms go to China to produce for export, they mainly invest in the Chinese special economic zones (SEZ).

41. Note that this shift for producing for the internal markets of Asia may also destroy jobs in the West—due to the reduction of corresponding European exports to Asia—although its destruction is less direct and probable than in the alternative case, when dislocated firms produce for exporting to the US and the EU.

42. When Western firms increase the GDP at home—not GNI—they are almost necessarily creating jobs.

43. Vide Rahman and Andreu (2006) and Andreu and Rahman (2009).

lower capacity to import goods due to their degrading growth rates—Chinese authorities have recently admitted that the growth model of China has in the last two decades been too much tilted to domestic investments and exports, and clearly has to be redirected to increase domestic consumption.

In fact, Chinese authorities have started shifting the demand structure, from high exports and investments and low consumption, to higher internal consumption (public and private) and lower exports and domestic investments, which is inducing lower GDP growth rates, today and for the next decades. Indeed, China is moving towards a new productive structure more in consistency with sustainable parameters. In our view, the entire restructuring of its aggregate demand should take place within the next 3-5 years.

Taking a closer look, one has to deduce that the internal saving rate of China, at times positioned over 50 per cent in GDP terms (53% in 2011), a rate even higher than its internal investment rate (48% in 2011),[44] will have to be reduced. Although the parallel reduction of the investment rate will significantly reduce the growth rate in future, keeping in mind the rest of the picture (comparative lower costs, salaries, etc.),[45] it seems that the reduced average annual growth rate of the GDP will not go under 7.5 per cent. This means that—taking into account the expected low or very low potential growth rates in the West (around 1.8%), due to expectable long period for adjusting and lower productivity growth—China will continue, although more moderately, with its rapid catching up process.

In brief, a sustained and rapid, although more moderate, industrial growth in China and a fast expansion of the services of India are rather

---

44. This unbalance between internal saving and investment—the former larger than the latter—is a circumstance that has amazingly induced a long-term creditor position of China at a world scale.

45. In the West, the media often present a list of problems of China that 'assumedly' may force a severe reduction of its fast GDP growth rate. Frequently, the rapid growth of wages in coastal regions is quoted, but this 'rapid growth' of wages would only be consistent—on average terms—with an observable wearing out of unproductive manpower attached to agriculture in China. Indeed, an assumption contrary to current observable facts is that in China still 50 per cent of the population live in countryside.

expectable in next two decades (2013-2033)[46] and this in consistency with a minor GDP growth rate in the West. Certainly, unless the West significantly increases its share in the exports of goods and services, the GDP growth rates registered in the West in the last two decades of around 2.2 per cent will dwindle to around 1.8 per cent (and the Eurozone to around 1.4%).

We have to insist that the last steps of globalisation in relation to the liberalisation of capital movements, carried out in the first 1990s and done in an asymmetric way[47]—more hasty in time than the historical dismantling process of the trade barriers—combined with the immobility of labour, has induced adjusting problems in the West that were foreseeable in advance. Mentioned exaggeration on the liberalisation of capital movements has finally been recognised by the IMF in the last days of 2012.

Indeed, we think that this operation of investing abroad at large scale was a wrong bet in favour of increasing Western GNI, that necessarily reduced the growth rates of the GDP and employment in the West. Calculated or not, and similar to what occurred with the creation of the very imperfect Euro-system, the initiative taken in the first 1990s for fast liberalisation of the movements of capital has resulted counterproductive for workers in the Eurozone and the West. Conversely the results may have been positive for workers in developing countries, as proven by the catching up growth rates exhibited by all sub-continental developing regions of the world in the period 1990-2010.

Really, if the intention of Eurozone and other Western governments had been to promote the catching up of developing countries, 'they could

---

46. This period could last more or less in function of: (1) the time necessary for the displacement of all the non-productive people from countryside to urban areas in China (and India), which mainly depends on the absorption capacity of redundant workers in agriculture, by industry and services, and (2) the moment of arrival to positions of convergence in terms of their ratios 'wages/productivity' in the West and Asia. Note that if the process of real wages/productivity adjustment accelerates in the West, the absorption capacity of industry and services in China and other places would be smaller. Consequently the shift of labour towards local industry would take more time in China, and corresponding GDP growth rate and growth of employment in the West would be either larger than expected or less negative.

47. This asymmetry refers to the existence of almost total freedom for exporting and importing capital in western countries, while many developing counties have kept prudence in authorisations for importing capital for protecting the domestic trade, industry, agriculture or mining, and also for exporting capital.

not have done it better.' But we suspect that they did not do so on purpose: they just committed mistakes by favouring some Western entrepreneurs.

Looking into the future, we recognise the urgency for a progressive and rapid adjustment in the West, particularly in the labour and financial markets. This means that slow and long-term adjustments in mentioned markets—as currently practised by the West in these or in other fields such as climate change and development financing—should be discarded because they could drive to a generalised failure in jobs creation.

As we have mentioned several times, the economic crisis (starting in 2007-08) is not merely a cyclical crisis as many others in the past. What we really have in front of our eyes is the beginning of a change in the historical turn of nations in charge, mainly due to the industrial shift to the East.

In other words, along the past five centuries (1492-today), some Western nations took advantage on colonised territories, particularly in technologies of navigation and war, thus enabling them[48] to reach political and economic domination. However, as foreseeable, and after half a millennium of supremacy, in the next two to three decades, the traditional 'hegemonic positions' of the West may quickly degrade, due to the expected loss of supremacy in economy and perhaps also in technology.

Globalisation and Reduced Quantitative Effects of the Economic Policy Practised by the West

Letting aside discussions on whether to apply Keynesianism (fiscal activism) or neo-classicism (implying fiscal austerity)—an option at times tinged with political ingredients, such as the desired size of public sector, or the respective short-term preference for employment or price stability—Western politicians should know that the potential effects of any fiscal action in the West is today much smaller than it was in previous times to financial globalisation and corresponding industrial shift to Asia.

Effectively, if a group of countries decide to increase their public expenditure for encouraging their economies (practising only Keynesian

---

48. Important Western nations, as f.i. Spain, France, Britain, Austria, Russia, etc., from time to time and for centuries, and just for exchanging leadership, became involved in wars against each other, in coalition or alone. After the First World War, and for most of the 20th century, global political leadership was shared by the US and the Soviet Union.

policies), and others not, the non-activist will mainly profit from the operation of the expansion carried out by the activists, if the non-activist group count with largely export-oriented economies.

In particular, if the Eurozone, as today defended by a majority of its members, would unleash a Keynesian policy in order to increase GDP and employment, one should accept that, if there is a group of countries—those of Eastern Asia, including China—whose exports to the Eurozone are significantly higher and growing faster than their imports from the Eurozone (both in GDP terms), the main beneficiaries when the Eurozone starts improving its rhythms of growth would paradoxically be the Eastern Asian countries.[49] This implies that, given the current structure and trends in the world economy, and along the period that the comparative advantage (low wages, costs, etc.) of Eastern Asians countries last, a next recovery of the Western economy promoted by means of fiscal action will *ceteris paribus* be less intense than in former up-turns.

Alternatively, continuation with just austerity policies in the Eurozone would *ceteris paribus* produce more stagnation than a policy of fiscal action combined with a decisive reduction of wages. This combination of fiscal impulse plus reduction of wages, although politically difficult to implement in the current power play in the EU, would have a higher potential for increasing GDP and employment growth in the West.

Unbridled Capitalism, Financial Deregulation and Western Degradation

Letting aside the industrial shift towards Asia—a structural change whose re-equilibrium process may take up to two and a half decades, thus progressively eroding the economic superiority of the West in terms of per capita income—we should not overlook another event that has re-accelerated the convergence process favourable to the emerging countries. We are here refering to the financial catastrophe felt since 2008: a catastrophe incubated

---

49. Note that the multiplier of the domestic fiscal policy of a country has to do—negatively—with its marginal propensity to import. Consequently, if a group of developed countries (A) imports 20 per cent of its GDP from another certain group of developing countries (B), while A exports little to B—f.i. only the 5 per cent of the GDP of the group B—the latter will *ceteris paribus* profit, if expansion starts in A.

after the first monetary reactions of the most important central banks of the West (the Fed and the ECB) to the severe fall of stock exchange that followed the outburst of the dot.com bubble at the beginning of the 2000s.[50]

Certainly, the same that democracy is the less inconvenient of the available political systems, capitalism, in its version of Social Economy of Market, is the less bad economic system we know.[51] Unfortunately, in both cases, most political leaders who have the tools to improve democracy and capitalism[52] are unwilling to do so in a determined way since they could individually lose more if changes were fully implemented.[53] This is why, in principle, radical or significant changes in the rules for modifying the financial system are not expectable: neither in the context of recent agreements in the G-20 nor in the context of eventual international treaties promoted by the current UN.

In fact, 5 years after the start of the crisis (2007-08), one of the major concerns of many national economic authorities in the West is still to solve the financial-banking crisis, without significant changes. Consequently, solvency problems and weakness of banking entities[54] have led to expensive salvaging plans undertaken by governments of affected countries, particularly directed to the big, so-called systemic banks.

---

50. The successive and successful reactions of the Fed—under Greenspan—when eventually the shares quotations at the N.Y. Stock Exchange degraded along his protracted mandate, made many to believe—against any logic—that the growth process could indefinitely continue without major corrections. The result was the formation of a big bubble in assets (housing) to internally compensate the shift of the industrial activity to Asia.

51. At times, capitalism generates economic cycles of high intensity bringing unemployment and humiliation to many families, and when it works without the existence of compensatory stabilisers (unemployment subsidies, etc.), it uses to induce a meaningful trend to the concentration of wealth and income in some few hands and to a rapid growth of poverty.

52. We are here referring to parliamentarians, ministers, executives in the ministries, executives in banks, etc. Indeed most of them are interested in not to excessively change the professional context in which they move, because if they did it, their personal economic expectations could dwindle.

53. Note that most politicians try to elude their return to their professional departure positions (as civil servants, lawyers, professors, etc.) at the end of their political careers. As a consequence, they are not fully independent in their decisions towards the private sector, as they consider it as the terminal station of their working lives.

54. From now onwards, when we mention private banks, we will be referring to all non-public entities that professionally practice 'universal banking,' that is to say, that they may practise all possible activities related with financial operations.

Implemented formulas for salvaging banks have been several and sometimes in succession, although almost always—particularly in the US—trying not to affect something that many consider as consubstantial to capitalism: the banks as private enterprises. Note that the cases in which the public powers have decided to buy shares with voting rights of banks to be refloated, and to enter in their administration in majority positions (nationalisations), have been scant.

Nevertheless, and as a matter of principle, neither the private property of some large banks near bankruptcy nor any other private property with doubtful future in other sectors of a mix economy of market should always be protected. In this regard, a first question to be considered is if the payments system of every country is a public service, or not. Next, if recognised as a public service, the question would be if it should be partially 'transferred' to the public sector or kept in the private one as it is today but, in the this case, under serious public supervision.

Today's Reality: The Payments System as a Public Service Managed by Private Bankers

Readers should observe that in our days, the payments system of every country is managed by universal[55] banks, mostly[56] private. Note that this payments system is of compulsory use by all economic players (individuals, firms and institutions). From the old system in which a good part of transactions were paid in cash or carried out with resort to commercial credit, as it historically happened till the second half of the 20th century— which made the corresponding central bank[57] the ultimate responsible entity of the correct working of the payments system—the world has moved to another very different situation. In the new context, with the support of information technology (IT), almost all important payment operations of all individuals and entities (private or public) are compulsorily realised through private banks.

---

55. These universal banks are old commercial banks, today authorised to also make operations typical of formerly specialised (investment) banks, thus they may intervene in any financial operation.

56. In many Western countries, there are banks or financial entities of a public or semi-public character.

57. Observe that till 20th century, it was not decided in many countries (including the US) that the corresponding central bank should be public and guarantied by the state. Indeed, the Fed was not born till 1913.

Logically, in this context, the interruption of the normal working of the payments system, due to the bankruptcy of a big entity or a group of them, has much larger economic destruction capacity than the interruption of any other public service. Indeed, as far as it has no substitutes, the payments system of any country—if starts wobbling—will have a larger capacity of fragilising the economy than any other shaking public service.[58] Concluding, the payments system is today a public service of compulsory use by all citizens, provided by private institutions, which are very fragile due to their high leverage: two traits that make that this public service has to be especially protected or supervised by the state.

However, along the last century, the tradition of private banks as administrators of the payments system has been kept as if nothing had changed in relation to critical subjects affecting the foundations of banking: the appearance of national central banks (for initially just monopolising the issue of banknotes),[59] the development of the monetary policy and macroeconomics, the national or international expansion of markets, the IT revolution, the process of globalisation, etc. Even more, it is our view that there exists a pact of silence for not discussing the issue, as if the survival of capitalism had something to do with the private or public ownership of banks which—among other things—manage a public service: the payments system of every country.

Certainly, current banks, private or public, not only manage the mentioned system of payments of a country, but also intervene in many financial operations alien to it (as avails, promotion of business, trading with foreign currency, with futures, options, etc.); operations which may at times induce significant losses. These losses—added to possible errors

---

58. Today, demonstrators in South European countries protest against the governments because they devote important quantities of money to save banks in crisis, while at the same time reduce subsidies or budgets to some public services (unemployment subsidies, public health system, education, etc.). Note that these two policies—of different costs and savings for the public sector—are simply not comparable: if the financial system collapses, the entire economy would collapse including the mentioned social services. Conversely, if some social services reduce their expenditures, or even disappear, the economy will not collapse because mentioned social services have substitutes.

59. In the 19th century and early 20th century, many Western private banks continued issuing notes.

in the management of the payments system as, for instance, irresponsible concentration of risks (mortgages), credits given to insolvent customers, undue lengthening of the maturity of loans, or financing of activities without economic future—may drag other banks in their fall, thus seriously prejudicing the working of the payments system, which is indisputable a public service.

This possible dominoes reaction is the reason why some banks are considered by many 'as too big to fall.' Consequently they 'should' be object of public support when they move fast towards insolvency. But this public support is nowadays inducing a great dissatisfaction due to the asymmetric treatment to the different entities (by size or by sectors). In fact in public opinion, today there are few defenders of the salvaging operations of big banks with public money, in particular, when these banks had earned lots of money in former cyclical expansion,[60] profits that besides were not especially taxed.[61]

Said all that, we have already arrived to the core of our story. In capitalism, there are two types of economic activities, those strictly private and those strictly public. In those strictly private, in which private goods and services are produced and sold (food, hairdressing, restaurant menus, cars, houses, planes, financial services, etc.), if a firm is successful, it will earn money, but if the firm fails, it will lose part or the total of the invested capital; capitalism is something as simple as that and most of us understand and accept it. However, some conceptual problems appear when it deals about big firms with huge payrolls, acting in mining, car manufacturing, etc.; in these cases, when losses arrive, public sector uses to supply funds (subsidies or soft loans) financed, provisionally or not, by the taxpayer in order to overcome adverse demand and massive job losses, or to help to orderly dismantle corresponding entities.

---

60. Part of these profits, based on defective accountancies, was just 'fabricated' and shamefully distributed to some bankers, 'members of boards.'

61. The idea for solving mentioned asymmetry, suggested by Geithner, former Treasure Secretary of the US, consistent on setting up a higher than normal rate in the corporate tax for big banks, seems to us a defective way of eliminating the differentiated-more favourable treatment to mentioned bigger banks.

The problem becomes even more complex when these big firms are big banks, whose main activity, based on 'trust,'[62] constitutes a fundamental public service (the payment system of the community), while they also realise other 'risky' financial activities strictly private,[63] and all that in a rather mixed way—that is to say, without setting up barriers of informative, financial and executive nature—assumedly to reach economies of scale, synergies, etc.,[64] Note that in case of separation, the realised activities would be safer and more profitable for the community than the current system of non-separation.

If besides these mixed activities, mentioned big banks had gathered, almost without legal limits, additional funds from other big national or foreign banks, the former could eventually drag the latter in their fall; hence, the picture of the bad organisation of the current financial system becomes clear. And let us not forget that, due to the non-transparency of banks accountancy and defective inspection by corresponding central bank, the possible entrance into a situation of insolvency of one of these big entities unexpectedly places the governments and supervising entities in a situation politically depending on failing private bankers, and not vice versa. In this regard, one should note that the failure of big banks is also a failure in supervision by government or central bank.

---

62. A bank with a ratio of cash-reserves of 2 per cent (or less) of its deposits, and with high leverage—that is to say with own resources of f.i. around 8-9 per cent of total assets—is an entity that, by definition, always moves in a delicate equilibrium, only sustained by the confidence of customers, confidence that may brake up in any moment. This is the reason why small errors combined with adverse economic circumstances may induce loses over 8-9 per cent of the assets, which will force the involved entity to be declared in situation of technical bankruptcy. Note that a fast growth of losses, although without arriving to the mentioned 8-9 per cent of its assets, may undermine the confidence and make that the cumulated losses quickly arrive to the fatal 8-9 per cent.

63. Among these private activities (services) of banks one could mention: capital underwriting and different trading operations in currencies, stocks, real estate, strategic raw materials including food, futures, options, etc., that, by their own nature, have a speculative character.

64. Corresponding barriers of responsibility, etc., initially set up in the US in 1933 by the Glass&Steagall Act, were also established in almost all Western world and kept working till the 1980s. Afterwards, in times of Pres. Reagan, for assumedly encouraging competition and efficiency 'at short run'—and for allegedly 'favouring all involved economic agents,' depositors and banks—former limits or separation of activities were gradually abated, which finally provoked a financial catastrophe. A catastrophe induced by putting sheeps (depositors) at range of wolves (certain bankers), without sufficient surveillance of 'distant and non-attentive' shepherds (central bankers).

In fact, if we would review the history of privately managed public services in the last 30 years,[65] we should expect that such a private management—almost always contracted for limited periods of time[66]— although 'nominally' trying to improve the efficiency of the service, have always focused on activities which could render high short-term profits, delaying at times long-term investments, while also sidelining less-profitable social services. All this has at times induced a loss in the quality of the service and a smaller supply of it, while increasing the instability of the service. In this regard, we have to recognise that, eventual failures of banks or a simple feeling that failures could become real, has in many historical occasions prejudiced not only the quality and the stability of the credit supply, but also the working of the payments system, that always should have remained stable.

In other words, we could say that the recent financial catastrophe in many Western countries was provoked by putting sheeps (naive depositors) at range of wolves (certain bankers), without sufficient surveillance of 'distant and non-attentive' shepherds (central bankers).

On the Separation of Banking Activities

Bearing in mind that current universal banks are entities, in which the provision of a public service of compulsory use for citizens—the payments system of a country—is mixed with certain financial services of a strictly private nature, it is clear that if authorities wanted a more stable payments system in a country or at a global scale, the first political option they should consider is the separation of the activities of the payments system from the rest, and to assign them to different entities, thus to a certain extend going back to times prior to the financial deregulation move initiated in the 1980s.

---

65. Among these public services rather deficiently administered by private sector, we could refer among others to the railways (the UK and Germany), to a part of the public health system today subcontracted in several countries, to the proliferation of private security services, etc.

66. This did not happen in banking. In fact the administration of the payments system as a public service was not explicitly given to private banks by authorities in any historical moment; it was given to them by the mere pass of time and the arrival of the information and communications technology (ITC) revolution, which made that the responsibility of keeping a healthy payments system moved from central bank to private banks. This case of an indispensable public service solely administrated by private firms is really unique in the West. And serious discussions on the issue—that is to say out of partisan politics, as we have attempted in the last item—have always been prevented or diverted by private bankers.

Note that this recommendation of separating banking activities is not new, as were not new the decisions made in the 1980s by most Western countries to return to a system of Universal Banking,[67] according to which all entities, including investment, saving banks, etc., could intervene in any financial business, irrespective of whether the latter belonged to the payments system or not (long-term investments or speculative operations, even with food). It seems incredible from the perspective of the healthy administration of a bank, that with the petty savings of a multitude of small naive depositors, a bank could start—directly or indirectly—gambling in the 'futures market' of cereals.

The way of fractioning the current banking systems—if in future this strategy were adopted, as it was widely adopted after the Great Crisis of 1930s—could be diverse. Logically, between the extreme position posed by Milton Friedman in 1953,[68] of radically separating the payments system operations (of any country) from the rest of financial activities, and the current situation of generalised universal banking—totally undesirable— many alternatives could be formulated.

Observe that Friedman proposed a payments system totally pure— with commercial banks only taking deposits and mostly investing them in public titles—thus diverting the rest of financial operations to the remaining financial entities which do not administrate the payments system (deposits). Evidently, a payments system as visualised by Friedman (served by *ad hoc* pure commercial banks) would be totally safe: the sole source of problems could come from competition for taking deposits, competition that could be modulated by the setting up of static or dynamic ceilings on the paid

---

67. The then called 'commercial banks' set up since 1933 in many Western countries, mainly administrated the payments system of the country; they just gave credits at short-mid term (mainly at 90 days), and accumulated important shares of public funds as a second line of liquidity. As a consequence, these entities would be very safe to the extent they kept an acceptable professional behaviour. However, in the 1970s, the growing number of investment banks that started giving cheque-books to their savers-customers, usable against their investments balances, woke up the aspiration of big commercial banks that started demanding 'deregulation' to compete with investment banks, which in those days grew fast. Commercial banks, after lobbing all across the West, achieved that, legally, any bank (commercial or not) could do any monetary or financial operation which, in a progressively deregulated context, would assumedly give to the big commercial banks a great advantage, given their bigger size per comparison to the investment banks, in general smaller.

68. Vide Friedman (1953).

rates of interests. The rest of banking-financial entities, not busy with the payments system, could profit from an almost total freedom of action under supervision (managed by the central bank or other supervising authority that should just impede to these entities to offer to the savers-investors non-sustainable remunerations).[69]

However, the proposal of Friedman of 1953 was too radical as to be accepted by the agents, then acting in the financial system. In fact, years before Friedman's suggestions, a non-radical separation of activities of commercial banks[70] from those of investments banks had already been legally accepted in the US and other countries. Certainly, mentioned non-radical separation of activities did not impede that American (and other) commercial banks continued realising loans at short-mid-term to the private sector, which, in certain cases of risk concentration could have induced (or would induce) the failure of the corresponding commercial bank. To avoid this possible concentration of risks, some limiting rules were formulated. And this, while an insurance deposit, introduced in the US in 1933, and later extended to most western countries, only was allowed to work in case of non-generalised bankruptcies and when it dealt about small entities.

Note that although mentioned non-radical separation of activities had produced—with exceptions—banking stability along 40-50 years,[71] it started being attacked in the 1970s and 1980s by the fundamentalists of efficiency in the short term, the neo-liberals, authors whose extreme liberal ideology occupied in those days almost all economic territories, and induced

---

69. Note that, if for example, a high proportion of entities offers annual interest rates of around 4 per cent to their savers-investors, and one or some others start offering substantially higher rates, as for instant 6 per cent, this strategy—if former situation was competitive—uses to be an indicator that the latter institutions are initiating a non-sustainable 'fuite a l'avance.'

70. Banks that only could invest in authorised public titles, being practically excluded the private ones.

71. Reaching this banking stability was precisely the aim of the Glass&Steagall Act passed in the US in 1933, and of other similar acts passed by parliaments in many other Western countries. Naturally, the cost of this stability was the development of certain inefficiency at short term, induced by the lack of competition among the different institutional segments of the financial system. However, mentioned laws generated indisputable efficiency at long term in the whole economic system, on promoting banking systems much more stable and safer than the preceding ones (before 1933), and than the current ones.

a banking deregulation movement[72] that finally undermined former banking stability. From the very start of the deregulation process, different scaring banking episodes in the Western world occurred. Among them we could quote the crisis in 1984 of the Continental Bank of Illinois, in 1995 the case of the Barings Bank, in 1998 the case of Long Term Capital Management,[73] and of course, the recent process of bankruptcies—sometimes not materialised due to governmental intervention—of an important number of big 'universal' banks, as well as the most important investment banks of the US (Lehman Brothers, etc.).

There is no doubt that concentration of risks, speculative attitudes, and subsequent banking failures, induced by financial deregulation, finally provoked a deep economic crisis which unveiled, with added dramatism, the underlying degrading economic trends of the West in comparison to booming Asia (ex Japan).

The Problem of Risk Concentration in Banking

On administrating the payments mechanism of the different countries, private bankers should remember that a great part of the money they administrate (including deposits) is not theirs. Deposits are property of depositors, who have carried their money to commercial banks not to let bankers freely speculate with it,[74] but to administrate it in the least risky and precise way, thus remaining safe and ready for withdrawal on demand, or at maturity. Indeed, depositors put their money in banks because they suppose that bankers are responsible administrators, and not greedy gamblers or simple malefactors.

As known, current 'universal' private banks receive funds from depositors and from other sources of financing—retailers or wholesale

---

72. In the 80s, the main deregulatory Acts in the US were "The depository and monetary control Act of 1980", and the so-called "Garn-Saint Germain Act of 1982". These Acts significantly diminished the distinction between banks (of deposits) and other financial institutions in the US.

73. An astounding peculiarity of the LTCM at the moment of its saving by American authorities was that among its partners, one could also find Robert Merton y Myron Scholes, two "top class economists" who had received in 1997 the Nobel Prize of Economics, due to their contributions on "financial derivatives" used for risk shifting.

74. If depositors were "risk lovers" they should not put their savings in deposits but in more profitable and riskier assets. But if they were not "risk lovers" and deposit their savings in current or saving accounts, it would be total abuse of confidence that their money was used by commercial bankers to intensively speculate with it.

providers, national or foreigners—which are invested in financial assets of different characteristics of return and risk. Due to their intermediary and transforming action, the banks use to lend at longer terms (than the average maturity of deposits and other sources of funds) to national or international borrowers, apparently solvent. But this transforming action has some limits and red lights that should not be crossed, if the entity does not want to run severe risks which may finally drive it to bankruptcy.

In this regard, bankers should not forget some basic principles of the theory of finances[75] that directly affect the protocol to which the bankers should always adhere in their professional activity as administrators of the payments systems of countries.[76] Such principles are basically two: (1) the existence of a direct correlation between the obtainable profit rate from a financial operation and the risk in which the investor-banker enters, this means that if, in a competitive context, bankers give credits for financing projects of expected high comparative returns, these projects will in general be of higher risk, and so bankers should charge higher interest rates, and (2) the average risk per invested monetary unity could only be reduced by distributing the investments in different productive sectors[77] or in different economic activities, in particular when the rates of return of the different financed activities were not co-related—that is to say, when they were independent—or even better, when their return rates were negatively correlated.

Conversely, if bankers invest the money received from depositors or alternative sources, in a disproportionate way, directly or indirectly,

---

75. In our view, when taking over, all members of the board of commercial banks (public or private) should make a formal declaration in a register (to be created) in the Ministry of Finance or in the central bank, expressing that they know and understand the scope and conclusions of the main basic principles of finance, mentioned in the text. Consequently, they could not allege any more in courts the lack of knowledge on financial principles. As a result, concentration of risks in banking should always be a punishable behaviour, at least from a civil perspective, because it is an attempt against the safety of the bank and its depositors. And those members of boards of banks who, at times, have till now alleged lacking of financial knowledge, apart from corresponding compensation to depositors and shareholders, should give back the salaries they received during the time spent in their postings.

76. And that although they administrate financial activities that are not part of the payments system of the country.

77. Diversification of investments in different maturities and territories or states will also contribute to the reduction of the average risk.

in one productive sector or activity, as for instance in housing, sovereign (public) debt of weak foreign states, or in one entrepreneurial group—own or of others—the arrival to a financial crisis of the entity will be almost guaranteed at mid-long term when the economic health of the massively financed activity enters into crisis.

Analysing other causes of the recent financial catastrophe, apart from the risk concentration in which many bankers entered in many countries (including the US, UK, France, Germany, Spain, Ireland, Netherlands, Iceland, etc.),[78] it is indisputable that corresponding central banks have also been responsible by action or omission of what has occurred: by action, on practising (2000-2003) a reckless policy of 'cheap money,' based on a downwards subjective evaluation of the inflation;[79] or by omission, by de-activating the necessary surveillance, and by omitting the eventual correction of entities with excessive concentration of risks.[80]

It is true that the recent and renewed widespread concept of 'economic freedom,' prevalent in the last three decades—that is to say, from the beginning of policies of Reagan-Thatcher till the arrival of the current financial cataclysm (2008)—made that just speaking about introducing significant controls on the activities of universal banks, was something totally out of fashion. Even more, for many the introduction of controls in banking was equivalent to introducing socialist ideas in the banking

---

78. Note that some German and French banks have also incurred in concentration of risks by disproportionally lending money to certain banks in Southern Europe.

79. The most important central banks in the West defined 'inflation' taking into account just the figures of the Consumer Price Index (CPI). As this indicator hardly rose in the early 2000s due to the cheap imports (at stable or decreasing prices) coming from Asia, Western central banks did not introduce in time the correction of the overdone growth rate of monetary circulation, which was used in some countries for financing (with mortgages) the purchases of residences (new and second-hand). This passive monetary policy of central banks—which provided all the money demanded by private banks to the current interest of intervention—resulted in rapid growth rates of the monetary aggregates and the prices of mentioned assets.

80. Note that, surprisingly and paradoxically, and conversely to what occurs today, the German masterminds of the statutes of the ECB—prone to protect the euro-system against inflation—did not make a fuss when the monetary aggregates, in the early years of the 2000, were growing in the Eurozone at rates that necessarily warrantied a high inflation (at least) in terms of the prices of assets. Probably, they did not protest because they 'thought' they could profit from the underlying inflation in these assets prices.

business. However, we have to remind that in those years Markowitz received a Nobel Prize of Economics (1990), mainly for his contributions (from 1952 onwards) on the convenience of distributing risks in portfolio financing.[81] These contribution and recommendations were nevertheless intentionally placed behind an opaque screen,[82] particularly in early 2000s in order to avert the reduction of the (apparent) high profit rates of banks in those days, always correlated with the realisation of riskier investments, and with high concentration of risks. Note—and this is relevant—that these higher but riskier profits of banks also increased, *via* incentives, the remunerations of top bankers, who recklessly encouraged this strategy, and this while the money of depositors became less and less safe.

On the Convenience of Introducing a Coefficient of Distribution of Risks

Although a higher ratio of capital for banks is important because it increases their own resources in terms of their assets, thus strengthening their resistance in front of future crisis—which is the road taken by the Basel III agreement in the context of the G-20 recommendations—in our view this measure is insufficient for averting the arrival to future banking crisis. To offset this insufficiency, we will here defend the idea of setting up a coefficient for distribution of risks.

Banks do not like that corresponding central banks impose ratios or coefficients on them, because these ratios always set limits to their freedom for investing the deposits they gather from the payments system. However, progressively in time, bankers have gradually accepted the existence of certain coefficients which ultimately favour them, since these coefficients have contributed to the stability of the banking system. We are here

---

81. According to the most famous publication of Harry Markowitz (1952), awarded Nobel Prize in 1990, to build up a balanced portfolio of investments for averting fluctuations in its value, the most important rule is the diversification of investments in different markets (assets) and maturities.

82. In front of these ideas of Markowitz, other contributions not fully profiled, made to believe that by means of operations with financial derivatives (futures and options) the risks of portfolios could be eliminated by their transfer to other entities in exchange of a price. All that, accompanied by the 'fallacy of composition,' made many bankers to believe that the risk would disappear, when in fact the risk just changed of place and responsible.

referring to the 'reserves coefficient'[83] and the 'ratio of capital,' both of which to be accepted by bankers, had to be placed at low or very low levels. On the one hand, the 'reserves coefficient' has for long been placed practically all over the West around its technical level, that is to say around 1-1.5 per cent of the deposits of customers, and on the other, the 'ratio of capital,' which after for long reaching minimum levels to enable higher leverage and profitability, has today (2012) been increased to around 8-9 per cent or more (Basel III agreement) to assumedly guarantee the banks survival in future severe economic crisis.[84]

After long intellectual battles fought in the 1960s and 1970s, other coefficients were finally abandoned in the 1980s by Western public authorities. We are now referring to the so-called 'investment coefficients' in strategic sectors that, although sounding to interventionism and socialism, contributed in many countries to the development of agriculture and certain local industries (also in the West) that, otherwise, would not have received enough financing.

But today, the current and long phase of cyclical downturn in the West, to a great extent provoked by the non-professional behaviour of many bankers, has again provided lessons on what implies violating the corollaries of the Theory of Finances, something that authorities should avert in future. Willy nilly, this means that at short or long term, central bankers will have to impose, and private bankers will have to accept, a new coefficient of

---

83. We are here referring to the traditional reserves coefficient, that is to say to the "relation between effective (cash) plus deposits in the Central Bank, and the deposits on demand of customers plus other liabilities changeable in effective to demand", and not to the currently under study 'liquidity coverage ratio constraint' (LCRC), a different concept than the 'reserves coefficient' because LCRC refers to the quotient between 'Liquidity'—an aggregate wider than effective plus deposits in the central bank, because it includes other forms of liquidity, particularly some public titles—and the 'average cash outflows' in a period of time (30 days) of the bank. In our view the latter coefficient is, and would be, totally ineffective because although the corresponding bank fulfill it, if in one moment it losses the confidence of depositors, the run of the latter and the bankruptcy of the bank will be a matter of hours. For a discussion on LCRC, vide Subramanyan and Van Hoose (2012).

84. In our view, the coefficient of capital, be this equivalent to 4 per cent, 8 per cent (of the assets) or even higher, cannot guarantee by itself a healthy structure of the assets of a bank. Even more, the larger the coefficient of capital, all the more the bankers will enter in higher risks for compensating the non-profitability—through lack of 'sufficient' leverage—introduced by a higher ratio of capital. Consequently, the introduction of a higher ratio of capital will always be required of complementary supervision.

distribution of risks. Note that the current Basel III agreement is just trying to introduce a liquidity coefficient, which seems to us a redundant way of reducing the leverage—additional to the rise in the capital coefficient—that in no case will stop future concentrations of risks and, consequently, eventual runs of depositors if they start distrusting corresponding banks.

Note also that, contrary to our recommended coefficient of distribution of risks, the so-called 'self-control,' so desired and caressed by commercial bankers, has not ever worked, as did not work either the 'undertones' of some central bankers, who in 2003-04—that is to say, several years before the bubble exploded—started warning on the birth of bubbles or exuberances in relation to the concentration of credits.

But we have to underline that the most important central banks of the world, the Fed and ECB, never shifted from successive 'sermons' based on finance theory, to an effective control of the concentration of the credit risks in certain economic activities,[85] a control that could have been simply executed by decelerating the overdone monetary growth of those days—absence of execution that by the way was never criticised by Germans in relation to the behaviour of the ECB—and/or by putting limits to mentioned credit concentration. However, as it has traditionally happened in the final phases of cyclical prosperity, and contrary to what one could have rationally expected, these supposedly 'independent' central bankers[86] did nothing, even in the years 2005-06 of fast inflating bubble, to stop a party in which the guests had drunk too much. Hence, the catastrophe finally arrived.

Note however that all these 'sermons' of central bankers could have been omitted, if at the same time a ruling coefficient of distribution of risks

---

85. Interventions of Greenspan in the Senate of the US were occasionally amazing. This man—for long considered as a guru at a planetary scale—declared one time that the Economic Theory has no accurate instruments as to delimitate if in any moment an economic bubble grows, or if it just deals about a mere structural shift of the economic activity and corresponding credit demand. Years later, when the bubble exploded and the current severe crisis started, Greenspan admitted, also in the US Senate, that he really had not understood the scope of what was happening in those days.

86. Independence was given to central bankers to act in the interest of the nation, thus protecting citizens from the biased behaviour of politicians in charge, who used to inject additional new printed (inflationary) money to the economy when elections were at sight. But it is a fact that this independence has not played a significant role because very often 'independent' central bankers do not dare to go against the executive and public opinion, which mostly prefer monetary injections and promotion of (inflationary) growth than cyclical corrections to recover prices stability or avert the formation of bubbles.

had penalised those that had not fulfilled mentioned coefficient, with nil access to liquidity of new creation. In such a case, the underlying arguments of the sermons—that never bind anyone—would have moved towards an intellectual debate on the structure of mentioned coefficient: a debate that beyond any doubt would have been very illustrative, resulting finally in the implementation of the coefficient.

This coefficient for limiting the concentration of risks may take several forms. Nevertheless, it is important to point out that the design of this coefficient—just applicable to commercial banks—will not be simple, because it requires to make previous relevant decisions concerning: (1) the optimum sectorial structure of the commercial banks portfolio;[87] (2) the period of revision of this optimum portfolio structure in order to adapt it to current needs; and (3) the amount (1%, 2% or 3%) of the allowed average deviation of every bank from the optimum sectorial portfolio structure per period of control.

Despite the technical difficulties that may emerge in the selection of the optimum structure of the portfolio—which should be differently defined in every country—academic economists and bankers, in the context of the G-20, should initiate a debate on the implementation of this coefficient, whose use will be of special relevance if authorities want to avert in future lethal credit concentration processes, as those observed in the last decade—on housing and sovereign debt—and in the whole history of banking.

Bankers are always complaining on the controls exerted on them by central banks, as if these controls were whimsical and their banking activity was strictly private, operating with strict private goods and services. But this is not correct; their activity induces perceivable externalities, due to the public service they administrate. Ignoring these externalities, bankers would prefer to have absolute freedom for sectorial changing their credit structure, as if they were administrating the assets of a portfolio company or an investment fund.[88] But to authorise this credit flexibility—or what is the same, not to put limits to the distribution or concentration of credit at short term—is itself a strategic error for two main reasons: (1) central bankers or

---

87. This revisable portfolio structure should be fixed for a certain period (one or two years) by the supervising institution or by the corresponding Central Bank.

88. These entities, in defence of their shareholders or participants may, at convenience, buy and sell their assets in any proportion.

supervisors should not permit arbitrary concentrations of credit, because this concentration is intrinsically dangerous, while every economic activity needs stable financial flows, and (2) because contrary to portfolio companies or investment funds, the money the banks invest is not property of bankers or shareholders but of the depositors.

Note in this regard, an economic activity—let us say housing—cannot normally develop, if in a year it receives 10 per cent of the available credit, the following year 20 per cent, and the next one just 6 per cent. Indeed every economic activity needs a different although stable flows of credit directed to it, including mild variations on a year to year basis.

Consequently, the setting up of mentioned coefficient of 'risk concentration' would automatically limit the formation of bubbles and avert the credit deficits suffered by some profitable sectors, as a consequence of the credit excesses in others. The existence of this coefficient would also avert the creation of non-sustainable jobs appearing in countries affected by bubbles, and even unfounded migratory movements induced by the formation of corresponding bubbles, always perverse from the perspective of the economic stability. Even more, this coefficient, if well defined, would limit from an additional historical perspective[89] the bankruptcies and the costly moves for the rescue of banks, always financed, at least initially, directly or indirectly, by tax payers and depositors.

Finally, we should add that, if certain banking entities would like to specialise in the financing of certain sectors, activities or regions, thus significantly separating themselves from the optimum portfolio established by authorities for commercial banks, they could do it but, of course, acting out of the payments system of the country. This means that they would not obtain financing from depositors-savers, from commercial banks or from the central banks, but from alternative sources of financing. In that case, the risks taken by these entities would not affect depositors, simply because they would not exist in their balance sheets, remaining in this case the payments system at the margin of any speculative or excessively risked activities undertaken by these 'specialised' banks.

---

89. Economic history has proven that most banking failures have been caused by concentrating risk in certain activities or productive sectors. In relation to the Spanish case, vide Alvarez and Andreu (1982).

On the Retribution Systems of Banking Executives

The astronomic and shameful retributions of bankers are also in need of urgent correction, because they are clearly connected to the extraordinary risks taken by banks. In particular, the short-term incentives payable to them at the end of the annual economic exercise should be eliminated because there is no warranty that operations with larger maturities than a year will finally result successful. On the other hand, the amount of these incentives should be reduced in relation to the fix salaries of executives. Even more, as their retributions with stocks dilute the relative amount of pure capital, thus in principle artificially reducing the prices of shares, bankers are inclined thereafter to restore or to increase their value by making the bank purchasing their own shares (buybacks). And all this while bank managers become important shareholders and exert options on stocks at the most convenient moment for them, often based on privileged information. These are additional defects that have proliferated in times of unbridled capitalism (neo-liberalism), especially in the last decade (2000), which still should be corrected in some countries.

Certainly, high salaries or incentives attributed to top level executives in the banking system should be related to a very real—and not imagined—'net' creation of value per worker.[90] To this respect, we have to point out that, any increase in salaries or incentives based on the rise of banking revenues per worker of one entity, but with a simultaneous proportional increase of risks, which means a zero-addition in 'net' creation of value ex-risks per worker, should be forbidden in those entities that administrate a public service, as the payments system of a country is.[91]

Former argument should take us to the more general principle that 'establishing incentives on non-sustainable activities' should be forbidden. In this regard we could wonder if a bank belonging to the 'payments

---

90. This 'net' creation of value refers to the value created minus the 'value' of the additional risk in which the corresponding bank could have entered.

91. In his first term in office, Pres. Obama pointed out that "it is difficult to limit the incentives of private bankers, when nobody speaks of limiting the incentives to high executives of industrial firms." But mentioned argument of Pres. Obama was mistaken because he did not consider that the private banks administrate a public service, very important and without substitutes, reason why their highest executives have (partial) responsibilities similar to those of ministers.

system': (1) should increase individual incentives, when increases in profits per worker come from dangerous concentration of sectorial risks; (2) if incentives should be created when actions undertaken by bankers could unleash other significant temporal unbalances in the accounts of the bank (as for instance, reductions of capital, taking funds at short term to disproportionally give credits at long term, exceedingly taking foreign currency loans to finance operations in national currency, etc.); and (3) if these incentives should be paid before the consolidation of the results of the undertaken actions. Our answer is negative in all three mentioned cases.

In relation with our recommendation that additional incentives to bankers could only be given for those 'net revenues' realised when the additional obtained profit offsets 'with advantage' the increased risk, we have to clarify that those increased risks, 'responsibly'[92] accepted, do not seem to have played in the past any role in the reduction of the self-planned and self-given incentives by the executives of the big banks. In fact, when a bank has earned money, the incentive has been for the executives, but when it has lost money, the shareholders and/or the taxpayers have been charged with the negative consequences of the increased risks: regrettably a very unfair result for the society as a whole, which does not follow the logic of capitalism. Note that, according to recent pratices, bank executives have mainly profited from the risks taken by them on behalf of shareholders and not from assumed personal risks.

Even more, we do believe that these incentives should have a limit in terms of the 'additional net value added' per worker generated by the bank in the last economic exercise.[93] Finally, we will add that the incentives to

---

92. 'Responsible risk taking' is something that belongs to the ethics of capitalism. If firms accept additional risks in exchange of additional profits, they will have to respond in case of bankruptcy with the loss of the capital of the firm. This is a basic rule of capitalism that however has not been fully accepted for the case of the big banks in many financial crises, in particular, in the last one.

93. It is our view that, in quantitative terms, distributed incentives to all the personnel—executives or not—in entities that participate in the administration of a public service of a country, should not be more than a small fraction (10-20%) of the 'additional' added value (net of the 'value' of the increased risks) reached by the entity in a certain exercise, once discounted the growth rate of monetary aggregates at a national scale. To this respect, one should not forget that the volume of the banking activity is to a great extent conditioned by the evolution of the monetary aggregates that ultimately depend on the deployed monetary policy by the central bank.

personnel—on the basis of variable retributions—should not reach but a small part of the total employees, and this while the evolution of wages of the rest of personnel should reflect the increase in productivity net of increased risks.

Entering now into the empirical evaluation of retributions of bankers, we will first refer to what has happened in the West with professionals and engineers as a whole,[94] whose median retributions have experienced in the last 2-3 decades a relative degrading (at times in absolute and real terms),[95] in front of the very high and rapidly growing retributions received by bankers that control the big banking entities.

The recent retributions of bankers not only are shameful themselves but also reflect a content of economic dominance that has little to do with the expectable competition in the labour market, and with the ethics of capitalism.[96] It is out of any economic logic that these top professionals in the banking business receive as retribution—including income in kind but excluding dividends as shareholders (owners)—figures up to a 100 times higher, or more, than those perceived by other professionals with similar degrees, working for the same bank.[97]

The arguments for justifying this unproportionate rise and level in the retributions of these top executives—already high in 1970s—have been several. Among them, the most quoted one refers to the 'fact' that these

---

94. This refers to all personnel in possession of an academic degree (in Economics or Banking), obtained from any university.

95. Former statement—reduction of median retributions—could be non-perceivable in statistical terms, given the fact that the observed annual average retribution of these professionals not only contains the wages of most of them—the majority—with a clear downwards trend in their real wages due to their relative overabundance—but also the salaries and retributions of top executives, that being a minority perceive retributions that have shoot up in last years, as if they were top stars of the show business, cinema, rock, sports, etc.

96. The ethics of capitalism praises those who work hard in their own interest and also in interest of society, but not those who work hard just for themselves but against the interests of society (causing bubbles and crisis), as it has been the recent case of many bankers. Even more, to work hard, in exclusive profit of themselves, while they compensate 'themselves' with salaries, pensions, stock options, life insurances, etc., in a disproportionate way and out of the logic of competitive markets, has nothing to do with the ethics of capitalism, but with non-acceptable excesses related with the 'stripping' of institutions, a behaviour which deserves social reproach.

97. "...sky salaries in financial sector have played an important role in the drastic increase of the personal income unevenness". Vide. Krugman (2009).

executives deserve a special treatment because they "create much more value for the shareholders than other employees."[98]

Nevertheless, such argument is far from correct, in particular in the banking sector. Anyone who has worked in a bank knows that the average level of professionals working in this activity is very high in comparative terms. Indeed, we have to underline that in the central administrations of banks there are many good professionals who, placed in second or third levels, are precisely those who normally design (adapt or copy) positive banking innovations and those who in the recent past, insistently warned against huge concentration of risks. Note that these good professionals only earn annual figures near—although superior—to the average individual retribution paid by the entity to employees. In opposition to this, and despite their huge retributions, many top executives have in the recent past launched 'fake or absurd' innovations[99] with very negative results for corresponding national economies.

Besides the argument of the 'creation of value,' other justifications as that of the 'entrepreneur-innovator' or the 'risks-taker' have also been used to defend the high retributions of top banking executives. In relation with the first argument, we have to underline that the so-called Schumpeterian entrepreneur hardly exists in the big financial organisations. In relation with the second—the special retributions of top managers as a compensation for the assumed risks—we have already said that this argument is clearly invalid, because those who belong to the board and general directors of big banks do not personally bear the risk of losses of capital, but the shareholders and the society as a whole.

The formation of retributions of top executives in banking or in multinational corporation (MNC) use also to be compared with earnings of

---

98. This creation of value uses to refer not only to the generation of profits but also to the rise of prices of shares of banks, etc. Following this logic, when the banking shares collapsed in 2007 and 2008, the top executives should have reduced their retributions or pay back the money they had received as short-term incentives. But, conversely, they continued auto-paying themselves and receiving these incentives, perhaps because, in their view mentioned incentives 'averted resignations' of top executives, and that others posted in their places—assumedly, of a lower professional category— could have additionally degraded the situation of the firm.

99. According recent remarks of Paul Volker, former Chairman of the Fed, the last authentic banking innovation he remembered was the launch of automated teller machine (ATMs) 30 years ago.

top sport stars, show business stars, film stars, opera singers, etc. However, from our perspective, the markets in which these stars move are perfectly transparent, being their retributions directly depending on demand.[100] It is true that these stars could work with the same intensity and dedication, for much smaller retributions than those they receive, given the high content of Ricardian rent of their retributions. However, while in the case of these stars very high demands are easily perceivable—their services are at times demanded by fanatic crowds[101]—the demand of top executives is opaque (not transparent) and frequently tinged with non-competitive components. Note that in the case of top executives, demanders are their own colleagues, members of the board, who will use the remunerations of the newly contracted to align them with theirs.

Definitely, retributions of top executives are decided by the board of the bank. These retributions are afterwards presented for approval to the shareholders in annual meetings, shareholders who normally lack power to revoke what previously had been decided by the board. This advantage of the board, combined at times with not sufficiently restrictive rules for companies, give the board members the opportunity of stripping the bank shareholders by means of paying to themselves disproportionate retributions.

Observe also—and this is perceivable in their speeches, declarations to media, etc.—that the top executives of banks are not precisely 'Nobel awarded' people with so special talents as to earn money in the proportions they do. In fact, most of them are easily substituted when they retire, pass away or resign, without any trauma for the firm. The contrary happens when in a football team one or two top players disappear or when the voice of a soprano fails.

Despite former arguments, one cannot discard the possible existence in the banking business of some few top 'star' executives, whose retributions should be comparable to the stars of sports, etc. It would deal about super talented people who frequently make decisions substantially different to

---

100. This does not mean that in all cases these demands are absolutely recommendable from a social perspective. What this means is that these demands are clearly observable, and depending on consumers, that at times pay extraordinary prices for attending a football match or a rock concert.

101. Note that in the world of stars of sports and show business, inheritance does not play an essential role; conversely in the world of executives and bankers to be 'son of his father' uses to count a lot.

those of their colleagues[102], and besides, in a successful way. Note that these people are not followers at all; conversely they act as pioneers in the actions or reactions they undertake, which mostly result successful.[103]

Responsibility of Bankers in the Current Crisis

Letting aside the industrial shift to Asia underlying the entire economic evolution in the West particularly along the last decade, it is our view that there have been three levels of responsibility in the generation of the current economic cycle in the West: private bankers, central bankers and governments. Of course, we have to insist that many private bankers have been mainly responsible for the current economic drama, regardless of whether the corresponding central bank had committed mistakes (by action or omission), or had not been enough diligent as to stop processes on which it lacked certain basic data, or because it had limited supervising competencies, or the latter had been bad formulated by the government.

There is no doubt that the responsible for the professional evaluation of taken risks, the concentration of these risks (as f.i. in the housing sector or in loans to certain foreign banks), the mistaken assignment of credits to insolvent people or firms (from a cyclical perspective), or for not co-assuring risks with customers, have been private bankers. Neither governments nor central banks were so directly responsible, and much less the individual borrowers, who in majority only dreamt of living in a better house. Consequently, they naively accepted mortgages offered to them by bank clerks,[104] who just followed orders of the management without any clarifation on the disproportioned risks the customers and the bank were assumming.

In our view, the responsibility of many bankers in the current financial crisis has been very serious: they involved their institutions in cases of severe professional negligence, and in some cases in frauds or crook behaviour. Nevertheless, one has to admit that negligent financial initiatives taken by many bankers became easier after the neo-liberal dismantling of

---

102. These colleagues could be the presidents of the boards of other banks or other MNC.

103. In this case, we would be talking about certain Schumpeterian entrepreneurs.

104. Sadly, when the financial crisis arrived, many of these clerks lost their jobs while many managers remained.

financial controls,[105] agreed by governments and central banks since the early 1980s. Even more, mentioned negligent financial initiatives by private bankers were also fed by the "moral hazard" provoked by the historical rejection of financial authorities to accept bankruptcies of big banks or financial institutions.

In case of bankruptcy (effective or imminent), and if the economic degrading of the bank had been provoked by proven professional negligence, all members of the board and top executives of the failed bank should be fired and respond in a civil way (as minima in front of depositors)[106] by bringing in all their available private possessions at the moment of the acknowledged failure, including those placed in fiscal paradises. We should not forget that, given the scant information the depositors had when placed their savings in an entity, any loss affecting them will never be their responsibility, except in cases in which they would have deposited funds at interest rates far over those of market, which would mean that these depositors had also entered in the game as gamblers.

Far from continuing receiving bonuses as a prize for their ineptitude, or receiving self-contracted millionaire compensations if fired, negligent or malefactor bankers should be expelled forever from the profession. Note besides that, in cases of technical bankruptcy, negligent banking executives should not have the same civil treatment than those who have speculated with their own money and lose it (individual entrepreneurs). Indeed, these negligent bankers, while also running a public service, have recklessly used the money of others—without explicit permit of the depositors—for entering in financial adventures that they did not understand, or they could not control.

Certainly, wrong or immoral behaviour of reckless or malefactor bankers—who *via* unfair and tricky incentives would disproportionally increase their retributions, while protecting themselves from the consequences of their possible inefficiency by means of getting armored

---

105. The non-existence of sufficient controls, although it makes the realisation of negligent or criminal actions easier, does not reduce the responsibility of those who acted negligently or in a culprit way.

106. Note that the shareholders appoint-validate the members of the board and their retributions in the shareholders annual meeting. So, mentioned shareholders may have difficulties to claim against the board on negligence or lack of knowledge of the profession.

contracts and high dismissal compensations that would 'prize' their eventual ineptitude or professional negligence—should not have been permitted at all.

Lessons for the Future: Towards a Correction of the Banking System

Once described the main problems that have driven important private banks in relevant nations to a situation of ruin or near-bankruptcy, or 'disguised' bankruptcies to keep corresponding banks alive, we shall conclude the chapter with some recommendations for future actions to avoid this type of financial problems.

First of all, governments should urgently clarify if banks, and what banks, do arrange a public service—the 'payments mechanism' of the community. The rest of banks or financial institutions not arranging mentioned public service (deposits) should no longer be defined and considered as commercial banks, nor being especially protected—through the deposit insurance system—since they do not administrate a public service.

Consequently, the sole banks that should have received bailouts as public support in recent crisis are those that operate the payments mechanism. But these bailouts cannot be provided to banks in problems without expelling their failed top executives, who have clearly proven their inability as managers, and at times their greediness or bad faith. For application in future, civil or penal responsibilities of bankers should be clearly profiled, particularly in relation with professional negligence. When professional negligence or criminal offenses are proven, applicable compensation or penalties—including jail service—should affect all members of the board present when a wrong decision was made.

We do also believe that the banking reform must be general and not particular, that is to say applicable on a global basis. In this regard, the recent attempt for banking reform by the G-20 could have been more positive, but unfortunately it was wrongly focused and is today almost stalled. For long the discussions in the G-20 were about dismantling fiscal paradises, reducing disproportionate incentives to the top bankers, and increasing the bank's capital ratio, and not at all on the fact that banks manage a public service and, as such, they should be more controlled, in particular in relation with the sectorial or industrial concentration of their risks.

Although along the current crisis, new money from governments or central banks has flown to private banks, this money, instead of automatically being used for increasing the volume of credit as requested by demanders of credit, was first used as a capital warranty. This was due to the limited funding provided by central bankers, always fearing to unleash inflation. As a consequence, the credits of banks have stagnated or shrank while these institutions have just gradually got rid of their toxic assets, a process that in some Eurozone countries has not finished and that may take an additional half decade, or more.

Regrettably, almost all banks and regulators seem nowadays focused on keeping the current system by introducing just minor changes, as those already mentioned (minor corrections on retributions of top executives, on fiscal paradises, etc.) while slowly increasing the ratio of capital. However, going back to a regime of separation, indispensable for isolating the public service—the mechanism of payments of a community—from the rest of (speculative or not) actions of bankers, has not taken off, although there are parliamentary initiatives in Britain, France, Netherlands and Germany which are proposing ways for separation of banking activities.

For most of the initiated actions by governments—mainly the modification of the incentives regime of bankers and the rising of the capital ratio of entities—one cannot expect the total elimination of risky situations. We do believe that with the simple modification of the incentives regime of bankers, the old overdone incentives for top executives will likely be re-channeled to other retributive items (fixed retributions, etc.). On the other hand, the increase of the capital ratio of banks cannot by itself eliminate the risks of failure. Certainly, the ratio of capital of entities should be considerably raised while the gambling margin of bankers in its different forms should be restricted with additional coefficients or limitative rules on financial investment. We are here mainly referring to a coefficient for the limitation of the concentration of credit risks by banks—as described lines above—and coefficients or rules on financing that take into account maturities of acquired and transferred funds (credits, etc.) to customers, while also considering if the acquired financing is in foreign or in national currency.

In summary, we think that if we want in future to minimise the risks of banking failures, the banking system should go—if possible at a global scale—to a separation of banking activities. Additionally, the coefficient of capital should be significantly increased and reformulated, taking into account much more intensively the maturity unbalances of assets and liabilities. Rules on financing in foreign currency and operations off-balance sheet should also be reformulated.

Besides all that, the supervising entities should establish a maximum coefficient of (annual or biennial) variation in relation with the structural changes of the credit supplied by commercial banks, most of times a clear indicator of having entered in dangerous speculative concentrations of risks. Finally, the incentives to bankers should be restated with decision and rigor and not just simply lengthening the term for their definitive payment. This limitation is too simple and too naïve if we refer to banks, entities whose basic raw material, the money, is ultimately provided by the central bank and depositors, and whose main activity is the management of a public service: the payments system of every country.

Indeed, the correction of the banking system in the West is one of the main political actions to be undertaken by Western governments. Otherwise, policies for softening the structural changes currently happening in the World or for alleviating unemployment will be rather out of range for Western governments.

4 Political Stalemate Prejudices Eurozone and Global Economy

Once discussed the main causes of the current economic slowdown of the West, particularly the industrial shift towards Asia and the financial crisis (provoked by unbridled financial capitalism), we will now focus on the wrongly conceived Monetary Union (MU) of the European Union (EU), which instead of being an instrument for improving the economic welfare of its members, as initially calculated by its promoters, has become the most important problem of Europe and the world at the end of 2012.

The Eurozone is today a MU formed by 17 countries of the EU-28, as an advanced group for finally reaching political unification, as hinted in the 1950s in the Treaty of Rome (1957). Although most EU leaders are aware of the dramatic failure of the MU, few EU politicians would publically admit that the EU project got totally derailed in the second half of the 1990s, when the single currency project gathered velocity. Although it became clear that some member-states of the then EU-15 did not want to enter into the MU (UK, Denmark and Sweden) while others were reluctant to implement some macroeconomic corrections to fulfill the Maastricht criteria, and others even falsified the figures to pass the exam for access, the MU project was pushed through.

Against this backdrop, the MU was devised without the complement of a financial union, that is to say, without a collective institution (a Ministry of Finance) for controlling the public finances in the Eurozone at all levels, and without the creation of a collective banking supervision system (a banking union), depending on the European Central Bank (ECB). As a consequence, the MU became a machine incapable for effectively working under adverse circumstances. Indeed, the signatories of the Treaty of Maastricht (1992) created a naïve mechanism that could work only in favourable circumstances but not in hostile ones, that is to say, like a car which can only be driven downwards, but not upwards or in rainy weather.

Indeed, under unfavourable circumstances like the current ones, the Eurozone leaders lack capabilities for efficiently reacting: either because they cannot give sufficient fiscal impulses to the economic activity (due to commitments in the Stability Pact), or because they cannot give sufficient monetary impulse at a collective scale, due to the anti-inflationary statutes of the ECB, and this while member-countries have no individual control on the common currency, thus depriving them from devaluation as an option for macroeconomic rebalancing. With all this limitations and shortfalls, the MU could not work but under favourable circumstances.

To make things worse, far from accepting the French proposals for fiscal harmonisation of the Eurozone—which would have meant a better economic integration for the MU—preference was given to fiscal autonomy of members and an indiscriminate mega-enlargement. In the years 2004-2007, the EU-15 was enlarged with 10-12 economically weaker new member countries (plus recently Croatia), to form the current indecisive EU-28.

One should also consider that before establishing the MU, Greece, Portugal, Ireland, and Spain were countries that kept rather healthy public finances, and a national currency whose devaluation had systematically solved their external problems (balance of payments) when appeared. In the context of the setting up of freer movements of capital in Europe (along the first 1990s), and with an 'unfounded' and wrong expectation of increased financial certainty with the arrival to a MU (1997-1999), the above mentioned countries entered in collaboration with investors-bankers of North-West Europe (among others France, Germany, Netherlands and Britain), all in all resulting in reckless debtor-creditor relations, which finally jeopardised savers-depositors-taxpayers in the whole Eurozone.

On the backdrop of degrading industrial activity in Europe (mostly induced by dislocation towards Eastern Europe, Asia, etc.), banks, either directly (local banks in Greece, Portugal, Ireland and Spain) or indirectly (local banks of France, Germany and Netherlands), initiated in the early years of 2000 huge violations of one of the main principles of finance by concentrating risks in housing (direct or indirectly), credit to foreign banks and/or investments in sovereign debts of weak states. Note that this concentration of risks coincided in time with a credit boom financed with the monetary facilities provided at very low interest rates by the ECB, which was not capable of foreseeing the big bubble it was co-creating together with reckless North-Western and Southern private banks.

So, one may conclude that in Europe both the North-West bank creditors and the South bank debtors recklessly gambled on: (1) an assumed everlasting economic progress in the West; (2) an indefinite growth of housing prices; (3) an endless maintenance of cheap interest rates; and (4) a wrongly assumed last resort, almost unconditional, to the ECB. Consequently both groups of top banking executives committed mistakes, either by direct action (Southern bankers) or by lack of accurate risks analysis based on excessive confidence in a Euro-system (North-Western bankers) that—as it had been devised—would not work under adverse circumstances.

Despite apparent 'economic miracles' in the first years of the MU (Ireland, Spain, etc.) which encouraged more countries to queue for access, first indications of bubbling were already patent in 2004-05 with exceeding growth in housing prices in several Eurozone countries, and an irresponsible concentration of banking risks, which materialised either in direct financing of new houses and apartments, or in economically unjustified projects of infrastructure by local governments.

Forgetting that they were also indirectly responsible for the financial crisis in Europe, the creditor countries of the Eurozone (mainly Germany, Netherlands, Finland, etc.) are now reluctant to pay without strong warranties any additional Euro for correcting in the South the depicted bank and public sector mistakes in the past 10 years. On the contrary, with the exception of France, they want to enforce austerity plans on the debtor countries, which not only are of difficult fulfillment, but also creators of a huge uncertainty on the future of the Euro-system and, consequently, on the progress of the global economy. Note that mentioned creditor countries do not consider penalising their own banks for their excesses in providing credits to Southern banks. Conversely they are forcing the population of

Southern states to pay also for the mistakes of the Northern banks,[1] which in fact acted as 'partners in crime' of the former ones.

In the 'good times'—that is to say, before the arrival of the crisis, and forgetting the need to urgently strengthen the Eurozone with more financial control and coordination by creating a common ministry of finance and a common banking supervisor—the Eurozone and EU leaders prioritised the redefinition of the EU (Constitution 2004, Lisbon Treaty 2007) in order to improve the EU governance. But the outcome was not more than a 'Penelope weaving' exercise, mainly encouraged by countries which had opted out from the Euro, to perhaps avoid real political progress in the Eurozone towards a political federation in which they did, and do, not believe.

Consequently, the very defective Eurozone governance in the last 5 years—just the first years of the economic drama—has kept the Eurozone practically adrift. Even more, since May 2012, leadership of the MU has fallen apart in two camps (France and followers against Germany and followers), which practised in negotiations a dangerous policy of brinkmanship, that in March 2013 started reducing its temperature.

Indeed, the inefficient system of 'unanimity' for solving serious problems, combined with successive temporal elections in Europe—which make important countries (Germany, France) to wait for momentous decisions—plus the problem of inconsistency in the governance of the Eurozone, in which non-Eurozone countries and the bureaucracy of Brussels also participate, could send the Eurozone to the boulevard of the broken dreams. Nevertheless, we do believe that the magnum problem created by the architects of the MU in the 1990s could be solved easily and without high short-term costs for the collective.[2] The most efficient solution would

---

1. It would be wise that governments of Northern countries, with the support of the International Monetary Fund (IMF), intensify their subsidies to their own banks with a part of the credits these banks gave to Southern banks—part that should be condoned to the latter—because the former were also co-responsible for the catastrophe. Indeed, this would be a European version of the Plan Brady, as applied to the debt crisis in Latin America in the 1980s.

2. Although many civil servants of the EU Commission, EU parliamentarians and Commissioners are constantly warning on the huge costs of moving towards a federation, be this of 28, 17 or a more limited one, the reality is that the most important costs they refer to are their own wages which they fear could disappear, and this while a federation would produce economies of scale of around 2 per cent of the joint GDP of the federated countries.

be the creation of a selective federation of interested Eurozone countries, whose political leaders would drive their populations to understand the signs of time, a time of larger political entities and more distributed political power at global level.

Stagnating Europe in the Framework of the 21st Century

From a political perspective, the first half of the 21st century will be a very different time in comparison to the second half of the 20th century. The latter was a period in which the so-called 'Cold War' (1947-1991) and its derivatives—tensions and faraway subsidiary wars—fully dominated the scene.

With all probability, the 21st will be a century in which a new concept of global democracy—for the provision of global public goods, and the correction of global externalities and global social failures—will call with insistence to the doors of the UN to finally practise democratic global governance. For similar reasons, it is expectable that several countries, today belonging to the Eurozone, soon decide to federate to bridge the democratic deficit of the current EU project. Indeed, and schematically, due to rule of 'unanimity,' the countries of the Eurozone are today just autonomous communities of a non-democratic pluri-state territory, more or less under the command of the largest member, and with constant interferences from non-Eurozone members of the EU-28.

In Asia, two emergent countries, China and India, that three decades ago hardly played any international role, are today nuclear powers that, counting with massive conventional armies and with economies quickly growing, are already claiming with strong demographic and economic arguments a more relevant role in global governance and, consequently, in all multilateral institutions and international negotiations.

In fact, in recent multilateral economic and political negotiations, be this commercial (Cancun, Geneva, Doha, etc.), or on climate change (Bali, Copenhagen, Durban, Doha, etc.), political elites of these two countries have already proposed solutions much more in line with their interests and the interests of the regions they anticipate to represent. And they are actually claiming the improvement of their representations in all multilateral institutions as the IMF, World Bank (WB), Security Council of the UN, etc., and in meetings of leading countries for the discussion of relevant affaires at a world scale (G-20, etc.).

In addition to these new emerging economic powers, Russia seems to have recovered in last years (as proven with the Georgia war in the summer of 2008) part of the influence in international politics it had before the crumbling of the Soviet Union. On the other hand, other important countries (Brazil, South Africa, etc.) are also calling to the doors of multilateral institutions. Even more, a second layer of emerging countries such as Malaysia, Vietnam, Indonesia and Thailand are reinforcing the call for improving representation in decision making in multilateral organisations. As a result of all these developments, the distribution of political power in the world is today under severe pressure to change.

Finally, we could mention a new process of restructuring in international aid, trade and investments, in particular referring to Africa.[3] Note that in recent years, mentioned economic flows are rapidly changing following actions undertaken by China and other emerging countries as development aid donors, and all that while the US, the apparent hegemonic power, although announcing a redeployment of its navy towards the Pacific, seems to stealthily retreating behind its own borders, due to economic slowdown at home and military failures abroad.

In the 'old continent,' citizens of the European countries continue enjoying comparatively high (but relatively declining) levels of per capita income, while expectations for their GDP growth rate in the next decades are weak. Indeed, their populations—with exceptions—have reached levels of quasi-stagnation, and their big MNCs have consolidated a maneuver for industrial investments outside the Eurozone that has generated more jobs abroad (Eastern Europe and Asia) and less in Western Europe.

---

3. The renewed interest for Africa, mainly developed by China, is non-violent, and consequently different to the old bloody colonialism practised in former centuries by European countries. Particularly, the Chinese know well the humiliation and crimes that foreign armies inflicted in the 19th and 20th centuries to China (respectively, the Opium War unleashed by the British in 1839 and the invasion of the Japanese, starting in 1937.

Concerning international political influence, the incapability of the EU to contribute—without the 'help' of the US[4]—to find even 'provisional' solutions for recent international conflicts (former Yugoslavia, Afghanistan, Iraq, Sudan, Egypte, Lybia, Syria, etc.) has become clearly perceivable.

Observe also that all European countries are small[5]—including the biggest ones—while continue ageing and, surprisingly, strongly 'fighting' against immigration. At the same time, they are embracing nationalism instead of merging sovereignties (constructing a federation), which assumedly would ease the necessary adjustments to solve the magnum global political and economic changes of the 21st century.

Despite the above described visible economic and political decadence of Europe, European politicians have till recently[6] hardly introduced in their analysis, speeches and writings comments on the economic consequences of the global industrial shift and the current political fragmentation of Europe, inducers of additional degrading. A future that, in the context of a global economy and high differentials in real salaries, unfavourable for Europe in terms of competitiveness in relation with emerging Asia,[7] will register with a high probability the following phenomena: (1) long-lasting lower GDP growth rates in the EU and growing internal distribution unevenness; (2) smaller job creation than in former decades, and huge unemployment if wages do not significantly decrease; (3) further ageing of the European

---

4. Certainly, solutions proposed by the US for the more thorny problems of mankind have mostly been 'non-neutral.' Nevertheless, these solutions have many times been supported enthusiastically by the UK and other European states, while the EU itself often turned a blind eye.

5. Of the 28 countries belonging to the EU, there are 5 countries of intermediate size at a world scale (with 45 million inhabitants or more), and 12 countries with populations of around 5 million or less, of which 6 countries have 2 million people or less. Paradoxically and, irrespective of their size, all of them purport to be equal to their partners in crucial decisions to be made (Treaty of Lisbon of 2007), reason why they claim 'unanimity' for deciding, while at times using their implicit 'veto right' in an abusive way.

6. Only in the first half of 2012, some European leaders have started insisting on the idea of 'more Europe,' and some of them have even started talking about the convenience to imitate the transit towards a political union. But no one has either defined the scope of this 'more Europe' or 'political union', or the road map to reach it.

7. Note that these differentials—due to the much higher salaries in Europe—although becoming progressively shorter, may keep its effectiveness for creating jobs (in Asia) or destroying jobs (in Europe) along a maximum of two and a half decades.

population and degrading of social protection; and (4) reduction of the European share in World exports and sustained increase in investments stemming from emerging countries.

Economic Performance of the EU and the Eurozone in the Last Three Decades (1980-2010)

Besides a hardly positive evaluation of the EU in relation to its foreign policy, it should be underlined that the EU has also exhibited serious deficiencies in its way of decision making (slowness) and in relation to its rate of economic progress, and this while it has maintained meaningful inflexibilities and segmentations in some important internal markets.

All this has made that, despite the cooperative formal 'effort' deployed by the EU members in the last three decades (1980-2010), with five enlargements of the Union—1981 (Greece), 1986 (Spain and Portugal), 1995 (Finland, Sweden and Austria), 2004-2007 (with 12 new members) and 2013 (Croatia)—and two significant moves towards a deeper vertical integration (the Treaty of the Single Act in 1986 and the final creation of the Euro in 1999),[8] its economic performance has been rather disappointing, an underperformance that has resulted compounded in the last decade (2000-2010).

While the GDP of the US evolved in the last two decades (1990-2010) at an average growth rate near 2.7 per cent, no European country[9]—except the (non-sustainable) economies of Ireland and Spain[10]—overcame or equated that annual rhythm of 2.7 per cent, in particular Germany and France respectively grew at average rates of around 1.3 per cent and 1.6 per cent. Even more, Germany, a country currently presented in media as the engine of the EU, grew annually only 1 per cent in the period 2000-2010.[11]

Although the smaller rhythm of economic progress of Europe in comparison with that of the US remained significant in the period 1980-

---

8. Originally, the Euro-system was designed in 1992 by the Treaty of the European Union, also known as the Treaty of Maastricht.

9. We are here referring to the countries that at the end of 1995 belonged to the EU-15.

10. As recently proven, the growth rate of these two countries was simply non-sustainable. Vide Andreu (2010).

11. Vide WB (2012).

2000—a 1.5 per cent lower in the Eurozone than in the US—when the crisis started in 2008, European growth differentials shortened in relation to that of the US but became unfavourably larger in relation to China and India, countries whose GDP grew in the period 1990-2010 at annual average rates over 10.7 per cent and 6.9 per cent respectively.

Although economic projections are never accurate, a simple linear projection till 2023 of the differentials prior to 2007[12] enables to reach *ceteris paribus* certain indicative conclusions: (1) in 2023 the GDP of China will be 65 per cent of that of the US, in front of 22 per cent in 2007; (2) at the end of the first quarter of the 21st century, China will have a GDP alike to the joint GDP of Germany, the UK, France, Italy and Spain; (3) in 2023 India will have surpassed the GDPs of Italy and Spain; and (4) the GDP of the five more important members of the EU, mentioned above, will be equivalent in 2023 to 70 per cent of the US GDP, instead of 82 per cent in 2007. This means that the EU will *ceteris paribus* continue losing speed not only in comparison to Asia, but also in relation to the US, certainly a worrisome expectation for the current and next generation of Europeans.[13]

Among the causes of the registered lower annual rhythm of growth in Europe, one may primarily find: (1) the small growth rate of the EU active population, an issue related to its almost stagnant population in combination with the new legal barriers to immigration; and (2) the reduction of the annually worked hours per active worker in Europe,[14] in comparison to the evolution of the annual hours worked in the US, UK or Asia. Note that these two are 'voluntary causes' of lower annual growth and therefore should not be subject of criticism.

Note that the European higher preference for leisure has negatively offset the positive effects of a greater productivity per worked hour in

---

12. These are projections realised using figures of the GDPs (calculated at exchange rates) recently published by the WB (2012).

13. Note that former comments have not been based on figures reckoned in GDP-PPP (purchasing power parity) terms, but on exchange rates. If we had operated in GDP-PPP terms, the results would have been much more unfavourable for the West and the larger countries of the EU.

14. In our view, an option for this working schedule would be acceptable if the EU population preferred this combination of income and leisure, while at the same time they behave responsible in relation to desired after-tax wages and public subsidies (unemployment, health, pensions, etc).

Europe, induced by the larger investment effort in countries of former EU-15 in comparison to the US. Changing the argument, we have to state that the high concentration of production and supply in certain industries and services in Europe, and the (at times) coordinated non-competitive actions of certain professional collectives (including trade unions), have been additional causes of the poor performance of the EU in last two decades.

As a result of some of the above mentioned arguments—mainly high concentration and oligopolies which induced a significant reduction of the EU competitiveness—the evolution of the EU exports in the last 10 years (2001-2011) has performed under the world average, although much better than Japan and the US but much worse than the low- and middle-income countries.

Nationalism in Europe will Finally be Defeated by Rationality

It is important to underline here that, since the birth of the Eurozone at the end of the 1990s, the EU contains major organisational problems that threaten any progress of the European project: proposals of Eurozone members for solving Euro-system problems—always of difficult formulation—are systematically hijacked by some EU members who are out of the Eurozone. A good example of this has been the recent proposal of the Germans to move forward into a selective federation in the Eurozone, for which several meetings among some Chancellors of the Eurozone have taken place on the basis of a German white paper. As soon as it was known, countries alien to the MU (deliberate out-opters, as Denmark or Britain) started claiming participation in corresponding meetings, or declaring them illegal in the context of the EU-28 organisation.

Similarly, the proposal for creating a Eurozone banking union, indispensable for solving in an ordered way the current and future banking crisis in the Eurozone, was brusquely opposed by the British as they considered themselves as the losers of the operation, since they currently enjoy the profits of London as a relevant banking centre not submitted to European rules. To safeguard their position, short-term oriented UK leaders would not mind blocking the resolution of the current Euro crisis, although at mid-term, mentioned solution would also favour them. Even more, despite its desirability, a Eurozone banking union could not work in the context of the current unanimity rule for decision making in relevant common issues, as formulated in the Treaty of Lisbon.

Nowadays, any attempt of Eurozone members to move forward towards more political integration or federation of Eurozone countries is obstructed within the EU-28 organisation and technostructure (Brussels and Strasbourg), alleging that it would be a *coup d'etat* against the EU-28. But the naked truth is that what the EU organisation primarily fears from this possible or likely political reshuffling are the outright negative effects on the non-democratic and costly bureaucracy of EU-28 and its[15] top executives.

Indeed many wonder today if the EU organisation is sustainable in the context of its current economic non-performance as proven by the comparative GDP growth rates at world scale. The problem of the EU today is not what it costs in relative terms (less than 1% of the joint GDP of its members) but the collateral damage that its inefficient organisation (Brussels and Eurozone) inflicts on the collective. Too much vetoes, too much individual interest and absence of a shared project, have created by alluvium an organisation that continuously multiplies its organs without delivering.

Besides the sure disappointing economic output that the Eurozone countries will harvest in the coming years as a result of the above depicted organisation of the EU-28[16] and the Eurozone, it is possible that growing neo-nationalism and anti-EU positioning among citizens in member-states may further compound the problem.

In brief, refusals to agree on certain issues by using nationalist arguments in the EU; practice of 'veto rights' when unanimity is compulsory, or future construction of minorities for blocking in cases in which

---

15. The innumerable committees and postings created by the EU-28 in the last 10 years are astonishing, since they are not delivering while creating additional difficulties for future efficient reorganisation. To create 28 positions for commissioners, one per member country, is a clear prove of the inefficiency and absolute lack of realism in the EU. The continuation of a rotating presidency after having created a post of a more permanent president 'to solve former problems of presidential short-term rotation' is another example of the EU nightmare.

16. The Lisbon Treaty of 2007 underlined—as demanded by Poland—that the new system of voting, applicable to issues decided by a system of 'double majority,' will not rule 'before 2014.' And this as if, today, the time was not a very important variable in decision making.

unanimity is not necessary (according to the Lisbon Treaty); maintenance of fiscal fragmentation of internal markets; and above all 'renouncing to the huge economies of integration' (up to 2% of the collective GDP) that could be obtained by means of the creation of a European Federation, are issues that—if not corrected—will favour the economic and political regression of the Eurozone and its member countries in the next 10 years, 2013-2023.

In fact, the internal battles in the EU-28 and the Eurozone—provoked by the lack of an accurate perspective on global developments in the 21st century by political leaders—are overshadowing the structural changes taking place in the rest of the world that all euro-citizens should know for adequately reacting.

Certainly, in a fast changing world in which the economic and commercial gravity centre is rapidly shifting towards Asia, keeping costly intra-European peculiarities and nationalism, induced by overdone and irrational attachment to the 'glorious' history of some European ex-Empires, today just nations with small and stagnated populations and low economic growth rates and expectations will only drive to a progressive (although relative) impoverishment of their citizens.

Conversely to the current trend towards the maintenance of a useless policy of keeping the *status quo* as defended by some disoriented countries of the EU, we do believe that rationality will finally gain ground and majority support. In this regard, we think that in some few years, or before if pushed by urgencies, certain national European communities—those whose politicians had explained their citizens the advantages of a new cession of sovereignty to a carefully selected collective—will discover that it is economically more efficient and politically more advantageous to put in common the administration and provision of some European public goods, than to do the opposite, as it happens today.

To this respect, we do believe that the construction of a European Federation by the economically more advanced members of the EU-28, all of them necessarily belonging to the Eurozone and all of them really interested in the new political union, is an urgent need. Note that this European Federation will have little to do with the current organisation, institutions and bureaucracy of Brussels, Strasbourg and other places. Note that citizens of the federated countries would have a direct democratic participation in the federal governance structure. Consequently, the former decision making of the EU-28, based on old treaties, will not be part of the Federation. Finally, a Federal Reserve Bank (FRB) of the Federation would succeed the current ECB which would be dissolved irrespective of the number of federated countries.[17] Former Eurozone countries, who stay out of the federation, would proportionally receive back their contributions and reserves formerly put at the disposal of the old ECB.

In such a context, the Eurozone members not interested or not selected (and consequently non-federated) could, if agreed, remain associated to the Federation for cooperation in political and economic affairs of mutual interest.[18] This implies that Eurozone or EU members not participating in the Federation could use, as any other country in the world, the currency of the Federation, but without either participating in the monetary and exchange rate policies, or in the fiscal policy, or in the defence and foreign policy of the European Federation.

Note that the advantages of this pro-federation operation would be huge for the federating countries. To start with, we have to underline that a Federation that gather 8-12 relevant states, could reach 'static economies of integration,' that in the field of defence would generate savings up to 1 per cent of the joint GDP of the Federation. 'Economies of integration' that could collectively reach savings up to 2 per cent of the joint GDP if—besides defence—were also put in common the foreign representation of the collective, the current ministries of finances, and the central banks of members to form a unique central bank (also supervisor) of a collective character. National parliaments would reduce their internal expenditures in proportion to competencies transferred to the Federation, etc. Observe that this figure of 2 per cent in GDP terms is much higher than that used in the 1990s (0.5% of the GDP) as a 'convincing argument' for the creation of a MU that, at the end of the day, has resulted unstable and inducer of negative results.

---

17. Disappearance of the current ECB and creation of the new Federal Reserve Bank of Europe (FRB of Europe) would be simultaneous, if a majority of the old ECB members wanted to move to the new FRB of Europe.

18. Member countries of the EU-28, not belonging to the Eurozone, could also keep their association and relations with the Federation, but of course, being out of the Federal political structure.

Finally, we will underline that in setting up a formal federation, interested countries would have to transfer[19] just an additional part of their sovereignty, since they have already transferred a significant and very perceivable chunk of it with the creation of the malfunctioning Eurozone. Even more, this additional transfer would occur in exchange of significant internal gains of a static character, and relevant dynamic gains of a global nature in the economic and political fields. Indeed, the creation of a selective federation will finally unveil the real advantages of a MU in a democratic context.

We have here to underline that mentioned movement towards a voluntary and self-selected European Federation or, alternatively, towards an economic and political degrading of the old continent as a result of keeping the current economic and political 'status quo,' are the two main available options at mid-long term. To the extent that the second one cannot work as proven by evidence in the last decade, a strategy for the reorganisation of Europe—towards a voluntary and self-selected federation—seems to us the sole reasonable option for European nations that want to keep relevance at a world scale in future.

Understanding the Accumulated Economic and Political Confusion in Europe

It is today accepted in Brussels, although not officially, that the EU is currently paying the price for the two main policy mistakes committed in the last two decades: (1) the implementation of a MU without a fiscal and a banking union, which finally—in the first serious economic slump—made the coordination of the collective monetary and individual fiscal policies in the Eurozone impossible, and (2) the overdone enlargement of 2004-2007

---

19. As it is well known and suffered by all, a huge part of sovereignty transferred to the collective in the Treaty of Maastricht of 1992 and subsequent rules was transferred in a regrettable and inefficient way. With this treaty, the members of the Eurozone gave to the collective a fraction of their national political power—their monetary and exchange rate policies—without transferring other powers (Fiscal Policy and Banking Supervision) indispensable for the efficient application of a collective Economic Policy. As a result, the Treaty of Maastricht implied a transfer of sovereignty of very negative consequences in the long term. Initial non-recognised inflation by rounding prices, lack of control of the assets bubble developed in the early 2000s, implicit support of non-professional behaviour of private bankers, and incapacity of the monetary system for sailing against the wind are circumstances that have produced the regrettable situation in which we are.

containing 12 countries, an operation mainly done for political reasons, which did not count with the difficult economic digestion by the EU of most of these new poor and politically underdeveloped countries. A digestion that would take a lot of years would complicate the decision making and would reduce the average speed of progress of former EU-15 members.

Years before reaching a final decision on the enlargement of 2004-2007, the European Council defined in 1993 the conditions that candidate countries should fulfill[20] for acceding to the EU and, in 1997, decided to select a group of six countries for entrance in the EU.[21]

After taking these careful steps and under the pressure of some member states (of the then EU-15) more interested in horizontal enlargements than in deeper integration, the perspective of the EU project radically changed: basically for political reasons, a decision for a simultaneous enlargement with 10 candidates to be carried out in 2004 was made. From our point of view, this was a mistaken decision[22] that awfully complicated the already required political restructuring of the MU at the beginning of the 21st century.

Note additionally that, at the end of 2002, when the decision for the omnibus enlargement of 2004-2007 was made, the internal economic and political situation of the Eurozone at 12 was delicate: the 'single currency' was already circulating but went hand-in-hand with a huge non-officially recognised increase of prices, based on exaggerated hikes in prices disguised of rounding, and on the rocketing increase of the residence prices, not included in the Consumer Price Index (CPI). Besides, the MU was planned

---

20. These conditions were: (1) attainment of democratic and stable institutions for guarantying the rule of law and respect to minorities; (2) setting up of a market economy that adjusts to the competitive game; and (3) full absorption of the set of rules of the EU, the so-called 'acquis.'

21. The six candidates then chosen were: Cyprus, Poland, Hungary, Czeck Republic, Slovenia and Estonia. Observe that in those days, most of these countries had a very low per capita income reason why, from our perspective, these countries should have not been included in the short list mentioned before.

22. To consolidate democracies in the east of Europe, there were several political actions at hand such as implementing preferential commercial agreements, increasing development cooperation and financial support for access to North Atlantic Treaty Organization (NATO); etc. However, Brussels, probably under pressure, finally preferred to give full access to the EU to non-mature candidates, thus creating at mid-term relevant problems in the fields of labour markets and the distribution of income, etc., but mainly in the governance of the Union.

for an indefinite period of time, when in fact the creation of a MU without the complements of a workable fiscal union and a banking union was an unstable stage on the road towards political integration, as warned in those days by many specialists on the issue.

Indeed, in 1992, the Eurozone candidates belonging to the EU-15 naïvely agreed to renounce to significant individual actions in the field of fiscal policy, and to fully renounce to individually managing their own monetary and exchange rate policies, while they put in common these monetary and exchange rate policies in the hands of a distant ECB, not prone to activism[23] but devoted almost exclusively to avert inflation or its acceleration (over 2%) under the surveillance—including scrutiny of technical details—of the German Government, always prepared to veto any 'assumed' diversion from the letter of the statutes of the ECB.

Observe that this system of 'single currency,' as designed in 1992, would only have efficiently and indefinitely worked—without the need for rapid progress towards a political integration—in an ideal, perfectly competitive, world. To the extent that in the EU and in the MU, this ideal world was, and is, far from reality—note that in the EU space there are many fragmented and non-competitive markets (such as those in the fields of labour[24] and services of diverse flexibility)—the need of practising active and coordinated fiscal policies[25] was and is essential what so ever.

In accordance with this need for coordination, national governments of the Eurozone subscribed the Stability and Growth Pact in 1997 but, shortly after implementation of the Euro, this pact failed to be accomplished. Complementary to the pact, and in an attempt to improve the functioning of the MU, the EU introduced in 2000 the Lisbon Agenda for encouraging

---

23. According to its short history, the ECB has behaved in a less flexible way than the Federal Reserve System (Fed) of the US—moving the interest rates much less times—while acting in a more conservative way. Since the initiation of the mandate of Mr Draghi, the ECB seems to have entered in a stage of more flexibility, although at times practising brinkmanship, perhaps under the pressure of Germany.

24. Early months of 2012 have finally proven the inflexibility of labour markets in Europe: a geographical area where workers and trade unions had always admitted devaluations of national currencies, but in which almost no one accepts today corresponding internal reductions of nominal wages.

25. Note that the coordination of economic policies in the current Eurozone is very complicated if not impossible: 17 fiscal policies have to be coordinated with one unique monetary policy, which at times results inconvenient for those members whose inflation or unemployment rates are meaningfully different than the average of the Eurozone.

microeconomic competitiveness among all EU members. However, the Lisbon Agenda never became more than a paper in the file.

Single Currency and Authorised 'Free Riding'

To keep full membership in the old EU-15, while remaining out of the Euro-system—as decided by the three unwilling countries and accepted by the rest—gave the deserters an important competitive advantage with respect to the rest: they profited from the stability of prices provided by the Eurozone, while keeping full autonomy in the development of their own monetary, exchange rate, and fiscal policies, thus behaving as authentic free riders[26] in relation to the provision of monetary stability in Europe. Even more, having full autonomy over their own currency, these out-opters also kept their influence in the decision making of the MU through their membership in the then EU-15. Note that this problem resulted severely compounded with the enlargements of 2004-2007 and the arrival of the financial crisis in 2008.

This implies in our view that, once the EU made the decision of moving towards the single currency, after a short period of time (for instance two-three years), the reluctant countries should have been invited again to enter in the Euro-system, or otherwise to move out of the EU political structure. Note that in the latter case, the out-opters could have kept a level of cooperation with the EU similar to those ruling in a customs union or in a common market. Note also that in the latter situation (ejection of reluctants), the following omnibus enlargement would probably have not taken place.

As the out-opters remained in the EU while interfering in the decision making of the Eurozone, and as the omnibus enlargement proposed by them became real in 2004-2007, thus increasing the number of *de facto* out-opters, the historical character of the EU project till the 1990s (advancing all together at the same speed) changed into a schizophrenic one, leading to an almost impossible decision-making in Brussels, and towards a

---

26. The UK and Denmark behave in this way—they do not share the costs of agreed economic adjustments—while Sweden enjoys 'derogation.' These three countries profit from the domestic monetary stability of the Union, without having transferred any sovereignty in relation to it. Even more, these countries may depreciate, at convenience, their own currencies, thus falsifying the degree of competitiveness of their exports to the Eurozone.

Eurozone crisis which is currently effecting most Western nations and many developing countries.

Different Aspirations of the UE-28 Members and Trend to a Breaking up of the Union

As a consequence of the methodology for progress applied by the EU in the last two decades—firstly by means of the 'voluntary access' to the euro by countries of the then EU-15 and secondly through the massive enlargement initiated in 2004,[27] a political reorganisation of the EU-28 towards a deeper integration, that is to say, simultaneously and by unanimity, is today practically impossible.

Even more, as many observers are suggesting in our days, the current and heterogeneous EU-28 will necessarily break, given the very different political aspirations of the divers countries belonging to it, and the difficult adjustment to the new gobal economic environment of the 21st century. Indeed, while some few of them want to continue being 'global powers' (France and UK)—which implies keeping defence expenditures (in proportion to their GDP) at pace with the world average—many others just want to economically benefit from their membership,[28] with access to wider markets of goods, services and financing from the EU and official postings, and this while they do not want to 'depend on the Union' in certain important issues, such as costly international policies and/or armed interventions abroad.

Against this pessimistic version related to the non-sustainability of the current EU-28,[29] our view is that mentioned 'natural trend towards rupture' will finally induce a good result for all: for those countries of the Eurozone that willingly opt to form part of a European Federation, thus progressing

---

27. Note that the positions of the UK in Brussels, frequently looking for a political balance that prevents a deepening in the cooperation progress of the EU, are frequently supported by some important members, including one of the recently arrived in 2004, all of them not very interested in being dominated by the great 'Centre-European States.'

28 Britain, in its relations with the rest of the EU-28, is a member almost exclusively interested in economic matters, defending them with its veto, and in averting political progress in the EU. In most global political matters, it solely follows the US.

29. In June 2012, the British Prime Minister announced the possibility of submitting to Referendum the continuation of Britain in the EU in 2017. Certainly, this threatening with opting out should not hinder the already planned action for creating a selective federation.

towards a deeper integration, and also for the rest of countries of the EU-28 and others, as we will explain below. Such rupture will finally clarify the political positions of every national community and will transform the current and disoriented European Project into another more mature, sustainable and transparent.

Last Proof of Inefficiency in the Governance of Europe: The Public Debt Crisis

Although the group of countries which belongs to the Eurozone is economically more homogeneous than the countries belonging to the EU-28, the reality is that the Eurozone countries could be divided in two big sub-groups: those who are today seriously indebted or lack economic growth capacity, such as Greece, Ireland, Portugal, Belgium, Italy, Spain, etc., and the rest which, being creditors of the indebted countries, are also running serious financial risks (of being not reimbursed in time by debtors).

Reflecting on antecedents and modern theory of the external public debt, we have first to affirm that the excessive accumulation of pending foreign debt was till recently a problem of 'developing countries.' Note that before the first 1970s, the external debt of developing countries was very low (in GDP terms), basically deriving from previous official loans (at low rates) coming from foreign governments or official entities as IMF, WB or regional development banks.

However, at the end of 1970s and early 1980s, Western commercial banks began to play a relevant role in international financing. These banks started loan operations with developing countries, in order to recycle the available liquidity excesses they had, coming from massive dollar deposits realised by the Organization of the Petroleum Exporting Countries (OPEC),[30] after their huge dollar accumulations produced by the price hikes following the two oil crisis of the 1970s (1973 and 1979).

Although at times the external indebtedness may be highly profitable for the promotion of economic growth, it may also originate substantial

---

30. Note that such massive additional deposits were a first derivative of the accumulation of foreign currency by OPEC, generated by the new (multiplied) oil prices induced by the two oil crisis of the 1970s: the so-called oil embargo after the Yon Kippur war and the Islamic Revolution in Iran.

problems when the terms of indebtedness become exaggerated or the financed investments do not deliver.

As explained in handbooks of International Economics, external debt problems may emerge: (1) when the amount of the accumulated external debt becomes high in terms of GDP or exports;[31] (2) when the financial sources move from low and long-term payable interest rates to high and short-term, or when the conditions of loans move from (low and) fixed interest rates to variable (and higher) rates, changes that could suddenly and significantly increase the burden of the debt service; (3) when an external shock that induces an internal recession (*via* exports reduction) suddenly appears, or when a revaluation of the foreign currency in which the debt was contracted occurs, as it happened along the 1980s with the dollar; and, (4) when a flight of local capital appears, and the owners—in front of a drastic devaluation of the local currency—rashly displace their capital abroad to redeposit it, or to pay for purchases of stocks or real estate.

Note that in the last two years (2010-2012), debt problems have also affected some countries of the Eurozone such as Greece, Ireland, Portugal, Spain and Cyprus. Observe that in all these cases, sales pressure of owners[32] of sovereign bonds in the secondary market, automatically inducing growth of yields to buyers, could have been de-activated with purchases of debt (in the secondary market) by the ECB. However, the latter has intervened in the national markets of bonds, rather scantly, reluctantly and occasionally in an indirect way.[33]

Fears to unleash a significant inflation in the Eurozone arrested the ECB to solve, at least provisionally, the indebtedness problems of certain Eurozone countries by means of giving them new special credits or buying

---

31. This is because in case of eventual reduction of revenues for exports, due to the fall of prices of exported goods of inelastic demand—raw materials or food—a loss of confidence in timely devolution of the borrowed money may appear.

32. When the confidence in one country starts vanishing, a downwards pressure in the price of its bonds in the secondary market will appear, due to the increased preference for liquidity of bonds owners, who on massively selling them, will reduce the value of the bonds in mentioned secondary market. Note that this operation, that automatically will raise the yield of buyers, will force in the same direction as the evolution of the nominal interest rates of following new emissions (growing risk premium).

33. These interventions have occasionally consisted of the provision to domestic banks of excessive liquidity that has been used to refinance public debt.

part of their debts, which would have implied the possibility of printing new notes in future.

Indeed, unleashing inflation is an unfair system for rebalancing the financial positions of debtors and creditors, but it is also a fast system that would have already enabled the distribution of the debt burden (of affected countries, debtors and creditors) among 325 million Eurozone citizens. Alternatively, the neoclassical system, used in the Eurozone for recovering lost equilibriums without resorting to inflation, may be fair for the creditors (rich or not), protecting them from inflation, but unfair with many innocent citizens of debtor countries, driving them through public austerity to massive and sustained unemployment,[34] and shrinking wages and welfare.

Observe that different sizes of public deficit and corresponding indebtedness in GDP terms, and their variability, should not be a matter of ideology at short term. At this term, choices for alternative deficits and corresponding indebtedness should be simple strategies either to keep lower unemployment rates, or alternatively, to reach lower inflation.

Now then, mentioned short-term differences will change into an economically and socially relevant matter, when as a consequence of successive fiscal movements (for instance along 5-10 years), the public indebtedness raises (or shrinks) significantly. The result of successively practising policies of public deficit in the Eurozone in the last decade, particularly after the 2008 crisis, is that a good part of Eurozone members are today caught in high public deficits and exaggerated indebtedness, while the inflationary solution (printing new euros for paying sovereign debts) is contrary to the statutes of the ECB.

Observe that the above depicted chaotic state of things in the Eurozone affects the international financial markets which, on the one side, includes the investors in public bonds (big pension funds, sovereign funds, relevant multinational banks, multinational investment funds, etc.) and, on the other, the demanders of funds, including the heavily indebted Eurozone countries.

The comparative stronger position of lenders-investors, accompanied by the 'advising' of rating agencies that just consider the capabilities of

---

34. This is because this way of rebalancing the public deficit and indebtedness, with reduction of public expenditure and increases in taxes, forces to fall the public expenditure and private consumption (two main components of the aggregate demand), thus increasing unemployment.

indebted countries to timely reimburse their debts, is the cause of the, at times, fast increases of the interest rates that most indebted countries have to accept when they try to refinance their debts. So, when a country, be developing or developed, and belonging or not to the Eurozone, starts crossing red lights,[35] the interest rates payable for refinancing will quickly increase, thus compounding the problem of the debt burden. The problem of the heavily indebted Eurozone countries is additionally complicated because their debt burdens are simultaneous, their economies are in weak growth or decreasing, and at the same time, they share a common currency that cannot be individually devaluated.

Very often, biased commentators suggest that higher interest rates, to be paid for refinancing when indebtedness is high, are due to the high degree of monopoly of lenders or speculators that unduly extract from sovereign states exaggerated margins. Although this statement may contain at times a certain doses of realism, the very truth is that not crossing the red lights— continuously surveyed by the rating agencies—may help to significantly reduce the burden of the debt in GDP terms. Note however that these rating agencies have too strict criteria for classifying the solvency of countries, and this while they are also part of the market (incurring in conflicts of interests), reasons why these rating agencies should not be private but more neutral and depending on a UN agency. Let us not forget that rating agencies, when exaggerate in their evaluations, produce negative externalities that an official agency could avoid, thus producing socially adjusted 'ratings.'[36]

Entering into details of the Eurozone case, we have to point out that the Eurozone countries that have 'no problems'[37] of indebtedness—the Northern ones—after a first stage of mild collaboration in the solution of the debt problems of some of the first indebted countries—by means of partially refinancing their public debt—seem today more reluctant to set up a larger and sufficient EU fund for rescues. Indeed, given the progressive increase of

---

35. Crossing a certain amount of public deficit (6-10% of GDP) and/or of indebtedness (60-100% of GDP), in a context of an economy that hardly grows or even decreases, will make it more and more difficult to reimburse creditors.

36. In March 2013, in the meeting for setting up the Development Bank of the BRICS, Russian president Putin called for the creation of national public rate agencies.

37. Note that the creditor banks (or countries) also run the risk of not being paid at maturity.

the number of indebted Eurozone members and the economic importance of them in the last years, this fund could be indefinitely insufficient, particularly, if the countries to be rescued have a small or nil capacity growth along the next 3-5 years, a circumstance that would increase their debt-GDP ratio, although the interest rates applied to them for refinancing would be low or very low.

Against this backdrop, it seems that there is no easy solution. The public opinion in the northern countries of the Eurozone is divided. Some citizens are pressing own governments not to support those countries that several years after the beginning of the crisis have not fixed their public accounts, while others opine that the errors of uncontrolled bankers, be these Southerners or Northerners, should not be paid by the local uninformed poor or middle classes of South and North.

In this context of lack of political cooperation and solidarity, it is possible that one or some of the heavily indebted Eurozone countries, and/ or one or some of those that cannot quickly recover sufficient rhythms of growth,[38] go out from the Euro-system, and proceed simultaneously to a drastic devaluation of their old (new) national currencies, and to a significant reduction of the size of social protection and actions of their public sectors. And all this against the official political *mantra*–supported by the technostructure of Brussels—that no country will ever have to leave the Eurozone. According to them, the departure of any country out of the Eurozone would initiate a serious and risky reshuffling of the EU, in which neither the EU politicians nor the Brussels bureaucracy seem to be interested.

---

38. For rapidly recovering a significant growth rate, they should resort to fast and deep reductions of public and private salaries and profits, instead of devaluating their currencies. These devaluations are impossible because they belong to the Eurozone. Mentioned reductions of wages and profits, if significant, would enable to reduce the costs of their exports and to quickly increase them, all this probably promoting a significant increase of the real GDP that would later produce multiplied and accelerated effects. Nevertheless, one problem of this initiative is that if several member countries (with homogeneous exports) do the same, the effect of the measure would be smaller.

Social Relevance of Public Deficit and Debt Accumulation

In the last years, the debate on the economic and social importance of the public deficit and the accumulated debt of states has multiplied its intensity mainly in the EU. In particular, since 2011, Germany is putting pressure on other Eurozone members in order that they comply in future with the so-called 'Golden Rule'—of nil, or almost nil, public deficit.[39] As the short-term correction of public deficits requires increase of taxes or reduction of public expenditures (including expenditures in education, health, pensions, etc.), an allegedly ideological debate has reappeared. It deals about the positive or negative effects of the reduction of public deficit on the social advances[40] reached in the last decades.

Before entering in the analysis of the economic and social incidence of public deficit and debt, one has to clarify the different intentions for payment contained in the budget. The most important refers to the way of paying the debt induced by successive deficits. There are cases in which those who issue public debt—mainly the state—are 'thinking,' if convenient and legal, in paying the debt by means of printing new money—an option which is not applicable to the countries of the Eurozone, because no one has individual autonomy for issuing euros[41]—or alternatively, paying the debt with own public resources (this implying more taxes or less expenditure) as promoted by Germany for the Eurozone.[42]

In fully independent states, high public deficits or debts could always be paid in the end with new printed money, combined with successive devaluations and other restrictive measures—as it has happened in financial crisis of many EU countries before the formation of the MU.

---

39. This has finally been approved in all the Eurozone countries in the summer of 2012.

40. Note that some of these social advances were not financially sustainable in several southern Eurozone countries.

41. To monetary effects, the current member-states of the Eurozone are provinces, regions, etc., with no capacity for issuing money.

42. In fact, if the intention was to pay with new money, the chosen strategy would in the long term take the country to higher rates of inflation. But this inflation, as it is well known, contains an implicit tax mostly paid by consumers of modest income, and this while inflation has an internal trend towards acceleration—the so-called 'galloping inflation' phenomenon—which in many historical circumstances has provoked real nightmares to governments.

However, in the case of the Eurozone members, which cannot devaluate the common currency, the solution of not (substantially) reducing public expenditure and not (significantly) rising taxes—that is to say, of (moderately) increasing deficits in order to avert additional social hardship— may imply fast growing of the debt (in GDP terms) if the growth capacity of the involved countries is almost nil or negative.

Deficit, Indebtedness and Reputation

Let us assume that the public sector of a country decides to have a certain public deficit for one or several economic exercises, and to issue a volume of public debt to get funds, that afterwards will be paid with non-depreciated money. In that case, if corresponding state wants to sustain its reputation of 'good payer', it will have to make sure that the relative volume of its indebtedness does not surpass a certain level (in GDP terms). This means, as mentioned before, that the accumulated debt should not grow from a moment onwards at higher speed than the GDP.[43]

Consequently, if for instance, a figure of 60 per cent in relation to the debt/GDP limit had formerly been established—as it occurs in the Stability and Growth Pact of 1997 agreed by Euro members—once arrived to that limit (60%) by accumulation of previous deficits, small additional deficits in GDP terms, even those cyclically induced by stagnation or reduction of the GDP, or by the rise of the payable interest rates on the debt, would force— not to overcome the agreed limit—to raise taxes or to cut expenditures.[44] But note that rising taxes or cutting expenditures may be inconvenient because they may reduce the volume of economic activity.

Observe besides that, for some citizens, cutting certain public expenditures may be 'unacceptable' if they have a 'social' content (such as unemployment subsidies, health, education and pensions). In this context governments will have to prioritise by cutting other 'non-social' expenditures (such as public investment in ports, roads, railways, etc.), while they necessarily will have to raise taxes to fulfill the budget deficit

---

43. A second criterion is that the net exports of goods and services, or the capacity for paying in foreign currency, will have to grow minimal at the same rate than the GDP.

44. In general, this has not been the case in relation with some Eurozone countries, either for lack of discipline or faith in the European Project. Note that this lack of discipline was also shared by Germany and France in 2003 in times of Schroeder and Chirac, indeed two not 'very conservative' leaders.

and indebtness restrictions as agreed (3% and 60%). As far as general tax increases on middle-class would reduce the aggregate demand thus increasing unemployment, socialist and social democrats will push for increasing income taxes on the rich, and at times including taxes on capital or wealth.

Note, however, that in the Eurozone, where there is no equal taxation among member states, rich people affected by mentioned social democratic solution could move to another EU country or even abroad, thus making former solution inoperant. Once again it is clear that the only way out to solve the problem of deficit and debt without impoverishing the middle class would be the establishment of a selective federation (and, then after, if convenient, paying the debt by printing money, as it has been partially done in the current cycle by the US).

However, as far as the Eurozone is not yet a federation, if a public sector wants to really pay its debts and keep its commitments, it will be better to behave responsible and not to exaggerate in issuing bonds beyond the limit of which no one will want to refinance the country anymore, as happened in the 1980s and 1990s in some Latin American and Asian countries, and as it has recently occurred in some southern Eurozone countries. This implies that, from a certain level of indebtedness (in GDP terms) onwards, new public deficit, large or not, and voluntary (structural) or not (cyclical), by possibly inducing a greater risk for foreign lenders as well as for nationals—being the latter who will finally pay—will not be recommendable and in no way will be 'progressive' as some socialist claim, but just irresponsible.

'Structural' Budget and Sustainability

This is not a place in which the so-called parallel action of the public sector[45] will be defended. What we will defend here is that, if an agreed limit of indebtedness to not surpass 60 per cent exists, a responsible government should keep along a normal business cycle an average indebtedness of

---

45. When the economy of a country enters into recession, the public revenues tend to shrink, thus *ceteris paribus*, inducing public deficit. In this context, attempts of reducing the deficit by means of cutting public expenditures induce reductions of the aggregated domestic demand, which reduces the GDP and the public revenue again. So, the cutting of public expenditures to reduce the deficit, provoked by the recession, may induce additional contracting of the GDP—the so-called 'parallel action of the public sector'—while increasing public indebtedness. The same counts for rising taxes.

around 50 per cent of the GDP, which—when the winds become seriously adverse—would give a margin for the realisation of offsetting budgetary operations, and for assuming meaningful cyclical deficits during 2 or 3 years.

But, attention, this 'common sense in the administration of public funds' is equivalent to a strategy in which—after arriving to mentioned 50 per cent—the budget structure of public revenues and expenditures should have, as an average, a structural unbalance that in GDP terms[46] should be moderately positive (surplus), and consequently significantly over -0.5 per cent in GDP terms as recently approved for the Eurozone. Note however that this authorisation by the Eurozone to member-states for maintaining a structural deficit of 0.5 per cent—a figure of mathematical foundation[47]— could only work—in consistency with the restriction of the 60 per cent—if the GDP would grow steadily though moderately, for instance at 0.5 per cent, but not if the economy was eventually in a slump down and generating additional high cyclical deficits on the base of former high indebtedness, already over 60 per cent of the GDP. In case of mentioned slump down, the relative size of the debt in GDP terms would rise crossing the barrier of the 60 per cent, and the default risk would start being perceivable.[48]

Certainly, if the structural unbalance of the public sector was systematically nil (equilibrium) or moderately negative (deficit) in GDP terms, and the level of indebtedness had already reached 60 per cent or more, the observed budget positions in years of full economic growth (on its potential) would be nil or moderately negative—which however could enable to minimally reduce the ratio of indebtedness to GDP—could not enable to create enough reserves to offset future cyclical deficits, typical of periods of

---

46. The structural budget balance is the balance that would result from applying the current structure of expenditures and non-financial revenues (mainly current taxes rates), to a situation of GDP of full employment. In all handbooks of Macroeconomics, it is assumed that observed budget balance is the algebraic addition of the structural budget—which may be positive or negative—plus the cyclical balance that necessarily will be negative or nil.

47. This figure comes from an equation that links the size of the debt with the size of the deficit, once introduced corresponding assumptions on the growth rate of the GDP and the established limitation of the relation of debt/GDP.

48. The limit for indebtedness of the 60 per cent of the European Pact for Stability and Growth could be risen up to 80 per cent if this figure was in general considered as admissible. Now then, the reader should know that, ceteris paribus, the higher the value of this figure, the larger will be the annual volume of interests paid by the public sector in relation with the total annual public expenditures.

economic slump. So, in the latter case, indebtedness could continue growing which, after crossing the barrier of 60 per cent, would be dangerous and (in the Eurozone) not payable without printing new money.

Concluding, we do believe that moderate indebtedness of the states, induced by previous public deficits—decided for implementing compensatory actions in front of adverse economic circumstances, when the states counted with a certain margin for increasing indebtedness (if this is under 60%)—may significantly help; however, we do also believe that high indebtedness, induced by reckless politicians that purport to sustain growing expenditures without raising taxes, or reducing taxes without reducing the public expenditures, has a propensity to generate problems that in the long term may be very serious.

To end our contribution to this debate, we have to emphasise that deficits are just instrumental variables, useful in certain moments of cyclical slump, but that should always be submitted to a severe control in order not to cross a certain level of indebtedness, considered as the limit 'accepted' by the International Community, at times reflected in agreed treaties (60%), as it happens in the case of the Eurozone.

As a result, we could say that what counts in the degree of the 'progressiveness of the public accounts' has to do much more with the size of the public sector (if it is well administrated), with the existence of progressive taxes—if that progressiveness does not result in economically discouraging—and with the size of the 'social expenditures'. A modern state that rationally and efficiently intervenes in social expenditures, that is to say in pensions, health, unemployment insurance, education, etc., financed with moderate progressive taxes, will be a progressive-reformist state. On the contrary, states whose size is small, revenue is gathered with regressive taxes, and that give unbalanced preference to the private sector in managing social expenditures, and overspend in defence and police, and consequently do not sufficiently finance social expenditures, cannot be catalogued as progressive-reformist states, but as conservative ones, although they accumulate intense deficits. Consequently, the size of the public deficit and/or indebtment is by no means an indicator of social reformism or progressiveness.

Finally, we do believe that politicians should keep their political principles (as for instance, for or against subsidies or taxes), but when they propose their policies, they should also include the financial support of their policies in consistency with bigger or smaller sizes of the public sector, and not just pure dreams built on public deficits that—according to some unreliable theories—no one will have to pay because the new public expenditures will finally result 'self-financeable' and consequently the indebtedness will not grow.

Could a Moderate Inflation be Socially Acceptable? Towards a Change in the Statutes of the ECB

In the context of the undesirable current economic situation of the West, we find a geographical space, the Eurozone that, containing 17 EU members with 325 million people and 4.5 per cent of the world population, is economically very important, producing near 20 per cent of the GDP of the planet, and exporting abroad—out of the perimeter of the Eurozone—a figure of around 13 per cent[49] of the total world exports. Note that these exports of the EU are today even higher than those of China—that has four times more inhabitants than the Eurozone—which just reach 10.5 per cent of the world exports.

However, and paradoxically, the Eurozone lacks efficient macroeconomic governance[50] due to: (1) the defective construction of the single currency system following the Treaty of the MU (1992); (2) the governance inconsistency between the EU-28 and the Eurozone; and (3) the rule of unanimity, indispensable in decision-making of relevant issues.

While in the Eurozone every member-state would keep a limited autonomy in fiscal policy—as agreed in the Stability and Growth Pact[51]— all of them renounced to manage their own monetary and exchange rate

---

49. If we included all the exports of the countries of the Eurozone, be these exports directed to the Eurozone countries or abroad, the obtained figure would be near 31.4 per cent. But note that for comparative purposes with the US and China, the relevant figure is the Eurozone exports to countries out of the perimeter of the Eurozone, a figure that is around 13 per cent, higher than those of China or the US.

50. And it also lacks efficient microeconomic governance, as proven in the report of Wim Kok (2004) on the working of the Lisbon Strategy of 2000 for increasing competitiveness, knowledge and jobs.

51. This pact 'forced' the ('observed') public deficits of the Eurozone members to not surpass the 3 per cent of their GDP. This rule was in principle connected with the wanted limit of the indebtedness of every member state, placed by the Treaty of Maastricht at 60 per cent of the GDP.

policies, delegating these policies to a distant ECB, which would not be involved in fighting against unemployment or low activity that because, according to the ideas of masterminds of the statutes of the ECB, monetary variables have little to do with the real economic activity. That is because they may have a significant and dangerous influence on the interests rates volatility and inflation.

Last statement, at times presented in a radical way and without any sequencing (mid-long term), has in our view a highly dogmatic and wrong content, based on defective 'monetarist' analysis. Note to this respect that the findings of monetarist analysis[52] founded on national figures of big countries, as the US, have not been so robust as to eradicate the activist monetary policy applied by the American Fed in almost all episodes of cyclical downturns of the last 65 years, including those occurred in times of conservative Greenspan as Chairman of the Fed.

Based on dogmatic monetarist analysis, German and other architects of the Euro-system decided a relative disarmament of policy aims (employment) and means of the ECB. Letting aside the scant movements of the interest rates of intervention by ECB—note that since its founding, in 1999, the ECB never implemented a categorical monetary policy—the authorised fiscal policy of the Eurozone members also evolved in a limited quantitative way (with authorised deficits up to 3% in GDP terms), and scantly coordinated. This lack of coordination became extremely patent when, after the appearance of the financial crisis in 2008, and following the recommendations of the G-20, every country of the Eurozone began to provisionally develop its own contra-cyclical fiscal policy, with deficits significantly larger than the previously authorised 3 per cent in GDP terms.

Note that mentioned voluntary disarmament of the ECB displays certain arrogance. Indeed, it seems that those who drafted the ECB statutes firmly believed that the absolute truth was with them and not in the statutes of other important central banks in the West or in Asia. The problem is that this arrogance may take the Eurozone and the EU to a long period of stagnation or slow growth.

Making an additional step in analysing the wrong foundations of the monetary policy of the Eurozone, we could suppose that the masterminds

---

52. Vide Friedman and Schwartz (1963).

of current ECB statutes probably were over-affected by the traumatic hyper-inflation experienced by Germany after the First World War. Note that, in those days, monetary control could not be accurately exercised[53]—simply because macroeconomic knowledge had not yet been developed—while Germany decided to partially pay the war-transfers (agreed in the Treaty of Versailles) with depreciating German marks.

Even more, mentioned masterminds, assessing certain monetary aspects of the economic history of Germany and thereafter extrapolating them to the rest of the Eurozone fell in a composition fallacy[54] that we will explain hereafter.

It is known that Germany, after the Second World War and during decades, practised a 'responsible' quantitative monetary policy for avoiding inflation, of so bitter memories for its citizens, and this while its fiscal balance positions were always remarkably moderate. The correlation between the practice of these non-activist monetary and fiscal policies and the rapid economic growth of Germany for decades 'enabled' mentioned masterminds to 'deduce' that it would be possible for the Eurozone to grow at any moment, and in an optimal way, without implementing activist policies.[55]

However, there are several details which may falsify former assumption and conclusions. First, one cannot overlook the fact that Germany received an extraordinary and long impulse from abroad, nothing less than from the so-called Marshall Plan.[56] Second, we cannot forget that after that

---

53. Note that, to a good extent, the German hyperinflation of the Weimar Republic had its foundation in the exaggerated war reparations imposed to Germany by the allies in the Treaty of Versailles. Note that these public transfers (reparations), induced public deficits (that were monetised) and inflation that forced systematic devaluations for increasing exports, thus generating a vicious circle.

54. The so-called 'fallacy of composition' is well known in the macroeconomic analysis, and defined as any incorrect generalisation of the consequences of certain individual actions. This is because, at times, what is true for an individual is not true for the collective.

55. Note that renouncing to an optimal growth at any moment is, by definition, an incorrect policy.

56. The effective incidence of the Marshall Plan in Germany has been modernly debated with more accuracy than before.

Plan, Germany continued growing fast[57] because its products were strongly demanded and exported basically to its European partners [European Economic Community-6 (EEC-6) and later European Community-9 (EC-9)]. Note that most of these partners almost systematically incurred in significant public deficits and inflation rates higher than those of Germany, circumstances that besides accelerating the German economic growth forced successive revaluations of the German mark, which reinforced its monetary stability.

More recently, at the beginning of 2011, Germany seemed to start going out from its former recession, again mainly due to the impulse generated by the public deficits of others—say the US, China, rest of Eurozone, etc.—deficits that, when started being cut-off in the US and in the Eurozone—as recommended by IMF—began negatively affecting the growth rate of Germany (with a stagnating or very moderate growth rate in the last quarter of 2012 and first of 2013).

Considering all this, one could easily deduce that the existence of different public deficits and inflation rates among trading partners may favour local economic growth rates of the more stable (less inflationary) countries. Conversely, we could also deduce that, if in the current slowdown, the US, China and the rest of the Eurozone countries had followed the same 'scantly activist' policy as practised by Germany, and they had not accumulated significant public deficits, the European economy, including Germany, could have for long remained stagnated in their levels of 2009 or even worse.

Note in this respect that while the German share in total world GDP is around 4.5 per cent,[58] its exports are near 9 per cent of total. This means that to a great extent its more rapid growth rate in certain periods may have been induced more by the 'expansionary' economic policies practised out of borders by commercial partner-countries than by the 'rigor' policies practised within Germany.

Taking into account the historical case of the German economy, we think that an exclusive focus in local analysis could have misguided the

---

57. This rapid growth rate was not continuously registered along the first five decades (1957-2007) of the EU, that is to say, since the creation of the EEC-6 in 1957 till 2007, and that because since the 1990s, Europe and Germany entered in a period of slow growth, in which the Reunification process of Germany had a significant influence.

58. German population is around 1.2 per cent of the total population of the world.

masterminds of the statutes of the ECB and the Growth and Stability Pact, leading them to the formulation of 'extremely limiting activist policies.' Consequently, to reach a higher level of efficiency and a better coordination of the monetary and fiscal policies, the statutes of the ECB and the Stability and Growth Pact should be democratically flexibilised[59] as soon as possible in favour of all citizens of the Eurozone and others.

Former consideration does not mean that, in case of significant figures of unemployment, the quantity of money should grow unrestrictedly. Nevertheless, we do believe that the monetary policy should be administered without any complex but correctly. Hence, while inflation (CPI, GDP deflator and asset prices) is kept at moderate levels, the ECB and the governments of the Eurozone could practise more activist (monetary and fiscal) policies. And if current problems were very serious—as for instance the existence of very high unemployment rates, unsustainability of some systemic banks, or appearance of serious problems in some sovereign debt markets—the ECB should have no doubts to act. Given the fact that transitory moderate inflation is a problem less serious than massive unemployment—due to the impossible recovery of the non-realised activity—the ECB should provisionally, f.i. for 2-3 years, allow moderate higher inflation rates—f.i. till 6-8 per cent—which always will be a lesser bad. This should not imply that the ECB should give unconditional and permanent financing to those in need, because the ECB will always have to keep its reputation, while it should also avert any 'moral hazard.'

Alternatively, if finally a voluntary and selective federation as that repetitively proposed by us since a decade ago (2002)[60] would become real, the current problem of inflexibility of the Monetary Policy, as practised by the ECB, and the limits (60%) of the pact for Stability, would automatically disappear.

---

59. In the current sequence of the financial drama we are living in, the rule of unanimity, applicable in the EU for relevant (international) issues, may progressively isolate Germany, a country heavily depending psychologically on its traditional anti-inflationary position. In the end, it would be totally irrational that in the Eurozone, there were a majority of countries suffering dramatic adjustments and fall of their GDP and employment, while a minority of 4-5 countries continues 'profiting,' *via* interest rates, from the problems of the others. This could be unacceptable, and the current Euro-system would finally prove to be non-viable. Even more, in the mid-term the 'winners' could not export to the losers by lack of demand of exports, thus all of them becoming losers.

60. Vide Rahman and Andreu (2002).

Contribution of the Created EU Federation to the Welfare of the Global Society

It is today of general understanding in the Eurozone that the creation of a Eurozone ministry of finance and a Eurozone institution for surveillance of the banking system (Banking Union), with competencies for enforcing the rules decided by 17 Eurozone members, would solve mentioned problems in the long term after being authorised by Brussels. However this pretended solution would not eliminate already commented problems of sovereignty and unanimity. There could be countries that would not accept the proposals of enforcement by these two new institutions, thus finally vetoing the decisions on competencies of the new Eurozone ministry of finance or of the banking union. Consequently, the Eurozone would return to the same deadlock in which it currently moves, be it with with 17 instead of 28 'veto-right' members.

In brief, it is clear that the creation of a European ministry of finance or a European banking union, although currently keeping the EU leadership busy, will not solve in the long term the monetary, fiscal and banking problems of the Eurozone, because the decisions to be taken are basically political and in need of moving from a unanimity to a democratic majority system (towards a federation). Alternatively, using technocratic appointments with long-term mandates and giving them independence and limits for their actions, as happens in the ECB, would condem the Eurozone to inaction and a further democratic deficit.

Having concluded that the options, as discussed in the former item (collective Ministry of Finance and Banking Union), will not solve the problems, we do believe that the most simple and effective way in front of the current Eurozone problems would consist in creating a new political entity (a federation), which besides counting with a common central bank and a ministry of finance, would in addition embody defence, international economic relations (trade and finances) and external representation of the federation in the federal unified budget.

In science, as in politics or economics, negative results of an experiment should take actors to new attempts for modifying or abandoning failed experiences. Indeed, the MU, the fourth stage of the Integration Process of Europe as suggested in handbooks of economic integration and conceived in the Treaty of Maastricht (1992) and complementary rules, has failed, and its continuation without serious modifications is today introducing much more obstacles than previously calculated advantages, and not only for European citizens, but also for the global society.

5 Global Problems to be Solved and Urgent Need for Restructuring the United Nations

Most nations of the world still do not live under what we have defined as mixed economies of market or social economies of market.[1] This means that although most economic activities in societies are carried out by the private sector—mainly devoted to produce private goods and services (like fruit, meat, haircuts, financial services, cars, planes, legal advising, etc.)— others, which should be arranged by the public sector (related with the sufficient provision or correction of public goods and externalities, and with the redistribution of income) are either still underdeveloped, or in process of privatisation or downsizing.

All in all, we find in different countries diverse combinations of public and private sector participations in GDP. These diverse positions, visible in countries like France on the one side (with extended interventionism), and the US on the other (with minor actions of the public sector, except in defence), have to do with the predominant understanding of citizens on what should be public or private, which depends on economic[2] and political history, population density, and wealth and income distribution.

---

1. A good introduction on the content of the public sector actions may be found in Stiglitz (1988).

2. The economic philosophy underlying public intervention has changed significantly in the last three centuries. In the 18th century—before Adam Smith (*The Wealth of Nations*, 1776)—the dominant position on public intervention was the convenience of promoting industry (mainly) in mainland, and encouraging trade with colonies (mercantilism). Smith, however, advocated a limited intervention of the public sector which should just promote the most indispensable public goods (government, defence, justice and police). The ideas of Smith played an important role along next hundred years and beyond (till our days). However, due to the proven negative distributive effects of traditional capitalism, a new breed of social thinkers appeared, as Marx, etc., who—as a remedy for the negative redistribution of capitalism—defended the

Although there are 'pure' public goods[3] whose public provision no one discusses, as for instance the national government, defence, justice, police, and some infrastructures,[4] there are other activities whose provision may be public and/or private, as for instance some levels of education, health, transports, communications, etc. It is precisely the different appreciation by citizens on effects and efficiency in the production and distribution (private or public) of certain goods what makes a mix economy of market more or less tilted towards public intervention.

Public action is normally based on the existence of market failures that not all societies fully acknowledge. Economic stability actions (such as modifying taxes, public expenditures, interest rates, etc.) undertaken by the state or the central bank to fight against cyclical fluctuations are based on the existence of a significant externality: the failure of the market system to keep full employment (due to inflexibilities, disappearance of favourable expectations, etc.). Other economic actions of the public sector directed to counteract externalities in many markets also exert a significant influence; to a good extent, the policies materialised in special taxes (on petrol, emissions of CO_2, etc.) or in subsidies (basic education, basic health, etc.) are based on the existence of respectively negative or positive externalities. Economic actions of public sector are also directed to change the negative distributive results of the pure economy of market,[5] in general prone to concentrate personal income and wealth in the hands of a small percentage of individuals.

---

ownership of capital by the state, which implies total interventionism. The result of the debate and actions and reactions between these two extreme and contradictory economic philosophies (Smithian and Marxian), including wars, is well known. Finally, in the second half of the 20th century, first Social Democracy (1945-1975) under different names arrived in many western countries, and then Neoliberalism (1980-2008) followed, although the latter is involved today in a 'forced' withdrawal.

3. Public goods have two critical properties: (1) it is not possible to individually ration their use by means of introducing a system of prices that no one would pay (the so-called 'free rider' problem) and (2) it is not convenient to ration their use.

4. Some infrastructures could be rationed, but rationing them would be inconvenient because in that case a good number of citizens would be excluded from their use, while the marginal cost of this use is nil.

5. Traditionally, the handbooks of economics used to say that in this case, the public sector acts to offset the social failures of the markets.

Apart from the debated scope for public intervention—related to market failures[6]—we have to underline that the public sector also contains some systematic failures to be considered. These refer to: (1) the limited information or understanding of the economic situation by governments, at times polluted with political dogmatism, as is the case today in the West; (2) the limited control on private reactions, following public interventions; (3) the limited control by government on bureaucratic growth and the trend of bureaucracy to expand action if there is available financing; and (4) the limitations imposed by the political process (term of elections, degree of decentralisation of corresponding country, etc.).[7] All these limitations— and at times related negative results of public actions—give supporters of non-intervention (neo-liberals) the opportunity of rejecting most public actions, by means of generalising negative anecdotes or partial political or institutional failures.

Recent Recognition of Global Public Goods and Global Externalities

During many centuries, the provision of the most relevant public good, peace and security (first regional and later global), was realised and developed, in a competitive and non-democratic way, by regional or global powers. This system of provision of peace and security has historically produced constant and sucessive wars whose results have never satisfied all contenders.

There are other global public goods whose understanding and provision have not been recognised by politicians till recently: we are here referring to the provision of a sustainable global environment, and a global economic regulation and control of certain global economic activities and transactions. The same could be said in relation with the so-called 'global externalities'—

---

6. In the working of capitalist economies, (full) academic neo-classical economists have long ago accepted the possible existence of five different forms of economic market failures: (1) lack of competition, including the existence of the so-called natural monopolies; (2) existence of the so-called public goods; (3) existence of externalities; (4) existence of incomplete markets; and (5) existence of failures of information.

7. Vide Stiglitz (1988: 5). We do believe that the political process is very important. The differences between the speed of economic development of China and India have a lot to do with the political process in India, in need of constant consensus among different regional political parties. The case of the inefficient political process of India has been recently overcome by the case of the EU, an assumed 'Union' of rich countries, practically without common governance.

mainly connected with the provision of natural resources, renewable or not—which till one generation ago, were not put on the table either.

Certainly, till the second half of the 20th century, no one dared to imagine that global environment and climate change would finally be problems that could indiscriminatedly affect all nations. But recent concern on mentioned issues has made that many countries—mainly the most scientifically advanced, particularly the EU group—started reflecting on what should be done to reach 'sustainability of the global environment.' And in fact, they have proposed some good ideas for the correction of the problem.

But in this field more than in others, the problem is that implementation of ideas has a cost, and when we talk about public goods, no one wants to individually assume such costs. Now then, as far as these public goods are of a national nature—f.i. national defence, etc.—the problem is usually solved by governments resorting to taxes that democratic parliaments legitimise. Conversely, if we talk about 'global' public goods—as f.i. global environment—in absence of a global parliament, efforts for its resolution will have to be 'agreed' among all nations. And here the problem starts.

On Main Global Public Goods

After taken for granted that 'national' peace and security, warantied by national defence, is a pure national public good, we should recognise that global peace and security is also a public good, this time referring to the protection of the global society. The main question in this case is who should decide—with legitimacy—what are the means and ends for getting or providing this global public good. Certainly, the foreseeable international economic evolution in next years, and subsequent changes in the political power in the world, point to the final arrival—in two or three decades—to a democratic UN which will have to decide on ends and means, on financing and implementation, of the new global public action for the provision of global peace and security.

All along the history of mankind on earth, and even currently, the provision of 'peace and security' have been carried out without the authorisation of citizens of the intervened nations, or without the consent of the contemporary regional society.[8] Paradoxically this provision was exercised through wars mostly undertaken by what we call today 'hegemonic powers.' As almost always, these actions of some individual powerful nations, acting alone or in coalitions—at times allegedly 'for protecting themselves' from 'possible' future military actions of others (pre-emptive wars), and in many occasions under the pretext of 'salvaging oppressed communities'—have lacked democratic foundation. Note that even when authorisation was given by an international organisation (current North Atlantic Treaty Organization (NATO) or UN), the undertaken military action also lacked democratic foundations and structure.[9]

Besides the provision of global peace and security, the global society should also provide a healthy and sustainable global environment, which is also another fundamental global public good, in this case indispensable for the continuation of life on the planet. But note that the attempts for getting a healthy global environment by means of voluntary arresting or reducing the emissions of greenhouse gases by the different countries, as 'agreed' in treaties in the context of the current UN, have failed. But at least, we have to underline that the global society is today fully conscious of the magnum environmental problems she is facing, something that for the time being is not the case with the provision of global peace and security.

Reflecting on global environment, we have to recognise that the understanding of the problem is not total, but soaked in multifaceted uncertainty. Really, if climate change had been provoked by mankind and industrialisation, then those who started or accelerated the industrialisation process should pay for what they did, making possible that the planet returns to its 'initial situation' or, alternatively, compensating the others. This would imply to know the historical emissions of every country which is not an easy task, although to some extent these historical emissions could be aproached by projecting the current ones backwards, with the help of the registered industrial growth rates of every country. This retrospective

---

8. Till recently, the concept of the global society did not exist; but in ancient times, it was possible to talk about regional societies (f.i. the Roman Empire, etc.), although at that time this concept had nothing to do with democracy.

9. Observe that in essence these institutions are not democratic at a global scale.

reckoning should end at a point in time in which nature would have fully absorbed by itself the CO_2 emitted by mankind activities.[10]

Former source of uncertainty has an evident economic effect. Indeed, if climate change would have been induced by mankind, there would be a historical debt of some countries, the industrialised ones, with respect to the others. If, conversely, the change had not been provoked or acentuated by mankind, or alternatively, it was not accepted as such, the historical debt would not exist or would not be recognised by the current industrialised countries. In this case, the industrialised countries would only accept to make efforts to control current and futute emissions, when proven. But accepted one thing or the opposite, the real or assumed historical debt is an argument that will be strongly played by developing countries in future negotiations because it favours them, and this argument will be played with more and more emphasis in order to avoid a catastrophe for all.

Although some stubborn scientists and politicians (ultra-conservatives) continue rejecting the case of the 'global warming' caused by the industrialisation process, the reality is that while the earth climate remained stable in the past 10,000 years, man-made greenhouse gases along the last two centuries seem to threaten former stability. Indeed, projections on future developments concerning climate change suggest that, *ceteris paribus*, average temperature will increase along the 21st century between 1.4 and 5.5°C. Note that increases over 2°C in the current century could lead to catastrophic rises of sea levels; rapid increase in the number of extreme weather events such as hurricanes, floodings and droughts; falling agriculture production; and probably famine and mass population movements.[11]

Due to the multiple direct and indirect effects of climate change, no one may be sure of the total cost of the earth warming. However, former

---

10. An additional problem to be considered is that, up to the moment in which the planet was not any more capable of absorbing additional emissions of CO_2, there were countries that polluted the atmosphere thus profiting from the rainforests of others and behaving as free riders, and this while the agrarian countries implicitly 'paid'—without noticing it—for correcting the industrial emissions of others.

11. These massive population movements would produce a magnum problem of human re-settlements, without any possible comparison with other former movements of people along history (not pre-history) of mankind. A world authority in this case would be absolutely indispensable to solve the resulting problems of land redistribution.

considerations on uncertainty should not drive us to inaction. Indeed, similar to the fact that the average expenditure in defence in the world is a figure of 2.6 per cent of global GDP—although the probability of being attacked is almost nil for most countries—individual nations should also invest an important rate of their GDP to fight against climate change, just to avoid eventual highly catastrophic results.

Note that according to some relevant reports, the annual costs of doing nothing to reduce emissions of CO_2 could range from 5 to 20 per cent of the total GDP by the end of the 21st century.[12] Consequently, it would be wise for the world to start spending a provisional figure that, for example after 10 years phasing, would reach a level of 2 per cent of the global GDP.

But given the current international political structure, multilateral but hardly democratic and scantly cooperative, the real difficulties underlying the pooling and management of mentioned volume of funds are, and will be, of an intractable political nature. Indeed, given the nature of the problem of climate change, and the possibility that individual nations behave as 'free riders,'[13] there is a scant probability that the international community tackles this problem by means of resorting to multilateral environmental agreements (MEAs), whose setting up has proven to be difficult and time-consuming, while bypassing them has been easy. The case of the failed Kyoto Protocol and the failure of other attemps for achieving agreements in other matters are patent proofs of the inefficiency of multilateral agreements negotiated under the umbrella of the current UN. As known, all MEAs used to be on minima and not on optima—for reaching wider consensus—while they are neither inclusive (many important countries do not sign) nor compulsory (no sanctions for non-compliance).

In this regard if the world does not progress towards democratic global governance (a new democratic UN) with capacity for enforcing matters assigned to it (including environment), the probability of successfully solving

---

12. Some few years ago, the so-called Stern Report announced that the cost of doing nothing along next decades could be equivalent, annually, to 20 per cent of global GDP at the end of 2100.

13. The possibility of different countries to behave as 'free riders' is twofold. Every generation of each country may be interested in passing the charge of the correction to the next one, and every country may be interested in passing the charge of the correction to other nations.

the problem of climate change and its derivatives (f.i. massive migrations to already inhabited countries) will be almost nil.

Finally, in relation to the quantitive targets to be introduced in global public action on climate change, it should be underlined that mentioned targets could adopt different levels. The target could be formulated in terms of nil additional warming—which would imply to leave the environment as it is now in order to stop global warming—or in terms of admitting additional global warming 'per period' of 1°C, 2°C, etc. Note in this regard that, the softer the planned correction is, with acceptation of higher warming in short periods, the higher would be the risk of a climate catastrophe.

To conclude our presentation of global public goods, we will finally refer to the convenience of establishing a set of global economic regulations, affecting the main global markets (international banking activities, capital movements, crude oil, strategic raw materials, etc.) and the so-called fiscal paradises, respectively, either for avoiding in future the misuse of markets by greedy adventurers in charge of some multinational corporations (MNCs) or governments [including sectoral governmental organisations, such as the Organization of the Petroleum Exporting Countries (OPEC)], or for stopping the development of international crime in its different versions.

Indeed, in the last 40 years, several sudden and sharp (up and down) movements in prices coming from the supply side in the market of crude oil have generated severe economic cycles (supply-side cycles), whose intensity should in future be minimised by democratic global governance in benefit of the global society. In this regard, the evolution of production and prices of crude oil should not be in the hands of some few individual large producer-exporter states (OPEC), which at times have operated monopolistic prices, or have used the commodity they produce as a weapon. The same could be said for the rest of strategic raw materials.

In relation to fiscal paradises, it is our view that corresponding global regulation should not only forbid the development of new paradises, but also include the establishment of a phasing period till the total extinction of the existing ones.[14] Recently, the G-20 introduced an increase in transparency

---

14. Consequently, governments should progressively deactivate the functionality of fiscal paradises in a maximum term of 10 years, by gradually illegalising the financial transfers—over a certain amount of money during a year—from normal banking areas to banks placed in fiscal paradises. Important movements of cash should be strongly penalised.

of fiscal paradises, although mainly for fiscal prosecution. However to the extent that criminal prosecution only unleashes when criminal activity is detected, fiscal paradises continue working, thus giving protection to former and new tax evaders, corrupted politicians, criminals devoted to drugs and human trafficking, mafiosi of different nature, etc. As it is clear that all this should not continue in a progressively more fair-democratic world, global society should fully eliminate these paradises, including the off-shore financial centres which do not comply with the rules enacted by future democratic UN.

Certainly, the existence of fiscal paradises is an international shame, only 'falsely justified' from the perspective of the 'lesser bad.' Its existence—according to its defenders—enables recycling money that otherwise would be in banking notes in boxes placed out of circulation. But this argument is just valid for those who negotiate with this dark or bloody money, and not for the rest of the legal society who annually losses—at global scale—fiscal revenues of US$ 280 billion,[15] and this while malefactors pay for time till the moment in which penalties for their former illegal or criminal activities are nationally or internationally out of prosecution (prescribed).

On Main Global Externalities

This is not the place for extensively explaining the logic underlying the problem of externalities, which is, as mentioned, one of the most important failures of markets. Although at times, in the context of very restrictive circumstances, it is possible to solve the problem of externalities with private solutions,[16] normally the public sector has to intervene.

There are several reasons that make government intervention indispensable. A first reason has to do with the fact that some goods (involved in externalities) contain traits practically identical to public goods

---

15. Vide Henry (2012). According to Henry, the current annually deposited figures in accounts in fiscal paradises represent an amount that jointly deprives governments all over the world from annual revenue of around US$ 280 billions.

16. It is possible to solve the problem of externalities with private solutions that enable to internalise the externalities, by forming economic units of sufficient size, or by the assignment of property rights. Alternatively, when the property rights are not defined, a private negotiation of all involved parties (small in number) could also solve the problem of internalising externalities (theorem of Coase).

(clean air and water), which necessarily imply the intervention of the public sector. A second argument refers to the existence of imperfect information that makes the arrival to an efficient private solution impossible. In third place, we have to add that if not all the involved owners become associated—as required to internalise corresponding externality—owners that do not join would behave as free riders, and finally, it must be underlined that keeping the 'associated' group united will require significant costs of transaction and information, in particular if the group is large. As consequence of the existence of one or several of mentioned arguments, the public sector will have to intervene.

In the case of public solutions for externalities, the government will use the markets for exerting an influence on them by using taxes and subsidies,[17] or will introduce marketable permits of pollution in combination with pre-defined pollution limits or 'caps.'

But note that up to this moment, we have not introduced the words 'transnational' or 'global.' Therefore, former concepts would be incomplete if transnational or global externalities generated by the economic activity of one or several countries, with spillover effects on other nations of the world, are not considered. Again, in this case, we could solve the problems by agreeing on taxes, subsidies, caps to be established, etc. The problem in this case, as in others, is that, contrary to what happens at national scale, it is probable that agreements result very defective in absence of a common authority (for all nations) in the world.

Indeed, in relation to the pure local or national externalities, as for instance the national environment, we may affirm that the above mentioned public solutions for externalities, related to aims and means, will be successful if applied in a democratic context. Note, however, that the level of exigency of the rules established for national environmental protection could be different in every country, and to some extent adapted to the feelings of own citizens.

Regrettably, this heterogeneity of national legislations induces some problems in frontier when productions that embody polluting processes

---

17. By introducing taxes when private firms produce social costs (f.i. emissions), or by giving subsidies when private firms produce social benefits.

are exported.[18] Nevertheless, much more complicated problems will appear when a part of the production of goods and services of a country induces negative spillover effects on the environment of neighbouring countries, or on global environment.

Letting aside the export problems induced by the existence of differentiated national rules on 'national environment,' what indeed seems inexcusable is the harmonisation of the national environmental legislations in relation to global environmental emissions, as defended by Tobin.[19] Undoubtfully, after an eventual process of harmonisation in all nations, there would be a single level of 'pollution tax,' that would everywhere equalise the marginal benefits and costs of polluting, thus enabling to reach efficient solutions for global environmental issues.[20]

Nevertheless reality has not followed—and is not following—the Tobin way towards the homogeneisation of taxes on global pollutants. This has happened because such homogeneisation of taxes is not only related with pure problems of efficiency and competitiveness among nations, but also with the indispensable downwards readjusting of the absolute standards of living of citizens, whose desirability is not shared with the same emphasis, either by all parties in every nation or by the different nations; hence our call for the establishment of a new World Environment Organisation (WEO) depending on a new democratic UN for solving these problems,. This WEO should also try to improve the management of common global renewable resources as f.i. fishing (in international waters) and rainforest, trying in the latter cases to fight against overfishing and overlogging, two exceeding activities with huge negative global externalities.

Besides the surveillance on the chemical content and fishing stocks of common sea water and oceans, a policy on human population should also be

---

18. Individual freedom for establishing different rules in relation to national environment could be used by the West as a base for supporting new protectionist rules on goods coming from (poor) countries, produced with highly polluting technologies. To this respect, vide Andreu and Rahman (2009b: 269).

19. Vide Nordhouse (1995) and Andreu and Rahman (2009b: 270).

20. Nevertheless, mentioned efficient solution based on equalisation of marginal benefits or costs has nothing to do with the per capita global pollution of every country, or with the per capita income of every country, two parameters absolutely relevant for fairly distributing the economic efforts of different individuals and nations to preserve the global environment.

devised by the new WEO. This is because, given the fact that the main cause of the global environmental problems is the growth of the population of the planet—and the wishes of all nations for reaching an economic 'affluency' similar to the current one reached by industrialised countries—mentioned population policy will be unavoidable. Indeed, a limitless population growth seems to be non-sustainable and, correspondly, limitations and conditions should be debated and regulated by a democratic UN.

The Basic Principle of Externalities: Those who Pollute have to Pay...'Just Proportionaly'?

In the context of the current multilateral institutions, once the targets have been established by consensus, the following step will be sharing of economic burdens, including the reduction or limitation of emissions at a consented rhythm to avoid additional global warming.[21] A conditioning variable could be the per capita volume of allowable pollution, which would depend on gross emissions and on ways of absorbing the CO_2 emitted to the atmosphere; absorption that will really depend on corresponding investments realised by every country in forest, compression and storage of CO_2, etc., or by the international community (global society). Note that up to now, all artificial absorption systems are still in an experimental stage.

Concerning distribution of burdens or investments to be realised for reducing or limiting the emissions of CO_2, Western countries seem to support the principle of 'those who pollute must pay.' But in our view this principle, perhaps correct for solving problems of 'national' pollution, should not be applicable to a problem affecting the whole global society, including in this collective both rich and poor nations.

In fact, within any country in which both rich and poor live, besides existing more or less sophisticated systems for controlling local emissions— as f.i. the setting up of physical limits to pollution, Pigouvian taxes to emissions, markets of pollution permits connected with caps established by governments, etc.—there also exist progressive systems of taxation and expenditure (f.i. public health system) favourable to the less rich, systems

---

21. Alternatively, the target for additional global warming along the 21st century could be established in just 1 or 2°C.

that may offset the failures of the public sector connected with the definition of permitted caps, taxes on emissions, etc.

Former consideration is relevant because to the extent that progressiveness has to play a role in this issue of global environment, the absolute volume of non-sustaninable emissions—the sole variable determinant of compensation, as defended by Westerners—will have to give primacy to other variables as the 'non-sustainable per capita emissions' and the 'per capita GDP' of every country. Note that former non-sustainable 'per capita' emissions refer to those that surpass sustainable per capita emissions, being the latter 'consistent with no additionally allowed global warming.' Diversity of non-sustainable 'per capita emissions' at a planet scale should play a role, which would imply to set more than proportional burdens to those who generate more non-sustainable 'per capita' emissions (in order to penalise their behaviour). Note additionally to this respect, that in our view, it will always be better for the global society to deal with those who do not pollute at all than with those who pollute a lot and pay a lot, because the latter induces high costs of administration.

On the other hand, for solving a problem that affects all citizens of the planet, the per capita GDP should play a fundamental role, because it would be unfair—when we are talking about the corrections to be implemented to waranty the survival of all human beings on the planet—that the rich did a lesser marginal effort per US dollar invested against climate change than the poor. In this regard, we should not forget that the rich have profited much more from the industrialisation process than the poor, while the rich countries—during colonialism—used to arrest or hinder the industrialisation of colonies.

As a result of all considered variables, the per capita burden to be distributed in future to solve the problem of climate change—basically to drive the evolution of CO_2 to the desired level—should be positively correlated with the per capita GDP of the diferent countries, although more than proportionally, and also in a progressive way with the volume of non-sustainable per capita emissions of the different nations.

Note in this regard that if the economic efforts were absolutely linear with the 'non-sustainable' emissions of the different countries—criterion defended by the West following the economic principle of 'those who pollute must pay'—then for solving the problem, we would just be taking into account in a proportional way the per capita non-sustainable emissions and the number of inhabitants of every country, and not at all either the different per capita GDP of every country or the differentiated per capita sustainable emissions, as a dissausive mechanism aimed at reducing the current polluting trend.

Having mentioned former aspects of the problem, some of them with a high content of uncertainty, one could wonder on the global economic effort to be realised in this uncertain context. Under these insecure circumstances, we believe that the global economic effort should be of a variable character: incremental if indicators of climate change would continue progressing in a direction opposed to that required, or de-cremental in the opposite case. As a reference to the relative effort to be realised, it is our view that, given its indispensable character and extreme urgency, the average effort should not be much smaller than that devoted today to military expenditures.[22] Hence, in order to arrive to a figure of f.i. 2 per cent the world GDP from the current small figure, a not very long phasing period should be established (less than 10-12 years). This is because continuing with the growth of CO_2 emissions over a longer phasing period could be extremely dangerous since the climate of the planet could enter into a stage of no return, if this is not already the case.

The next question to be discussed in this matter is also nuclear. It refers to in what forum and with what legitimacy 'corresponding authorities' would establish the conditions to solve the problem. Till some few decades ago, the environmental problem either did not exist or the people had not noticed its existence. But today the problem is in front of us all and looking for urgent solutions. However, the current methodology for resolution—the MEAs—is clearly not appropriate.

Indeed, to reach internacional treaties or agreements (MEAs) at a planetary scale among the near 200 countries that currently belong to the UN—for which the decision-rule is consensus or 'unanimity' and not majority—the arrival to efficient global agreements is practically impossible. There will always be countries with strong arguments (or just pretexts)

---

22. According to the last figures of the WB (2012), the average of military expenditures at a world scale was 2.6 per cent in 2010.

that will reject to agree with certain powers. On the other hand, as the political-domestic circumstances in front of every national government will be different, and the economic conditions facing every country will be variable, different governments will have different sensitivities in relation to the efforts to be realised in relation to climate change. These differences will drive them to the joint formulation of agreements on minima and not on optima at a global scale. Even more, these agreements on minima will require an extended time-period for discussions, inconsistent with the required urgency for the formulation of an optimal agreement, while they will lack capacities for control and enforcement.

Former arguments force us to declare most of past international agreements on environment, realised under the umbrella of the current UN as inefficient, because they have been excessively time consuming, have generated agreements on minima and not on optima, have not been inclusive (all countries not participating), and have been neither controllable nor compulsive.

On the Foundations of Public Action at Global, Regional and National Levels

From the moment in which a new democratic UN starts working, this organisation should intervene with public action on global public goods and global externalities. Note that when one of these phenomena exclusively affects the inhabitants of one country, it is the national public sector of this country which should be called to administrate the issue. However, if a problem (as f.i. acid rain) only affects two or more neighbouring nations, the solution should be regional, because the rest of the world should not pay for administrating the provision or correction of regional public goods or regional externalities. Notwithstanding this, a relevant UN agency should necessarily supervise the regional arrangements for the provision of regional public goods or correction of regional externalities.

The principle that every public problem (be this a public good or a single externality) should be exclusively solved by one public administration is also fundamental, because it enables to treat the problem in the most efficient way and to avert duplicities. To ilustrate this principle, we have to underline that the provision of global peace and security—a clear global public good—should be done in the future just by a democratic global government (the Executive Council of the new democratic UN), and not individually by member countries or groups of countries (coalitions), and not only from the perpective of the different financial capacities—certainly only the new UN should and could finance a multilateral, neutral and functional army to provide global peace and security—but also from the view of legitimacy for formulating aims and means in the interest of the global society.

Climate Change and Human Resettlements

Letting aside the current growing illegal migrations, induced by the huge economic inequalities among nations and the restrictive rules for access of foreigners to jobs in rich countries—and all that in a context of full and live information of the poor in developing countries—we will now focus on the massive human resettlements that may probably become a priority in some few decades, if climate change continues with its current negative trend.

Indeed, although the current volume of displaced people[23] in the world, mainly coming from economic-ethnic civil wars, has reached millions, this phenomenon could in future become an almost irrelevant precedent in comparison to the immigration and resettlement problems that climate change may provoke in next decades.

In fact, according to most—not all—scientists, if the average temperature of the planet rises in the 21st century more than 2°C, seas will meaningfully raise their level, provoking floods in seaside cities and areas. In large countries, this will provoke significant internal migrations. In the smaller, overcrowded or estuarial countries,[24] displacements—in some cases of a massive nature—will necessarily imply migrations to other countries. In

---

23. The current displaced people (by wars, ethnic cleansing, etc.), amounting at around 20 million—and living in neighbouring countries, normally in tents—uses to be subject of several forms of abuse.

24. *Ceteris paribus*, one has to expect that an estuarial country like Bangladesh, today with a population over 170 million people, in which during monsoon season up to one-third of its surface is flooded, may as a consequence of climate change experience severe worsening. This could imply that Bangladeshi migrations to other countries will become a necessity. Observe that from a global quantitative perspective, 200 million displaced along three decades, due to climate change, would mean an average of 7 million per year, a huge figure of people to be resettled in inhabited territories without creating political and economic problems.

drier areas, forced external migrations could be the result of the persistent reduction of water availability induced by climate change.

In absence of a global authority, one cannot imagine what could happen on the planet if the future amount of international displaced people by climate change reached additional figures of around 200 million people (as forecasted in 2008 by the International Organisation on Migration, a figure equivalent to 2.8 per cent of the current global population). We do believe that in that case, the induced problem could be unbearable if such movements of people had to be realised in just two or three decades—when the problem became observable but unsolvable—and if migrants should have to be resettled in already inhabited territories. Note that in such circumstances, and for the first time in modern history, a mega-movement of people would take place just for surviving.

In the absence of a global authority with enforcement capacities, including an efficient and professional army, a factual or attempted massive displacement of people towards neighbouring inhabited countries could be considered as a *casus belli* at the receiving end. This could trigger even preventive military actions for the defence of own territories. Indeed, mentioned massive migrations provoked by climate change could drive, in absence of democratic global governance, to an unprecedented political and humanitarian catastrophe.

Note additionally that since the initial environmental problem was partially ignited by rich countries, future Western actions to resist sharing negative consequences of global warming—by means of not accepting (or not financing) migrations forced by climate change—would be an unbearable and egoistic political positioning, from the perspective of democratic global governance.

Non-competitive International Prices and Necessary Reforms

In relation to the provision of global public goods, we have mentioned the case of global economic regulations, at times connected with the existence of certain degrees of monopoly on relevant goods traded in the world.

In fact, when one starts analysing certain international markets—as that of oil or other strategic raw materials—whose supplies are concentrated in a small group of producing-exporting countries, one should expect that neither the produced quantities are the optima from the perspective of the economic theory of the non-renewable resources, nor are current prices consistent with sustainable global supply and demand. And that because 'market prices' could be coherent with a non-sustainable suply, while these prices could have been formed in a market not free of 'hoarding operations' realised by certain MNC, or even by national superpowers,[25] that is to say, in a market with artificially increased or reduced demands.

Ultimately, neither the production of these raw materials (crude oil, gold, platinium, diamonds, etc.) nor the international prices formed in corresponding markets will be optimal because we are talking about the provision of goods that, although private, induce significant externalities while containing a meaningful degree of monopoly. Besides, this degree of monopoly could be temporary variable and therefore could at times generate global economic instability and often long or deep economic cycles.

The Crude Oil Market as a Particular Case of Necessary Global Economic Intervention

Entering in the example of crude oil, and trying to analyse the traits of its international market, we have first to state that the global demand of this good should adjusts to what the global society needs in a context of environmental sustainability. This means that the global demand of crude oil should be free from excesses of consumerism, which are taking us to global warming.

In relation to the oil supply, we should also consider: (1) at what level the supply should be placed to form with the sustainable demand an optimal and sustainable price; (2) how that (sustainable) supply could adjust to changes, due to short-term political phenomena—as for instance, a revolution in a producing country or a technological innovation (fracking)—or to certain fluctuations of the demand provoked by short-term meteorological variations; (3) who could control these productions, and how, in order to avoid sudden and deep fluctuations in the international prices,

---

25. Remember that, at a national private level, maneuvers of 'hoarding' were in other times, and even today in many poor countries, a reproachable behaviour defined in the penal codes. In a parallel way, public hoarding by individual countries could be reproached in future by the new democratic UN.

as happened in the past when OPEC, which having a strong control on production and exports, enabled or provoked the generation of deep business cycles; and (4) what could be the convenient level of expenditure in research for a progressive substitution of crude oil by other less polluting energy resources.

Note in this respect that since the beginning of the Industrial Revolution in the 18th century, but particularly since the motorisation started at the begining of the 20th century, till the 1970s—when the Report of the Club of Rome was published—no one protested with enough intensity against consumption excesses and energy wasting observed in the production, distribution[26] and consumption processes of goods and services.

Monitoring the reality of the oil market and by-products, we may also find that this market is not competitive at all, thus not being efficient either at short term or at long term.[27] Indeed, in last decades, the supply in this market has been prone to the abuse of disseminated consumers of the world, who, through imitation, and despite the rocketing prices of oil (from 1973 onwards), have individually continued consuming in an overdone way, and this while no Western government reacted with adequate substitution policies for changing the existing habit of individual transport. Even more, contrary to common sense, in the mid-1980s, most governments promoted individual transportation which experienced a boom. The inefficiency of the oil market also became patent when in other years oil prices went down too far,[28] certainly under those advisable for economising the use of crude oil.

On the Foundations of the Reshuffling of the Oil Market

First of all, we should point out that fundamentally this market is still organised in a similar way as it was several decades ago. However, one should note that the world economic structure has radically changed in the last 30 years, with many developing countries embodying to the group of fast

---

26. Freedom for commercial distribution—as it occurs in capitalism—uses to generate important extra cost, thus being at times highly inefficient. For instance, in the developing world, it is frequent that food exports are first sent to the metropolis for thereafter to be re-exported to neighbouring (developing and developed) countries of the first exporter.

27. As remarked by Joseph Stiglitz in his publication *Globalisation and its Discontents* (2002: 174), international cartels should be declared illegal at a global scale as they are illegal at national level in countries such as the US.

28. Note that this happened in certain moments along the 1980s and 1990s, thus encouraging artificial cyclical expansions.

growth, as it happened with China and India, which jointly contains around 37 per cent of the planet's population. Note that these large populations legitimately aspire to become fast track consumers of industrial goods, the same as the rest of citizens of dynamic countries of South-East Asia, Latin America or Africa, and they imitate the negative habits of consumption in the West, particularly in relation to urban developments based on the massive use of motor vehicles.

Leaving aside the development of new mining techniques, this massive use of vehicles means that the demand for crude oil is probably growing today at non-sustainable rhythms, due to the fact that these growth rates are much higher than those of oil production capacities with available and expected technologies, and acceptable costs per extracted barrel. However, mentioned rapid growth of the oil demand, even if matching production was available, would not be sustainable due to the CO_2 emissions generated by its overdone consumption.[29]

Obviously, if mentioned (non-sustainable) trends of the global demand became real, the demand-supply unbalance would economically favour the current oil exporting countries, a situation which besides being wrong would be unfair. But note that all this could occur in a world that in some decades will change into being governed democratically,[30] reason why mentioned unbalanced and unfair results could politically and economically be arrested in just two or three decades.

The simple possibility that abrupt rises in oil prices may happen in future, as a consequence of eventual abusive restrictions established by suppliers, or as a result of the ultra rapid growth of the demand, is a clear indicator that this market should be reorganised as soon as possible in a sustainable way in consistency with the political advances foreseeable for the 21st century.

---

29. Note that besides emissions, cars will also produce overwhelming congestion, due to excessive number of cars circulating at the same time in many cities, cities whose 'centres' were designed, for other purposes, many decades before the last boom of motorisation, occurred in the last third of the 20th century.

30. If democracy is a political system prone to the distribution of wealth, there is no doubt that when the global society reaches global democracy, democratic UN will take mankind towards more egalitarian positions. This should be recommendable after centuries of concentration of the wealth in industrialised countries, particularly since the initiation of the Industrial Revolution. For comparative figures, vide Maddison (2001).

A last question to be discussed is if, in a world of 7,000 million people grouped in 193 countries (represented in the UN), most of them highly dependent consumers of oil, the level of their per capita income and wealth should extremely depend (or not), among other causes, on geological circumstances that have placed some oil producing-exporting countries in an oligopolistic position in relation to consumers, which are the majority. In this regard, we do believe that any abusive or defective administration of the oil prices should be averted in future by means of the intervention of an agency of the new democratic UN, and not by a self-regulating organisation of producers-exporters (OPEC), whose errors in productions and prices are at times compounded by the degree of monopoly, and the derivatives of armed actions undertaken by hegemonic powers. In this field as in others, we do believe that keeping self-regulation—in this case referring to the producer states (OPEC)—without counting with the interests of consumers and the general interests of the global society, is highly dangerous and prone to abuses.

A Specialised Agency of the New UN for Administrating the Oil

Let us now look into the real nature of OPEC. Certainly and by definition, the OPEC is 'an international Cartel' that, as other producers' organisations today existent, is not consistent with the principles of sustainable global capitalism. Indeed, to be sustainable, global capitalism should avert the current non-competitive structural behaviour typical of certain relevant markets which, as the oil one, have a clear propensity to: (1) induce unfair distribution of wealth among nationals of producing countries; (2) induce cyclical fluctuations at global scale that may be dangerous; and (3) generate monoculture economies (petroleum but also gold, diamonds, etc.) which uses to hinder domestic development of democracy due to the absence of diversification of productions.[31]

---

31. In our book *Global Democracy for Sustaining Global Capitalism* (2009b), it was pointed out that one of the main conditions for sustainability of democracy is that it must be supported by a market economy and that the different productions of that market economy should be enough diversified. Conversely, when certain productions (oil, gas, gold, diamonds, etc. or even banking in fiscal paradises) individually generate more than 50 per cent of the annual GDP of a country, the generation of political clientelism is almost warranted, and this clientelism usually tends to progressively position these countries away from democratic behaviour.

Indisputable, the volume of petrol to be produced at a world scale should be democratically decided by the UN, on the basis of the current technology of extraction and official geological reports on proven reserves in the world. And all that in consistency with an expectable demand of oil that should depend on sustainable economic growth as desired by the global society.

As a result of former considerations, this democratic UN should organise an agency for defining prices and productions as well as for arranging a follow-up of the quantitative evolution of the strategic deposits kept by national governments, and all that for avoiding dangerous short-term fluctuations in prices, and averting the promotion of artificial 'supply shocks' and crisis that so much have hurted the global economy in the last decades. In case of productive problems generated at short term in a relevant producing country, the agency would authorise increases of production in other countries while the initial political problem is solved by peaceful means in the troubled country.

In the reorganisation of the oil market, one should not discard that the UN would establish a worldwide ecological tax on petrol, replacing the current ecological taxes of the different states. The revenue of the new tax could be directed to increase the sustainability of the planet, while it could reduce the volume of the direct contribution of members to the annual budget of the UN.

Reorganisation Problems in Other Global Markets

The former is not but one example of formation of prices and productions in one market of strategic raw materials. In principle, we could say the same in relation to other markets in which agricultural products, cereals, sugar, coffee, etc., used for human nourishment, are interchanged.

In this regard, we should underline that, despite the global population growth, the supplies of some of these products have recently been reduced at a world scale, due to the shift towards the production of biofuels. Encouraged by profitable prices, this prioritisation has been done by some big agricultural firms or governments, which has favoured the consumers of fuel by means of increasing fuel supply and reducing its prices. This has been done in such a way that, those with more acquisition capacity at a world scale—most of citizens of the industrialised world—with their 'exaggerated needs of fuel,' necessary to continue with their non-sustainable way of living, have indirectly induced that the poor of the world become poorer—due to the increases of prices and the scarcity of basic food.

We do believe that, given that this negative income redistribution—*via* prices—could induce social unstability, as it systematically happened all along the 19th century and first third of the 20th, the priorisation between agricultural production of food and biofuel should be defined by an agency of the new UN (WEO),[32] and not by individuals (producers) or national governments.

In addition, and in connection with the formation of prices of certain agricultural products (basic food such as cereals, etc.), we do believe that the financial speculation on basic food realised or encouraged by subsidiary companies of banks, should also be controlled.[33] Certainly, although processes of buying and selling futures on cereals may reduce the intensity of fluctuations of mentioned prices, they may also contain speculation for unduly increasing profits.

On the Exploitation of Natural Resources in the North Pole

Following former discussions on natural resources, we could now wonder on the legitimacy of the current spontaneous appropriating process of potential mineral resources deposited in the North Pole,[34] unleashed by some neighbouring countries.

Indeed, the urgent positioning of the different intervening countries in relation with the mineral deposits in the North Pole—consisting of temporarily gaining preferent positions without any legitimacy—reminds us of the disastrous outcome of the division of Africa at the end of the 19th

---

32. Current Food and Agriculture Organization (FAO) could pass in future to depend on WEO.

33. It has been recently known that certain major banks, as for instance, Barclays, Goldman-Sachs and Morgan-Stanley, be this by themselves or by setting up subsidiary companies, have dramatically entered in these future markets of cereals, obtaining important profits (Barclays, the leader bank in these operations, has declared to have earned 500 million sterling pounds in the last months). Vide *The Independent*, September 1st, 2012.

34. These mineral resources could become exploitable when the melting of the current polar ices in the North Pole, induced by the global warming, becomes a consolidated but undesirable fact.

century, when Western countries, in full colonial euphoria, and without even knowing either orography or dwellers of territories, distributed sub-Saharan Africa among themselves in a reckless and irrational way.[35]

It is curious that now, more than one century after the so-called 'scrambling for Africa,' we are again observing a pre-snatching of the subsoil of the planet—in this case the marine beds of the North Pole—in a pure political power play among competitors, and certainly realised with bad style. Note in this regard that, although the world is today progressing in a totally different political context than in times of the Conference of Berlin in 1884—with much more countries governed in a democratic way and with extractive technologies reachable for all—contenders in the scrambling for the North Pole do not look for consensus but to gain a favourable position in front of the others.

Observe that, similarly to what occurred in sub-Saharan Africa with a shameless distribution of formally confiscated territories—which by the way were not at all property of European countries[36] and mostly were not *terra nullius*—the marine beds of the North Pole are neither property of the candidates who dare to declare their right to distribute the new 'beds,' nor of others who even without being 'hinterland countries' or just with overlapping 'territorial waters' also dare to take part of the spoils of this part of the planet.

We have to acknowledge that historically, in absence of democratic global governance, the so-called 'territorial waters' were defined in an arbitrary way,[37] according to the political influences of the then strongest nations. Contrary to this behaviour, we do believe that in the 21st century,

---

35. This distribution became a fact in the Conference of Berlin, held between November 1884 and February 1885. Attendant nations were: Germany, Austria, Belgium, Denmark, Spain, US, France, UK, Netherlands, Italy, Portugal, Russia, Sweden and Turkey. No African country attended the meeting.

36. Note however that in the Berlin Conference two antithetic concepts linked to colonialism were extensively discussed: simple Annexing *versus* Protectorate. Note that the latter at least respected the 'long-term' sovereignty of the inhabitants of every territory.

37. Letting aside the Roman Laws, which declared the seas as free, and other minor theories, the world had to wait till 1930 for a definition of 'territorial waters,' year in which an *ad hoc* international conference held in The Hague established 'territorial waters' within 12 marine miles. Half a century later, and due to an initiative of certain Latin American countries, the Conference of the UN on the Sea Rights (1982) declared an 'exclusive economic zone' of countries that would reach till 200 marine miles.

the natural resources of the North Pole or other today non-accessible places (such as part of the South Pole) should not be object of appropriation by individual nations, but by the global society and its legitimate representation.

We do believe that the current world cannot enable a new unequal and unfair distribution of the resources of the subsoil of the planet in remote and till now unknown and unexploited places, particularly, in a historical time in which these extraterritorial resources should be administered by a democratic UN representing the global society.[38] Note besides, that the administration of this extraterritorial wealth could give the new UN an important financial capacity as to decisively intervene in other problems as collective UN defence, development financing, financing of environmental sustainability, climate change, etc.

Summarising, all mentioned problems related to the production and pricing of crude oil and other strategic raw materials, to the appropriation of *terra nulius*, as marine beds in international waters, as well as those coming from the current non-democratic administration (at a global scale) of goods which generate global externalities of a negative character—as overlogging tropical forest or over-exploitation of fisheries in international waters—are issues whose exploitation and administration could significantly improve if the 193 nations of the world, reorganised in a new democratic UN, would set up a new *ad hoc* agency (WEO) in which all mentioned relevant aspects for the sustainability of life and biodiversity were decided, controlled and enforced under surveillance of the UN army-navy.[39]

Urgent Need for Democratising the UN and Underlying Economic Trends to Convergence

As we have already mentioned, the convenient democratisation of the UN will not occur in some centuries, but in just 2 or 3 decades. This relatively short period for major political global change has been deduced from projections into the future of certain economic aggregates, based

---

38. This is alike to what is done by most of states that administrate the subsoil of their territories.

39. We have already pointed out that agreements or international treaties among equals— which require consensus—use to drive to soundly failures, and this while the global problems of the planet continue gaining intensity, due to the growth of population and the global per capita consumption of energy and food.

on oficial figures published by the WB[40] and International Monetary Fund (IMF), referring to the last three decades (1980-2010). Mentioned projections are pointing to a continuation of the rapid convergence in the next 2-3 decades.[41] This convergence is also consistent with the recent acceleration of history and politics initiated in the early 1980s, and easied by the appearance of new technologies of information and communication. Although believing that a *sine die* continuation of current political and economic structures in the world is a general psychological behaviour of those in power, we insist that main developments and trends point out to the opposite.[42]

We do think that in the next 2 or 3 decades, several convergent movements of relevant macroeconomic magnitudes among the countries of high income (all together) and the rest of developing ones (of low and middle income) will take place. This will mainly happen because while the magnitudes of industrialised countries will continue their comparative decline, those of the rest—the developing ones, including the 'emergents' — will quickly increase,[43] although more moderately than in the last 2-3 decades.

Obviously, when these processes finally induce economic equality (or almost), the traditional assymetric positions in economic negotiations of the West with the rest of the world (still based on dominance) will have to be abandoned and substituted by economic parity and democratic representation. These changes will force radical reforms in the statutes of

---

40. The Graphs which prove the current mentioned economic trends were presented by Rita Dulci Rahman and José Miguel Andreu in the UN in New York, the October 19, 2010, when introducing their book *Global Democracy for Sustaining Global Capitalism: The Way to Solve Global Problems* to the managers of the UN Division "Analysis and Policy of Development". This exercise on economic trends has been repeated 2 years later with same results.

41. And this irrespective of what is happening in the middle of 2013: stabilisation of the Western economies and transitory weakening of emergent countries as India or Brazil.

42. Many top professionals of any field, although recognising that in the last few years, there have been deep changes in their activity, when questioned about the future they 'surprisingly' consider that the changes to come will be mild.

43. These convergent movements refer to the following magnitudes: (1) the aggregated GDP of the countries of high income in comparison to the aggregated GDP of the rest (developing countries); (2) the aggregated industrial productions of these two groups of countries; (3) the evolution of shares in international trade of goods of these two groups of countries; and (4) the aggregated defence expenditures of these two groups of countries.

all multilateral institutions including the UN, which will necessarily change into democratic. Consequently, the General Asembly of UN will have to change into a Global Parliament in which global issues will be debated and decided by majority. A Global Government (or Executive Council)—subordinated to the Global Parliament (the new General Assembly)—will substitute the current Security Council and execute the resolutions adopted by the General Assembly.

Note that the creation of a democratic UN will enable to recover former economic rationality—lost when national capitalism progressed towards globalisation—on certain issues of the global agenda already mentioned (global economic regulation, correction of global externalities, and better international distribution of income and wealth).

We have to insist that changes in relation to the economic power of the different (important or not) countries in the world have significantly modified the political shape of the world in the last three decades. And we are convinced—based on economic arguments—that mentioned trends will continue and will probably induce major political changes in future, mainly resulting in the democratic reshuffling of the UN.

From the perspective of the economy, and given the stepping up of the growth rates of China, India and neighbouring Asian countries, two essential phenomena have become observable and will become progressively clearer. Although the most important of the two, the fast economic structural change favouring developing countries, has not been object of meaningful attention by Western politicians and academicians—who have mainly been (and are) busy with the most urgent consequences of the recent spectacular downfall (2007-08) and difficult recovery of the GDP in many Western countries—the reality is that the currently observable 'structural change' is a historical phenomenon that will likely overturn the relative importance of many Western European countries. Indeed, Western politicians, without forgetting the current cyclical and institutional (EU) problems, should focus their attention on microeconomic issues related to competitiveness of East-West, thus trying to achieve a soft landing for the West by minimising the speed of their relative economic decline.

In this regard, we should not forget that what is happening today in the world economy directly points to a radical change in the historical importance of the different parts of the world. Certainly, and for centuries—perhaps from the 16th century onwards—the technological, military and navigation advantages of the West gave the different countries belonging to this geographic area[44] the opportunity of 'civilising' the others while extracting from their territories raw materials (gold, food, etc.) and even slaves at low cost.[45] This was generally done by means of the establishment of an asymetric way of trade, eased through political and military domination, which served colonisers in the 18th and 19th centuries[46] to finance their industrialisation processes.

But mentioned historical background and following economic derivatives are today rapidly changing. First of all, in the last 65 years, the world population has multiplied almost by 3, moving from 2.5 billion in 1945 (end of the Second World War) to 7 billion in 2011, certainly a rapid increase mainly concentrated in developing countries. As a result of this massive and biased population growth, only around one billion live in the West, this just representing around 16 per cent of the total world population.

One should not forget that population is the basic parameter of democracy. This is the reason why today it is very difficult for the West—without losing its face—to reject the proposals of an overwhelming majority of the world (84%), or to impose their (at times) irrational views on the others. We are well aware that, in the long run, current unfair economic and political *status quo* could only be maintained by means of military actions or intimidations on (today mostly democratic) developing countries, but this would be in contradiction with what the West has preached in favour of democracy along one century. Nevertheless, we do believe that these possible threats are quickly losing credibility because the most important 'leading' developing countries (China, India and Russia) have comparatively big armies and are nuclear powers, while today, despite of UN efforts, nuclear weaponry seems to be proliferating.

---

44. Note that these few Western countries insistently tried to lead the group, getting involved in wars against each other or in coalitions, mainly among Spain, France and Britain.

45. Up to well advanced the 19th century, slaves were considered merchandise and cargo in international trade. On this issue on the cargo treatment of the slaves, the reader may see the interesting film titled "Amistad," directed by Steven Spielberg.

46. We have to affirm that in the 19th century, Spain, with its internal political disputes (three civil wars), lost the opportunity of generating quicker industrial development.

As it is well known political hegemony requires, among other conditions, a supporting economy growing at high speed. But this fast growth will not be possible in future in relation to most European countries already developed,[47] irrespective of whether they remain independent and keep their current small sizes, or if they federate.[48] Note that, *ceteris paribus*, the most important contributor to the growth rate of a country is the shift of workers from sectors of low productivity—agriculture—to those of higher productivity, as industry and services. But in fact, the very developed countries only have 2-5 per cent of their active population in the primary sector, reason why they have no margin for important intersectorial transfers of human resources. In future, and for similar reasons, the additional embodiment of women to active population will not significantly count either in already developed countries. Finally, we should not forget the relatively higher investment capacities of China and India—much higher than those of Western countries—as indicators of their higher growth capacities.

Former arguments, plus lower comparative population dynamic in Europe, will *ceteris paribus* exclude France, Germany and Britain as main actors in the future, reason why after the next three decades, the sole Western global actor will be the US. Now then, if some 8-12 Eurozone countries finally federate, this federation would accompany the US among the top group of leading countries of the World, which at the end of the first half of the 21st century, or perhaps before, will be formed by China, the US, the European Federation and India.

All these circumstances taken into consideration enable to predict that there is no future for the current UN as it is today organised, with five veto owners with capacities to stop any discussion or proposed resolutions, although the latter were supported by majorities. Agreements by consensus

---

47. One should not forget that along the last 20 years (1990-2010), the GDP of Germany—the so-called 'the economic engine of Europe'—grew at an average rate of 1.3 per cent, while France did it at 1.6 per cent.

48. If some of them federate, they could get important economies of scale and synergies amounting up to 2 per cent of their GDP, without counting other dynamic advantages coming from the larger negotiation power of the federation. Vide Rahman and Andreu (2005). Despite of it, we consider that even the formation of EU federation will not change the current economic trends that will induce the reshuffling of the political structure of the world.

(such as MEAs) in most of urgent issues (as environment, global economic rules, administration of sustainable fisheries in international waters, rainforest keeping, control of international monopolies, administration of strategic raw materials, exploitation of continental platforms in arbitrary defined territorial waters, etc.) will surely fail, which will further undermine the current global governance capabilities of the UN, and compound the already degraded habitability of the planet. This will finally force the democratisation of the UN.

From our perspective, this democratisation process will take place in little time, 2 or 3 decades as a maximum. Rather before than later, current main countries of the world will start negotiations with emerging countries on new statutes for a new UN based on democratic principles, and on a new UN agenda founded on the recently appreciated global needs to be provided by the global society.

Of course to enforce decisions taken by the UN Parliament or by the UN Government, a UN army-navy will have to be created to be constantly deployed in all continents and oceans. This army-navy should be neutral and professional, depending exclusively on the UN and financed by it, and should defend and support the interests of the global society in issues as peace and security, global environment, global economic regulation, positive or negative global externalities, global distribution of income, fight against air and sea piracy, etc.

6 | Economic Changes and the Political Scenario of the World in 2040s

After the West, basically Europe, abandoned feudalism and time later mercantilism, the relations among their economic agents started being organised in the context of a system of production, financing and interchange that was finally named 'capitalism,' today also known as 'traditional capitalism.' Under this economic system, the state or authorities in charge hardly played any role in the definition of the economic aims, because according to what was then generally understood (Smithian Economics), the available natural resources and the individual decisions of investment in agriculture, industry or in the service sectors, realised in a context of freedom of contracting and exchange, would determine for the better the economic trajectories of individuals, firms and countries. Only some few interventions in internacional trade—mainly asymmetric protectionism and rules relating to colonies—or in some prioritarian activities or industries, as defence, infrastructure, transports, etc., were exceptions to the general rule of free private economic initiative.

However, mentioned freedom of competitors, be these workers, consumers or producers who started the economic game with different departure positions—this is to say, with more or less material or intangible assets, as properties, education level, health situation, etc.—quickly drove the majority of non-owners to economic subordination. And all this induced unbalanced personal income distribution resulting in political non-sustainability, even in the case of coexistence of primitive-traditional capitalism with fragile national democracies (as in the case of the French Republic born in 1789).

In this unstable sociopolitical context of the 19th century, 'socialism' appeared. It emerged first as an ethical-political concept, and later, in the second part of the 19th century and first decades of the 20th, as an alternative economic system for modifying the harsh reality connected with the induced negative income distribution. Both concepts, 'socialism' and 'socialist economy,' although containing significant advances in relation to certain social aims, also included huge mistakes connected first with the behaviour of individuals, mostly prone to defend own interest and individual accumulation, and second in relation to the capacities of public economic planning. This collective planning—aiming at defining and controlling all productions, prices and wages—after some decades of difficult praxis in the 20th century, was sidelined due to the rapidly changing reality, impossible to be systematically re-evaluated and controlled by a national centralised authority.

'Traditional capitalism,' to which socialism tried to substitute, was not a perfect system either. Along the 19th century and first third of the 20th, 'traditional capitalism' moved through stages of rather slow and cyclical growth, while inducing unfair personal income distribution in the context of some primitive 'democratic systems', practically insensitive to the hopes of majorities (who lacked voting rights, etc.). Indeed, along the last decades of the 19th century and first third of the 20th, 'traditional capitalism' proved its good working in microeconomic adjustments, because it was much more flexible than its alternative, the central planning system, initially developed in the Soviet Union after the Revolution of 1917. However, in the 1930s of the 20th century (period of the Great Crisis and Depression) 'traditional capitalism' delivered a dramatic proof of its bad macroeconomic functioning, comparable to the bad macroeconomic performance of current neoliberalism, as designed today by the EU under the direction of Germany.

With independence of the theoretical assesment of interventionism, based on the application of the Keynesian model, the reality is that in the period 1950-1973—the so-called 'Golden Age' of capitalism—the economic growth rate of the world was the quickiest in history. However, even in this age, two underlying interconnected problems were already dangerously progressing: (1) the explosive demography in many countries, that would multiply per 2.8 the planet's population in the period 1945-2011, and (2) the induced explosive growth in the consumption of raw materials—in particular of crude oil—for the production of energy, fertilisers, manufactures, services of transport, shelters, etc.

Note that the spontaneous and explosive economic dynamics, on which capitalism[1] had evolved in the Golden Age, could not be sustainable at long term in a limited world; and much less when a 'new version of unbridled neoliberal capitalism,' coexisting in some countries with the traditional one, became 'global.' Note that in the current global economy, many relevant economic decisions are defined and controlled by huge multinational corporations (MNCs), global banks or even by small oligopolistic (oil exporting) states, and not at all by the main national governments.

Indeed, we have arrived at a time in which the sovereignty in markets is to a large extent exerted by producers—not by consumers—in particular by those who have the supreme power in the big MNCs, including banks, or in certain states producers of strategic raw materials. Note that this power is almost absolute in front of the scant international power of most national consumer states, firms or individuals, who difficultly may defend themselves against at times the agressive and selfish behaviour of these MNCs, oil producing countries, etc.

These MNCs and selected states also use to defend the existence of fiscal paradises or off-shore financial centres to which annually around US$ 280 billion is diverted, a figure representing 0.5 per cent of the world GDP. For comparative purposes, one should note that the Official Development Aid (ODA) is today far lower than mentioned annual transfer of money to fiscal paradises. In 2011, the total ODA was just US$ 131 billion.

Consequently, given the current overwhelming problems of mankind, and the lack of adaptation of the national political decision-making to the wider geographical playing ground of 'global capitalism'—which has again negatively modified personal income and wealth distribution, this time at internal scale—the traditional states will necessarily have to give up part of their sovereignty to a multilateral power, capable of solving the current common problems of humanity and besides, with democratic legitimacy, which will finally drive the global society towards the democratic reorganisation of the UN.

In brief, capitalism, including its traditional and global versions, both of them liberal, counts with the advantage of its flexibility and adjusting

---

1. Capitalism, as practised in Western Europe from around 1955 to 1980, was mainly a softer version of former 'traditional capitalism,' due to the inclusion of a public social protection system (welfare state).

capacities to the changing circumstances but today is in need of controlling at short-mid term two of its main unpleasant derivatives: human suffering, provoked by the consideration of labour as a commodity to be purchased as cheap as possible, and overconsumption. These are characteristics that induce unfair distribution of income and reckless overuse of natural resources, two negative results that the global society will have to correct.

Global capitalism has again become a blind machine that *a priori* does not know where it is going to in terms of demography, energy consumption, food prices, global warming, long-run administration of natural resources, renewable or not, etc. Therefore, the so much respected 'invisible hand' by neoliberals has turned in current times of global unbridled capitalism into an 'irrational hand.' And that while it paradoxically induces 'certainty' on the probable direction of the personal income and wealth distribution: towards concentrations of income and wealth against the less rich or the poorest in all societies. These are reasons why developments of global capitalism should be controlled as soon as posible by a supranational authority with competencies on all those matters imposible of being controlled by national states or small groups of them.

In consistency with the future existence of supranational authorities and public activism, we have to insist again that the economic system of the future will be the social economy of market. Any alternative option, in favour of a central planned economy discarded decades ago, or in favour of an uncontrolled neo-liberal economy, as that essayed without success in the past 30 years, would drive us to a magnum catastrophe.

Different Interests of Developed and Emerging Countries

From the 16th century onwards, incipient traditional capitalism in connection with mercantilism and colonialism, basically developed in Europe, for long divided the world in two main categories of countries, colonisers and colonised, next to some isolated, ignored or undiscovered countries. Following two major decolonisation cycles in the 19th and 20th centuries and the Russian Revolution in 1917, mentioned classification changed into countries belonging to the Western capitalistic sphere, countries belonging to the Communist-Socialist Eastern block, and other countries self-defined as non-aligned Third World countries.

After the First and Second World Wars fought in different parts of the world but actually dealing with the disputed hegemony among European countries (and Japan in Eastern Asia), the second half of the 20th century witnessed a new phenomenon: the appearance of subordinated wars in countries in which the Cold War materialised (far away in Africa, Asia and Latin America/Caribe). A particular case, which represented a turning point in the involvement of the Western societies in the Cold War, was that of Vietnam, since the development of new communication technologies (TV and video) made that reports on real battles could be transferred directly into the living rooms of families having relatives or friends at the battle ground. Similarly, in the Eastern block, the invasion of Afghanistan in 1979 by the Soviet Union progressively lost societal support in Russia, preceding the call for withdrawal from Afghanistan (1989) and from the arms race with the West, while demanding more funding for internal economic development (Perestroika).

In the last decade of the 20th century, two important new developments changed the economic global framework. Although favourable for the richest strata of the Western population, these developments would undermine the capacities of the West, in the long run, to keep the rest of the world under political control. The first of them was the rapid development of information and communication technologies (ICT). With full information in real time and with the facility and cheapness of communications, it is not posible any more to keep people uninformed. This access to total and live information by the poor has already undermined the capacity of non-democratic governments to *sine die* sustain in power, and the ability of Western internally democratic countries for behaving in an autocratic manner in territories, or with populations, in other continents.

The second refers to the globalisation-liberalisation of finances. This globalisation of finances, directed to enable the free movements of capital at short term (using modern ICT) or long term (foreign direct investment; FDI) among the different countries in function of the different profit rates to be obtained, would severely and negatively affect the employment in the West, particularly of the youngest generation. As we have explained before, the free movements of capital would favour: (1) savers-investors of the most advanced countries, thus *ceteris paribus* moderately pushing for increasing their gross national income (GNI), and (2) the workers of countries with smaller labour costs in proportion to their productivity (workers of emerging countries, mainly Asians).

Consequently, what is today happening in the world in relation to the industrial production shift towards Asia and the acceleration of raw materials extraction from Africa and Latin America are effects that were clearly predictable when, at the begining of the 1990s, mentioned new economic initiatives were adopted in the West. Nevertheless, no government officially showed or proclaimed any concern for mentioned negative but expectable effects.

In parallel to mentioned initiatives, and following the end of the Cold War, the West also tried to expand democracy to some countries that had not experienced this political system of governing, particulary those formerly belonging to the Eastern block or those placed in North Africa and the Middle East. This was done because Western countries thought and expected that, after the arrival of democracy to these countries, a better understanding with them on economic and political issues would enable a significant improvement of the general security, and an increase of the economic influence of the West. However these naïve expectations have been falsified by facts in the last two decades, following the industrial shift to Asia and the financial crisis in the West. Even more, recent political developments in North Africa and Middle East—the so-called Arab Spring—have proven that supporting uprisings against dictatorships does not automatically produce secular democracies.

Note additionally that the West realised its bet for democratisation without taking into consideration that demography always plays an essential role in democracy, be it at national or at global level. Certainly, when the existence of collective needs—related with global public goods, global externalities, etc.—was felt in the last decades, the population of the emerging and developing countries, nothing less than 84 per cent of the total of the world, started demanding to have a say in the formulation of global policies to apply, thus rejecting the existing self-appointed global governance of Western leadership, which till today prioritises the interests of only 16 per cent of the global population against the interests of the 84 per cent majority.

Global Economic Convergence and Development of Global Democracy

In parallel to the progress of commercial and financial globalisation in the last decades, the world started appreciating the existence of some needs of collective nature. To the extent that the provision of these needs became more or less urgent, richest Western countries took the initiative for starting global discussions (several summits and global conferences under the umbrella of the UN or its agencies) in order to develop global policies and to program some interventions.

However, the results of these meetings, except for human and social rights (child vaccination, women's empowerment, basic human rights, basic education, etc.) have been mainly disappointing. Regrettably, the continuation, and at times aggravation, of the main conflicts and global problems in the last 60-65 years, has also proven that national states (or coalitions of them) have been, and are, incapable of solving them.

Undoubtfully, the same as happened in the second half of the 20th century, when many national governments introduced national corrections to some negative traits of capitalism in their societies (national public goods and externalities), the global society should have started time ago correcting some negative characteristics of global capitalism, resorting to democratic global governance.

Instead of that, self-appointed global leaders [veto-owners in the Security Council and board and top executives of the World Bank (WB), International Monetary Fund (IMF) and World Trade Organization (WTO)] have cosmetically improved the coordination of their applied policies and, very hesitantly, have also marginally improved the "representation" of some emerging countries in certain discussions and forums, enabling them to accede to corresponding meetings, and all that without transferring sovereignty to one superior (global) government and administration, capable of implementing global efficient solutions, with democratic legitimacy, for counteracting inconvenient global decision-making carried out by MNC and other factual economic powers.

Foundations for the Democratisation of the UN

To be consistent with former considerations, we have to affirm that the reorganisation of the UN will have to result into a global parliament with supremacy on its own Global Government or Executive Council, and all that in order to provide with waranty and 'democratic legitimacy' the global public goods, as well as to correct or control the global externalities, the international monopolies, and the inter-regional distributive unbalances. Note that, as a consequence, the current Security Council, with its non-democratic structure and decision-making, seems to be condemned to disappear, as well as current biased rules for board representation and appointments of top executives of IMF, WB, WTO and others.

Contrary to approaches referring to a mini democratisation of the UN, developed in the last decade—mostly of a normative character and irrelevant due to its marginal meaning and contributions—we do believe that the UN will become really democratic as a consequence of the recent and ongoing changes in the economic structure of the planet, and those to come in next decades. In particular, we will refer again to the fast shift of the industrial production to Asia, to the relative gearing up of the economic growth in Emergent Asia, to the structural change in global and mutual commerce favourable to developing countries, and to the relative decadence of the West, even in sensitive issues as defence.

These overwhelming changes, already underway, will progressively condition in the next future all the economic and political negotiations among nations. We do believe that after few decades, two or three at most, these negotiations will finally be realised on the basis of parity.

This being said, we could now wonder when mentioned change of the UN towards democracy will occur. To this respect, we do believe that this will happen when the costs of defining and administrating the global public goods, the global externalities, etc., by the current leading intervening countries, become unreasonably high in comparison to the advantages to be obtained. Note that the same rationale underlied the end of the colonisation process.

Conversely to what many conservatives think, including most authorities of self-appointed leading countries, this will not happen after 2 or 3 centuries, but in 2 or 3 decades, a short period induced by the expected economic convergence—in absolute GDP and trade terms—among the current richest countries of the world and the rest,[2] a process that, on the other hand, is (and will be) consistent with the recently perceived acceleration of history. Accordingly, those who believe that the 'history of the world' ended with the fall of the Berlin Wall, favouring forever Western dominance, were and are simply mistaken.

Rapid Changes in the World Economic Structure as Stimuli for the Creation of a Global Democracy

Global economic changes, those already occurred (in 1980-2010) and those expected to happen in the next 2 or 3 decades, will take us to a structural rupture of the current economic power sharing in the world and, as an automatic derivative, to a radical political change. To start with, we will quote the conclusions reached by the famous study *Dreaming with the BRICS*, released in 2003 by Goldman Sachs. According to this study, the economic dynamics in the world would produce in 2050 a picture unimaginable at mid-20th century. Remember that in 1950, China and India were two nascent states embedded in deep poverty and backwardness. However, a hundred years later, in 2050, China, the US and India, by this order, will be the economically and politically most important countries in the world. Behind them, but faraway in their economic capacities and also in politics, would rank Japan, Brazil and Russia. Finally, in the last wagon of powerful countries and by this order, would be placed UK, Germany, France and Italy.

In our view, the results of former analysis (of Goldman Sachs), although endowed with a certain internal consistency, did not count with two economic and political phenomena that would affect the future composition of the leading and the last groups of countries of the study. It deals about: (1) the foreseeable birth of a selective EU federation, today not easy to profile concerning its components, which will induce that this EU federation join the group of leading countries next to China, the US and India, and (2) the necessary transformation of the UN into democratic, for

---

2. This expected economic convergence refers to the evolution towards equality (in absolute terms) of the shares of developed and developing countries in selected economic variables. This means that the shares of developed and developing countries will within 2-3 decades reach 50-50 per cent in terms of GDP, industrial production, exports of goods, military expenditures and so on.

administrating the global public goods and externalities with legitimacy and efficiency. The latter will be a radical change that will make that the current political influences—today still based on political dominance and economic supremacy—pass to depend on the demography and knowledge of the different countries or groups represented in the General Assembly.

In relation with the second phenomena, many Western commentators suggest that the UN should not democratise till the moment in which large populated countries like China have become democratic. Otherwise, according to them, non-democratic China, with 20 per cent of the population of the planet, would obtain a huge influence in issues of the Global Agenda. And they are right: such democratisation process cannot occur today but may happen in future when China complies with the underlying conditions for reaching an internal acceptable democracy. In this regard, we do believe that in 25 years, horizon 2035-2040, China will have a per capita GDP of around US$ 25,000-30,000 (constant US$ of 2007) and an extended middle class, who with their political demands will force the appearance of a 'sustainable democracy,' a circumstance that by itself, and *ceteris paribus*, will make possible the democratisation of the UN. Referring to other important countries, we have to underline that India is democratic from its very birth in 1947, and other countries with significant populations (Russia, Brazil, etc.), although at times contested, are also democratic. Let us not forget that Western democracies are not perfect either.

Radical Changes in the Economic Structure of the World in the Period 2010-2040

We have already clarified that the prognosis made in 2003 by Goldman Sachs with a horizon of 2050 has already been falsified by reality. Certainly, the new economic events of the decade 2000-2010, particularly the Western financial mishap, whose effects have been felt in a very different way among developing and developed nations, suggest that the convergence process as predicted in 2003 will be shorter in time. This forces us to make new economic projections.

To make a prognosis on the economic structure of the world in 2040, one should at least prolong the trends of the last 30 years (1980-2010) into the next three decades. But before doing so, we will successively present the growth of output (GDP) of the different economic regions of the world along the period 1980-2010 and then the evolution of the GNI of the different regions and main countries of the world in the last 10 years. Note that the used GDP and GNI data are from the *World Development Indicators* of the WB (2012). Finally, we will present some simple projections, with a horizon 2040.

Table 6.1

Average Annual GDP Growth of the Different Regions of the World (%)

	1980-1990	*1990-2000*	*2000-2010*
World	3.3	2.9	2.7
Low income	4.5	3.2	5.5
Middle income	3.3	3.9	6.4
Lower-middle income	4.1	3.8	6.3
Upper-middle income	2.7	3.9	6.5
Low and Middle Income	3.5	3.6	6.2
East Asia and Pacific	7.9	8.5	9.4
East Europe and Central Asia	(..)	-1.8	5.4
Latin America and Caribean	1.7	3.2	3.8
Middle East and North Africa	2.0	3.8	4.7
South Asia	5.6	5.5	7.4
Sub-Saharan Africa	1.6	2.5	5.0
High income	3.3	2.7	1.8
Eurozone	2.4	2.0	1.3
Other Relevant Countries			
United States	3.5	3.6	1.8
China	10.1	10.6	10.8
India	5.8	5.9	8.0
Brazil	(..)	2.7	3.7

Sources: *World Development Indicators*, WB (2012; 1992).

To start with the comments directly extracted from Table 6.1., we have to firstly state that the GDP growth rate of the world in the last three decades has been very similar, as an average: around 3 per cent, although mildly decelerating in the last decade 2000-2010 up to 2.7 per cent. Note that at the autumn of 2012, the GDP growth rate of the world was around 3.3 per cent, a figure—that in comparison to the average GDP growth rate of the last 30 years—is not expressive at all of a global economic crisis.

Observe also that the disparity of the GDP growth rates of the different regions or groups of countries, along the last 30 years has been spectacular in a double sense. On the one hand, there have been regions that, starting the 1980s with an average rapid growth rate, stepped up their growth till 2010. The case of East Asia and Pacific[3]—commanded by China[4]—that moved from growth rates of 7.9 per cent to 9.4 per cent, and that of South Asia—led by India—that in the last decade geared up its growth rate up to 7.4 per cent, are good examples of growth accelaration. Contrary to these positive economic trends, the evolution of the Eurozone has been clearly disappointing: it has economically progressed at a deccelerating speed, reaching in the last three decades respective and successive average growth rates of 2.4 per cent, 2.0 per cent and 1.3 per cent. This is certainly a trend towards stagnation, whose speed in the period 2000-2010 cannot be explained just by the financial crisis.

The consequences of the so-called financial crisis have also been significantly felt in the US, which after growing for 20 years (1980-2000) at an average rate of around 3.5 per cent—mildly above the world average—its average GDP growth rate in the first decade of the 21st century dramatically halved (till 1.8%). This is a figure that proves the failures of the administration of this country, mainly along the Bush era, which were induced by the economic housing bubble, the pre-emptive wars and some biased fiscal policies, mainly favouring the rich via tax reductions and, of course, by the industrial shift to Asia. Both the housing bubble and the pre-emptive wars in a context of inmoderate tax reductions contaminated the Eurozone and drove the EU to worse results than those of the US, due to the larger inflexibility of its markets, mainly the labour one, and its very deficient common governance.

After two decades of economic and political chaos (1980-2000), 'East Europe and Central Asia,' a region mainly represented by the Russian Federation—following the wake of a recovering Russia under Puttin-Medvedev—obtained in the last decade 2000-2010 an average GDP growth rate of 5 per cent, thus totally changing the messy economic performance of the decade 1990-2000. Note that the GDP growth rate of the region during the transition period (1990-2000) was negative (-1.8% under Pres Jeltsin).

---

3. This includes the low- and middle-income countries of the region.
4. Of course, as explained in Table 6.1, the GDP growth rates of China along the last three decades overcame the figures of the total region 'East Asia and Pacific.'

At a minor scale, the economic figures in the last three decades in the Latin America and Caribbean (LAC) region, have also registered an accelerated rhythm of growth. Particularly in the last decade (2000-2010), while the West decelerated, LAC grew at 3.8 per cent. Even more, in the last 20 years, LAC grew over the world average. A similar process of acceleration in the figures of GDP growth, although more pronounced than in former region, may be found in North Africa-Middle East, a region that grew at 2.0 per cent, 3.8 per cent and 4.7 per cent in the three consecutive decades.[5] Amazingly, sub-Saharan Africa also experienced an accelerated growth in the last three decades, which peaked in 2000-2010, with a growth rate of 5 per cent as an average.

All in all, and in particular in the last decade 2000-2010, the low- and middle-income countries have by far surpassed the growth rhythms of the high-income countries. But the most surprising of the diverse GDP growth rates of developing and developed countries in the last three decades has been its progressive divergence. Specifically, in the decade 1980-1990, the growth rates were similar (3.5% and 3.3%, with a disparity of just 1.06 favourable to 'developing'). But in the next decade (1990-2000), the growth rates were already different (3.6% and 2.7%, with a disparity of 1.33), and in 2000-2010 the dispersion became more than outstanding (6.2% and 1.8% with a disparity of 3.4).

All former reflexions indicate that in the 1990s of the last century, a process of rapid economic convergence between 'developing and developed countries' started. And all sourrounding figures and data suggest that the current accelerated catching up will probably continue at least throughout 2 or 3 additional decades. Note however that this observed economic convergence process of nations is just aggregated; consequently one cannot deduce that mentioned convergence has had a significant influence on the level of life of all citizens living in developing countries. Indeed, many of them have been left behind in the process of development, or remain economically exploited or excluded.

---

5. Probably, after the beginning of the Arab Spring (2011), this region has entered into a chaotic economic situation with collapsing industries, tourism and security.

Table 6.2

*Economic Shares (%) in Total GNI of the Different Regions
of the World, 2000-2010*

	2010	2007	2005	2000
GNI (billions of US$)	62,565	52,850	45,135	31,315
Low income	0.7	1.4	3.0	3.2
Middle income	29.6	23.4	18.0	17.0
Lower-middle	6.5	12.3	10.5	7.4
Upper-middle	23.1	11.1	7.5	9.6
Low and Middle I.	30.3	24.8	21.0	20.3
East Asia and Pacific	11.6	7.9	6.8	6.3
East Europe and Cent. Asia	4.7	5.2	4.3	3.0
Latin America and Caribean	7.2	6.2	4.9	6.1
Mid East and North Africa	2.1	1.6	1.5	2.0
South Asia	3.1	2.5	2.3	1.9
Sub-Saharan Africa	1.6	1.4	1.2	1.0
High income	68.9	75.0	78.9	79.8
Eurozone	20.4	22.0	22.3	21.1
United States	23.4	26.3	28.6	30.7
Emergent countries				
China	9.1	5.9	5.0	3.4
India	2.5	2.0	1.8	1.5
Brazil	2.9	2.1	1.5	2.0

Source: *World Development Indicators* (2002; 2007; 2009; 2012).

Obviously, when the growth rates of the different regions (or countries) of the world experience serious divergences among each other, as we have observed in Table 6.1, this will necessarily modify the structure of GDP and GNI in the world. In particular, we will refer to the changes registered in the last decade, a decade (2000-2010) in which the West, in front of a falling industrial production due to the industrial shift to Asia, selectively developed an intense speculative bubble on housing which, easied by main central banks, and financed by greedy and unprofessional bankers, finally exploded producing a catastrophe.

Indeed, most of the period of 2000-2010 was dominated by extreme interpretations of the capacities of unbridle capitalism, "necessarily conducive to a continuous economic growth, and to the final disappearance of economic cycles," as assumed by some wrong or 'Wall Street captured' academicians who, while turning a blind eye to market failures, ruthlessly attacked any intervention by the public sector, including infrastructure development and maintenance. As assumed, reducing taxes and public expenditure—except the military for keeping dominance—would give more space for action to the private sector which, liberalised from public controls, would reach an economic bliss. The reality, however, has proven that such economic bliss was merely a dream, and that most liberising policies essayed under unbridled capitalism were simply a suicidal race towards the cliffs.

The results in just 10 years—'the decade of the broken dreams in the West'—are already at sight (Table 6.2.).[6] Starting with the evolution of the structural share of the high-income countries, we have to underline that in the period 2000-2010 they have lost almost 11 points in their global GNI share, while the low- and middle-income countries increased their global quota by 10 per cent points.

Note that mentioned convergent trend in GNI of developing and developed countries favourable to the former, has a clear correspondence with the evolution in the world exports, which was extensively commented above. In fact, as the West has lost competitiveness, its exports and consequently production have relatively dwindled. This has profited developing countries which in the last decades, particularly in the last one, seem to have received a strong tale wind, due to factors already analysed (lots of transferable population placed in rural areas with nil marginal productivity, transfers of women to active population, high propension to invest in physical and human capital, high rates of internal saving, significant reception of private capital from the West, etc.).

Observe that most losses of the West in the period 2000-2010 have occurred in the last 3 years (2007-2010), the initial years of the so-called financial crisis. Note that in those three years, the high-income countries lost more than 6 per cent points of their GNI share, while the low- and middle-income countries won in that period 5.5 per cent points. In this period of crisis, China moved from sharing 5.9 per cent of global GNI to 9.1 per cent, this means that in the middle of the 'global crisis' China increased

---

6. Table 6.2, has been constructed with the figures of the World Bank (*World Development Indicators*), Table 1.1 titled "Size of the Economy", taking the 4th column "Gross National Income Atlas Method". If we have used the GNP in PPP terms, column 8th, the result would have been more favourable for the low- and middle-income countries

its GNI share by more than 3 per cent points (50%), practically the same as East Asia and Pacific. Conversely, East Europe and Central Asia, mainly the Russian Federation, also received an economic blow, while the rest of low- and middle-income countries increased their share in global GNI.

One could also deduce from Tables 6.1 and 6.2 that while the Eurozone has grown in the period 2000-2010 at an annual rate of 1.3 per cent while the US grew at 1.8 per cent, the lost of share in global GNI of the Eurozone should *ceteris paribus* have been higher than that of the US. However Table 6.2 clarifies that the drop in global GNI share of the US has been much more significant than that of the Eurozone. This probably indicates that the Eurozone has increased its creditor position—for instance investing much more in the industrial shift towards East Europe and Asia than the US— while the US has enlarged its debtor position.

The case of Europe and that of the US also proves that the initial attempt by Western governments to increase their share in world GNI through capital transfers to cheap-labour developing countries has failed: freedom of capital movements from the West to emerging countries, far from contributing to increase the GNI share of the former, has ultimately reduced it, due to significant reductions in GDP share, following the increase of Western imports from emerging countries and the parallel reduction of Western exports, both in GDP terms.

If instead of focusing on the last decade, we would go back another 5 years, till 1995—note that in these years the 'rapid industrial shift towards Asia' was starting—then one would find that the annual gain of share in GNI of the low- and midde-income countries along the last 15 years has been around 0.77 points. Note that if this annual gain in share (0.77), more conservative than that of 1.0 points registered in the last decade (2000- 2010), was multiplied by the number of years resting to 2040, we would find that around 2040—if not before—the GNI of the world will be distributed 50-50 per cent between developing countries and today's high-income countries.

Doing similar projections we find that East Asia and Pacific could generate in 2040 around 19-21 per cent of the world GNI, LAC 8-9 per cent, South Asia 7-8 per cent, East Europe and Central Asia 7-8 per cent, Middle East and North Africa 5 per cent, and sub-Saharan Africa 3 per cent. And this while the the US could move down from its current quota (2010) of 23.4 per cent of the total GNI to a figure of around 17-19 per cent. In the case of the Eurozone, whose economy is today totally wrapped in uncertainty, and its performance up to 2040 will depend on whether it federates or not, we may say that in the case of federation the current group of the Eurozone could reach in 2040 a figure mildly lower than that of the US, around 13-16 per cent of the world GNI. Japan and the European Immigration Countries (EIC) (ex-US) would complete the GNI of developed countries (50% of the total).

Main Traits of the New Democratic UN

In relation to the basic profiles of the new democratic UN, which according to our reckoning will start working in 2-3 decades, we do believe that the new Charter of the UN should adjust to the following democratic traits and principles:

(a) Initially,[7] the General Assembly consisting of a rather proportional representation of populations of member states of the UN will act as a sovereign World Parliament in relation to its limited but relevant agenda for global governance. Its decisions will be adopted by majority, normal or reinforced. The Government of the UN, its Executive Council, will necessarily act in accordance with the principles defined by the General Asembly.

(b) The new Executive Council of the UN—sustitute of the current Security Council—delegated by the General Assembly for dealing with all issues (urgent or not), could count with 24 members appointed by the General Assembly [8 larger nations with long tenures status (10 years), 'but without veto rights,' and 16 with rotating short tenures (2 or 3 years)].

(c) The UN will necessarily create an army-navy for its own service. These armed forces, besides being professional and neutral, will generate meaningful economies of scale, mounting around 1 per cent of the world GDP. The UN army-navy will also induce a great

7. Note that after 2 or 3 decades of working, when global democracy has already become consolidated in the new UN, the distribution of the seats in the General Assembly should be proportional to the electoral support of the different global political parties, and not any more depending on the population of the different member countries.

saving to the current police-states (US and main North Atlantic Treaty Organization (NATO) members), which will finally be freed from their current direct implications and responsabilities. Note that mentioned economies of scale would enable the whole of UN member-states, to annually save around US$ 600-625 billion, a figure that could be devoted to finance the fight against climate change, the correction of global externalities, or to finance development of least development countries (LDC).

Member states will finance the UN army-navy more or less in proportion to their GDP. Professional armed forces of the UN will be permanently deployed in all continents and oceans in order to rapidly intervene in cases of conflict, piracy or natural catastrophes.

(d) In order to sustain dignity and prestige of the new democratic UN, we do recommend the expulsion from the UN and all its agencies of countries that disobey or act against democratic resolutions of the new UN.

(e) Some agencies of the UN will have to be reorganised [IMF, International Labour Organization (ILO), etc.]; others will have to be created ex-novo [as the World Environmental Organisation (WEO), the Global Economic Regulations Agency (GERA), and the UN Institution for Development Cooperation (UNICO)]; and others will re-embody (as the WTO). UNICO, to which will embody the WB system and the United Nations Development Programme (UNDP), will be an organisation that will play a decisive role in development cooperation, as an intermediate target for reaching Peace and Security.[8]

Ways of Democratising the UN: New Voting Systems and Global Agenda

We are sure that if current economic circumstances persist—and all seems to point out that mentioned economic environment and trends will keep although some UN members may develop soft forms of protectionism—current global governance, inefficient and non-democratic,

---

8. For a description of the functions of UNICO, vide Rahman and Andreu (2004).

will progressively degrade and its credibility will finally fade away. And that while the situation of the remaining important problems of mankind— such as peace and security, climate change, global economic regulation, administration of natural resources, etc.—will probably worsen or stagnate.

Taking all former arguments into consideration, we are sure that in a moment along the next 2-3 decades, the most important powers of the world, as China—which will already be democratic—plus the US, India, the European Federation (if created), the Russian Federation, Brazil, Japan and other countries, will find it indispensable to meet in an intergovernmental conference in order to make a proposal to the global society for the complete reorganisation of the economic and political relations in the world, by means of introducing democracy in the UN as the sole system for reaching an efficient and legitimate governance for the implementation of the Global Agenda.

The initiators of the new UN should agree that rich countries will have to pay contributions, at least initially, more important in GDP terms than the poor.[9] With these new economic contributions, plus additional revenues such as global recharges on inheritance tax, global eco-taxes, and resources deriving from the exploitation by the UN of *terra nullius* (North and South Poles), etc., the new UN will finance the global public goods, the correction of global externalities and the income gap, as well as the new army-navy. Note however that these initial increased contributions will time later tend to dwindle to the extent that the economic gap (per capita GDP) among nations decrease, global warming flexes down, and the needs of the new army-navy of the UN become less pressing due to growing sociopolitical stability in the world.

In relation to voting procedures, two systems could be considered. There could be a normal system of voting in which 50 per cent plus one of the votes issued in the Parliament of the UN will be sufficient to produce an oficial decision which will bind all members and a reinforced voting in which 66 per cent of the issued votes will be required. Reinforced voting could mainly be used to introduce corrections in the Charter, or for decision

---

9. The less developed countries of the world will have to pay more taxes or contributions than those currently paid, which are almost zero. They cannot expect to form part of a new democratic UN without practically paying anything for it.

making in certain matters related with peace, security, international operations with refugees, migrations to inhabited territories induced by climate change, interventions of the army of the UN in countries which systematically and massively violate the human rights or practise ethnic cleansing, etc. Of course veto rights or blocking minorities should not be accepted, as they are not democratic.

Additional issues, to be discussed when the Provisional Charter is elaborated, could be the extension of the agenda of the new UN, and the enummeration and definition of the agencies to be developed for reaching the aims assigned to them. The agenda of the new UN should be fully detailed and profiled in order to avoid problems in future.

Ways and pre-conditions for access to the new democratic UN, conditions to remain in it—particularly in relation to the individual asigned contributions and their punctual payment—and the causes of expulsion, basically disobeyance to Resolutions of the UN—should also be clearly specified in the provisional Charter.

The organisation of the UN and the relations among its different organisms—the General Assembly, the Executive Council, the army-navy, and agencies—will have to be profiled also in the new Charter. It would be important that the volume of the represented global population in the new UN would reach a figure of 90-95 per cent, and that no one of the big current powers would remain at the margin of the organisation.

According to the Charter, a well-profiled UN agenda should establish the limits of action and intervention of the UN. Actions and interventions that in no case would affect issues related to culture, language, religion, etc., of UN member states, except in cases of barbaric or irrational behaviour, endorsed by a 66 per cent of the issued votes in the General Assembly.

The Charter could also establish an initial limit of the national expenditures in defence—perhaps up to one per cent of the GDP of members—in order to avert rearmament. The former accumulated arsenals—nuclear or not—will enter into a situation of first freezing and then reduction, effectively controlled by the UN. To oppose to such controls—the same as would happen if a country disobeys any resolution of the UN—would imply the expelling of this country from the UN and all its agencies, including the economic ones.

It is difficult to accurately define the common interests of most of countries on the horizon 2040, but it is sure that peace and sustainable economic prosperity, combined with a more balanced distribution of income, and a healthy environment, will continue being the main objectives of the global society.[10] After a predictable cyclical process of political convergence due to democratic alternation, most countries of the world—and the world as a whole—will finally adopt the Social Economy of Market (or Mix Economy of Market).

When the first General Assembly of the democratic UN will be constituted, its two first activities will be: to approve the final Charter, and to convalidate (or not) parts of the former legality of the old non-democratic UN.

Finally, to shift the siege of the UN out of the US, for establishing it in a more central-located and well-equipped place around the Mediterranean Sea (as f.i., Nice, Florence, Palma de Majorca, etc.), would be by itself a democratic initiative adopted by the new UN, that, besides, would be economically convenient for the majority.

The Economic Costs of the New Democratic UN

Till this moment, we have focused our analysis on why and how a new democratic UN will finally substitute the current one. In following lines, we will enter in a first assessment of the initial economic costs of the operation. The new budget of the organisation—although far from high in comparison to the value of the provided global public goods, the improvements realised in the correction of global externalities or global monopolies, and the achieved progress in relation to the reduction of the economic gap of the poorest countries of the world in a reasonable period of time (25 years)—will nevertheless present a significant change in its figures. This will be due to the rational and efficient pooling of certain activities till now not realised by the UN, but (although in different proportions) by national members. Note that, amazingly, the UN spends today (2012-2013) for its Regular Budget a very small figure (around US$ 5.5 bn), equivalent to 0.01 per cent of the

10. We do believe that in these days the old battles on pure ideological-economic principles, related to the assumed 'necessary efficiency' of all liberalised markets, and the alleged "inefficiency" of almost any public intervention, as defended by extreme neoclassicals, will finally be confined to the files of history.

world GDP,[11] indeed, too little money to do more than speaking, debating and often wasting time.

To begin with, we will refer to the costs of the new system of provision of peace and security. As formerly suggested, it will be indispensable that the UN counts with an own and professional Army-Navy, deployed on all continents and oceans in order to quickly deal with conflicts, violence, piracy, human and drugs traficking, or natural catastrophes. To the extent that the current defence expenditures of the different countries of the world are, as an average, around 2.6 per cent of their GDP, we do believe that—taking into account the huge economies of scale to be reached by means of the organisation of the UN army-navy, which will necessarily be not nuclear—a military expenditure by the UN equivalent to 1 per cent of the global GDP will be enough to fulfill its targets. Observe that this figure would be equivalent to US$ 600-625 billion (of 2010), a figure almost similar to the current expenditures of the US in defence. Note however that this global expenditure in the UN Army-Navy will not depend anymore on the disproportionate endeavour of one sole nation[12] as it happens today, but on efforts of the global society as a whole.

If we now refer to the suggested expenditure to be devoted to development financing (ODA)—a budget that would indirectly but significantly support the cause of peace and security—we would arrive to an annual figure equivalent to 1 per cent of the global GDP,[13] a significant figure that would enable to solve the problem of poverty and to significantly reduce the income gap of LDC in one generation. In order to fulfil this target, the new UN agency (UNICO) busy with this activity would have to annually count with a mínimum figure of US$ 600 billion (of 2010), equivalent to around 1 per cent of the global GDP. Note that this figure would imply almost to multiply the current effort devoted to development

---

11. Note however that this figure does not include the programmed budgets of the agencies.

12. The mere fact that one nation in the world (US), with less than 5 per cent of the global population spends in defence almost the 55 per cent of the total military expenditures of the world, is a clear indicator of the "intention" of this country for *sine die* keeping military supremacy.

13. This is a figure equivalent to the 2 per cent of the GDP of donors, as defended among others by Tinbergen, J. and by us in (2004) in "Responsible Global Governance: A Programme for World Stability and Institutional Reform."

financing by around 4, while distributing it in grants. Financing of UNICO could come—as we have explained and justified in other places—from a recharge at a global scale on the inheritance tax.

In relation to the necessary expenditure to be realised for fighting against climate change—and in order to modify the current negative course of this phenomenon in a context of uncertainty—we have already mentioned the convenience of (initially) spending per annum a figure of around 2 per cent of the global GDP. Note that this figure should be administered by the WEO, and initially attached to a not long phasing period for accomodation.

To the extent that the former three ways of expenditure will be the most outstanding of the new democratic UN, while the rest would only be subject to marginal corrections, we do believe that the budget of the new democratic UN will initially mount up to 4-4.5 per cent in terms of the global GDP, a figure mounting around US$ 2,500 billion, similar to the GDP of France.

In the long term, we do believe that the expenditures in army-navy of the new UN will enable the countries that currently and willingly play the role of policemen of the world[14] to become liberated from their current 'voluntary' responsabilities, thus saving a lot of money: perhaps one-two points, or more, of their GDP—in particular the US—savings that could be devoted to internal activities (promotion of infrastructures, education, social security, public funding for political parties and democracy promotion, etc.), or to external ones.

Certainly, the advantages harvested by UNICO activities in the fields of education, health and infrastructures in countries or regions currently less developed would be huge, actions that, besides avoiding social unstability and reducing the probability of local wars, would significantly increase the rhythms of growth of the low- and middle-income countries.

More important than former expenditures would be those devoted to the fight against climate change, whose effects—if nothing or almost nothing was done—could condition for the worse, according to available projections, the evolution of all economic and political variables in the world.

---

14. These countries are basically the US and some NATO members.

Summarising, with the arrival of democracy to the UN, we do believe that the current UN budget could increase around 4-4.5 points in global GDP terms; a raise that far from being an additional burden for member countries would certainly be a blessing for the world as a whole; a world that could become more balanced, more peaceful, fairer, and consequently more livable. Conversely, to refuse to do this effort would be extremely shameful, wrong for world leadership, and inefficient for the global society.

Towards the Disappearence of Hegemonic Powers

Contrary to what was believed by some US neo-cons in the first years of 2000—nothing less than the arrival of the 'End of History' with a unique permanent power in charge, the US, and the rest of nations subordinated to the latter—we do believe that with the arrival of global democracy to the UN,[15] the history of hegemomic powers will finally reach its end.

In our view, the historical conditions for reaching and keeping a sustainable hegemony were: (1) to be in possesion of a great technological, and if possible exclusive, military advantage; (2) to have a powerful economy growing at high speed—more than those of rivals—to *sine die* warranty military superiority without strangling the consumption of the population; (3) irrelevance or neglect of the human rights in subordinated nations; and (4) absence of a rapid dissemination of information on committed atrocities. Note that the existence of these four conditions made it easy to abuse people or assets in subordinated nations, without political costs for the dominating countries.

However, these four conditions either have already disappeared or are going to disappear in the next three decades.

Besides the degrading of these four conditions, we should not forget that keeping the position of hegemonic power, being very costly in human and material terms, only may be justified facing own voters—democratic or not—if the exerted domination materialises in economic or politcal advantages. If these advantages were not attained, or became degraded or

---

15. There are intellectuals who believe that capitalism, after defeating socialism in 1991 with the disappearance of the Soviet Union, and after becoming global, has also defeated democracy (in 2008). Indeed, a very pessimistic analysis in which MNC—and not global democracy, a democratic UN—would substitute national governments.

sine die interrupted, the economic incentive to continue as a hegemonic power would disappear, and the extraordinary power annexed to it would vanish, as it happened in 1989 with the Soviet Union, and some decades before with the British Empire.

Therefore, we do believe that the concerns of the West, or even its fears, in relation with the possibility that China will become the next hegemonic power, are unjustified and present an unrealistic view on what is economically and politically coming. For China, as for any other important country in the world, to be a hegemonic power in future will not be profitable, due to its foreseeable great costs, its scant results and the parallel loss of prestige in function of its predictable successive failures. Undoubtfully, much more important for China and other emergent colossus will be the establishment of democratic global governance through the democratisation of the UN, because its UN membership will endow China with a significant influence in global governance, due to the size of its population (19.5% of the world), a crucial variable in any democratic organisation.

It is very important to underline that in our view those non-democratic countries with a population over 70 million inhabitants[16] should first reach internal democracy before being part of the new democratic UN. In particular, the case of China is essential. But in this regard and conversely to the views of those who proclaim that China will never become democratic, we dare to affirm that, within 25 years—a period along which this country will probably count with a per capita GDP of around US$ 25,000-30,000 (of 2007)—the extended middle class in China will bring democracy to the country. This has always occurred in prosperous societies with extended middle classes, and the case of China will not be an exception.

Concluding, if the current economic trends in the world continue in the next 2 or 3 decades, moving in favour of developing countries to finally—around 2040—reach economic parity with those developed, most important Western countries could progressively consider that it would be convenient for them to renounce their privileges and extraordinary powers in current UN System (veto-rights) in order to endow the UN with capacities to democratically solve the pending global problems. On the

---

16. This is a figure equivalent to one per cent of the planet population.

contrary, if veto-owners continue trying to keep their extraordinary powers, this exercise will become a boomerang against their own interests, due to the growing economic and political costs of sustaining mentioned powers.

It would be very positive for the global society as a whole that the self-appointed global leaders at the end of the Second World War would finally renounce to the extraordinary powers they assumed in 1945. This move would also be consistent with the principles and ethics of democracy, which the West constantly preach and defend, but hardly practice in international and global relations.

7 | Summary of Economic Findings and Political Recommendations

Along this book, we have dealt with several issues, namely: (1) the causes and evolution of the current 'financial crisis,' with special reference to the incidence of this crisis in the Eurozone; (2) the future of social democracy and of the social economy of market; (3) the European problems induced by the mistaken construction of the Monetary Union in the last two decades, and the inconsistency of governance between the over-enlarged European Union (EU)-28 and the Eurozone; (4) the global problems induced by the defective (or absent) administration of the common global needs—as the provision of global public goods, the correction of global externalities and the improvement of the global distribution of income—and the recent acknowledgement that such problems will have to be solved by means of democratic global governance; and (5) the political re-organisation of the UN on democratic bases, mainly induced by the structural economic changes following the industrial shift towards Asia and the current crisis, changes which will progressively induce the disappearance of hegemonic powers.

The Economic Situation of the Planet: We are not in a Global Crisis

According to our findings, the current economic drama induced by three main developments—the industrial shift towards Asia, the financial crisis started in 2007-08 and the failure of the Eurozone to react on the economic drama—has produced diverse results in the different regions of the world. Indeed, one has to certify that in the last 5-6 years, the results have been very unfavourable for Europe while North America is showing today (Autumn 2013) a still slow recovery. Conversely, in the period 2008-

2012, the 'economic drama' has just slightly affected the main developing and emerging countries, which continue with fast—although moderately declining[1]—growth rates.

Mentioned negative economic developments observable in the high-income countries (the West) in the last 5 years have been the result of different causes that have mutually reinforced each other:

(a) the most visible, and insistently repeated, is that referring to the excesses committed by private bankers who, particularly in the US and the Eurozone, and facing a relative degrading in the demand of credit by their industrial sectors, opted—aided by the cheap money injected by their respective central banks [Federal Reserve System (Fed) and European Central Bank (ECB)]—for concentrating their financial investments in real estate activity. Note that other European private banks in f.i. Germany, France and the Netherlands indirectly participated in mentioned overfinancing and overconcentration of risks (investing in foreign public debt or in credits to foreign banks). But, as it is well known since the first writings of Markowitz (1952), such risk concentration could result in a financial catastrophe as it finally happened, although some banks had taken measures to technically transfer corresponding risks to other financial entities.

(b) The correction of the cyclical fall, initially assumed as the unique cause of the current drama, made that in 2009 an extended group of countries (G-20) met in London to take 'coordinated' action by planning a generalised Keynesian impulse. However, in 2010, private rating agencies and financial multilateral institutions (International Monetary Fund; IMF) started recommending a fast reduction of the deficits of the most indebted countries of the West, because they feared the possible development of a significant inflationary process, subsequent to the planned fiscal push and

---

1. The case of India, reaching recently (Autumn 2013) a GDP growth rate under 5 per cent—interpreted by some EU analysts as the end of the Indian Dream—is not but a growth deceleration coming from the restrictive monetary policy implemented to promote prices stability. Anyway a growth rate of 4.5-5 per cent in Europe or in the US would be a huge success for politicians. Even more, these analysts should not forget that, once reached prices stability, the Indian economy will progressively return to around 7-7.5 per cent of growth rate, which is the current potential growth rate of India.

corresponding growing indebtedness. But this recommended fast reduction—as had happened in former expansion—was not followed by all involved countries at the same speed. Indeed, the coordination of policies in the West was impossible because the US put into practice a sort of moderate Keynesianism, while the main members of the Eurozone, having no individual capacities for modifying the monetary policy and exchange rates of the Euro, were 'implicitly' forced by Germany to individually accept neo-classicism, or just reductions of fiscal deficits and pending debt. In particular the mismatch between the governance of the EU-28 and the governance of the Eurozone gave the opportunity to member-countries, not belonging to the Eurozone, to excert their influence to hinder the implementation of correcting policies as designed by the Eurozone, such as the creation of a banking union or a joint ministry of finance. Consequently the Euro-system, far from becoming a system for rapidly recovering economic equilibrium when losing it, became a nightmare of governance, thus *sine die* delaying the exit from the crisis.

(c) Regrettably, former mentioned causes of the current economic drama—overfinancing of real estate and subsequent bankruptcies and rescue of banks in the US and Europe, plus misconstruction of the Euro-system—are not the sole causes of the current depressing situation. There is an additional, important and long-term force that is making the exit of the West from the crisis much more difficult, and that conditions the strength of the next economic recovery in the West, which necessarily will be weak. We are here referring to the industrial shift towards Asia. This is a shift that, after changes of speed of economic growth in the West (relatively declining) and Asia (accelerating) in the last three decades—and its likely continuation in the next decades—will induce a reallocation of the economic gravity centre of the world, displacing it to Asia. This industrial shift will finally be followed by a change in the political power structure of the planet. Certainly, the average annual growth rates in the successive decades of 1980, 1990 and 2000 of the low- and middle-income countries (respectively 3.5%, 3.9% and 6.5%) in comparison to the decelerating growth rates of the high-income countries (respectively 3.3%, 2.7% and 1.8%), are proofs of the progressive convergence between developing and developed countries, and of the fast relative economic decline of the West. If we would compare former figures provided by the World Bank (WB) with those of the Eurozone (respectively 2.4%, 2.0% and 1.3%), we would have the complete gloomy picture in which Europe currently moves.

As far as the last and more prolonged cause of the current economic drama—the industrial shift to Asia—is not explained by governments to Western citizens, the latter will not fully understand the new unfavourable economic picture in which they move (and will have to move). It mainly concerns the recent change in the direction of the 'East-West' trade, which is restraining and will restrain the exports of the West and will favour its imports from the East, thus inducing in the West lower rhythms of growth than in the past, and consequently, inducing serious difficulties for job creation in Western countries, unless real Western wages experience a significant decrease.

The new geographical redistribution of the world trade and its consequences on regional employment, already perceived in the first decade of the 21st century, with developing countries gaining quota and the high-income countries losing it, is at the end of the day a problem of competitiveness, and not so much a macroeconomic problem as many Westerners tend to believe. Given the difficulties for rapidly and significantly increasing the productivity of labour in the West, unless western wages rapidly degrade for gaining competitiveness against Asians exports, difficulties for competition in the West may be of long duration, perhaps up to two decades more.

Note that this indispensable increase of competitiveness in the West with respect to Asia was till recently unnecessary. First, because the Asians were not so well industrially equipped and second, and consequently, because the Asians did not significantly export to the West (note that China entered in the World Trade Organization (WTO) in 2001). Current industrial and trade shift towards Asia was ignited by the liberalisation of movements of capital which enabled initiatives for Western industrial dislocation towards Asia in the first 1990s. Surprisingly, this change did not alarm either Western governments or citizens till mid-2000s.

Liberalisation of capital movements in the West accompanied by very stringent migration rules towards Western states plus the traditional inflexibility of wages in continental Europe—induced by the long-term trend of growing wages in the past—have produced what we have in front of our eyes: that the wages that the Europeans receive every month are by far not competitive, and consequently cannot sustain if countries want to recover economic equilibria. However, this is something that few politicians dare to explain to citizens.

Indeed, the productivity per worked hour in the EU, although higher than that of Asians in most activities, is not capable of offsetting the difference of the paid wage per worked hour—much smaller in the case of Asia—and the number of yearly worked hours by Asians, a figure much higher than the European one.

In this context of concealed or censored reality, some political parties in Europe try to convince the people that, merely by increasing public expenditure, reducing taxes and accepting some inflation, while ECB sustaining the acceptability of the public debt of some members, they may again push the Eurozone economy to past (2007) prosperity, thus increasing jobs and wages. In fact, it is a miraculous and amazing approach to Economics, mainly supported by certain unionists who reject reductions of real wages and reversal of welfare state levels in the West; and despite that, regrettably but inexorably, these cutbacks will have to occur—as they are already occurring—as a consequence of both globalisation and corresponding convergence processes.

On the other side of the political spectrum, extreme neo-liberals and other rightists claim that important and fast reduction of public deficits and indebtedness should take place, while internal wages should severely degrade *via* full flexibilisation of labour markets, efforts that, assumedly, will make Europe in the long run—although without specifying how long is the log run—return to the economic prosperity and employment levels of 2007. Indeed this is a 'solution' with huge social costs and short-mid term negative implications in societies.

Note that far from the two explained incomplete analysis and recipies, we do believe that the West should implement a mix of them, but much more adapted to the needs of the 21st century, that is to say adapted to the real picture in which the West moves: in the middle of an overwhelming long-term economic change, favourable to developing countries.

To clarify our view, one should observe that in the 1970-1980s, the economy of the world entered into a process of structural change—accentuated in the 1990s (liberalisation of capital movements) and 2000 (China and WTO)—placing the West in front of an unexpected, although (many years ago) predictable, historical turning point. Let us not forget that, from the times of the start of the Industrial Revolution and even before, the main Western countries enjoyed technological, navigational and military advantages that—in a non-democratic context and absence of human rights—were used to colonise and economically exploit many subordinated countries.

Nevertheless, since the information and communication technology (ICT) revolution in the 1980s and the liberalisation of capital movements in the 1990s, mentioned advantages, including military, started dwindling. All this, accompanied by the huge amount of transferable labour force to non-agricultural sectors in the large Asian countries and others—around 500 million people in China and India altogether—and by the wearing out of the higher growth capacities of most advanced countries, is today inducing a trend towards economic equilibrium (50-50%, foreseeable in 2-3 decades) among developing and developed countries in terms of GDP, industrial production, exports, military expenditures, etc.

The historical rebalancing of the world economic structure—already underway—will have significant political consequences for the West. During the entire period towards re-equilibrium, whose duration will mainly depend on the speed of real wage reductions in the West, the economic growth of the West will be weak or very weak. This means that the longer the period of adjustment in wages, the larger will be the unemployment rates and the underuse of human capacities, particularly those of youngsters. Conversely, the shorter the duration of the adjustment period of wages in the West, the faster will be job creation, be it with lower wages and significant adjustments in lifestyle.

As a lateral result, it seems probable that a faster adjustment in the West will induce a worsening distribution of income (with profits growing while wages contracting), which in our view should be corrected by public action. Note however that since the deficits and indebtedness are high and in need of reduction for restoring more balanced income distribution, public action should favour social expenditure in provisional detriment of f.i. defence, non-urgent public investment and mainly redundant administration.

In brief, unless Western workers accept significant lower wages accompanied by a new life style (greener, more collective in consumption, etc., which will contribute to a more sustainable planet) they may have entered in 2007-08 in a 'long boulevard of broken dreams.'

To conclude, we do believe that, after 5-6 years of economic drama in many western countries, the world today—as it has occurred in the last 20 years—is more in a phase of economic re-structuring in favour of developing countries (China, India, Brazil, Indonesia, Vietnam, South Africa, etc.) than in a generalised crisis disturbing more or less equally all regions of the world, as many Western politicians pretend, just to shield their own confused policies.

To illustrate this conclusion, we should remember that long before the liberalisation of capital movements and after the Second World War, i.e., in the period 1945-1990, most Western countries registered internal experiences whereby in the middle of long periods of prosperity, some of their territories, after for long having been prosperous at national scale, were left behind. Similarly, at a world scale, next period of global prosperity will probably be one of mild growth for Europe, thus inducing relative decline in this continent.

On the Future of Social Democracy and Social Economy of Market

As known, social democracy is a political doctrine placed between communism and capitalism that, after the last step towards globalisation— the liberalisation of capital movements—has paradoxically become rather empty of practical economic content. To the extent that social democracy was born in the West in the context of modern national capitalistic states, it inherited 'nationalism' as a relevant trait, thus fighting for better redistribution of income 'just' among national citizens, while favouring the development of national social economies of market. Indeed, after the Second World War, social democracy worked acceptably well in Western

Europe for several decades, precisely when capital movements were very limited among nations, and the international trade was not so extended (globally) as it is today.

The problem of the social-democratic movement today is that it cannot systematically go against national entrepreneurs—for improving the lot of national workers—because under pressure, capital may rapidly be relocated abroad which would destroy national jobs. On the other hand, the social democracy movement cannot go either against global competitiveness among nations by pressing for reintroduction of protectionism, because in that case, it would prejudice the lower middle clases and poor people of the West, who could no longer buy cheap manufactures and food coming from Asia. Note, additionally, that such protectionism would also hit hard the poorest people of developing countries by repressing the creation of jobs in these nations, as it happened during the long colonial period.

So, once the economic playground has become global, social democracy should adjust to this new global picture. Among the necessary adjustments, we do believe that social democrats should promote social economy of market in larger political unities—be this by promoting federations of states, by enlarging regional cooperation, or by pushing for the creation of democratic global governance—in order to introduce a superior control on the working of relevant international markets, today practically unbridled. Otherwise, the maintenance of the current geographical ('national') fragmentation of political power combined with liberalised (globalised) capital movements would induce an indefinite continuation of sovereignty of markets, many of them monopolistic, and at times over-speculative, and consequently inefficient and unfair.

To the extent that there are today emerging developing countries with much smaller real wages and social protection than those of the West, social democrats of emerging countries should also impulse the increase of wages and social protection in their countries, while Western social democrats should collaborate in the control and gradual moderation of real wages, while cooperating in the official fight against inefficient social protection in the West, and all that for progressively achieving global economic equilibrium and a fairer and more sustainable life style for all.

With the arrival to larger political units, and in particular with the institutionalisation of democratic global governance, social democracy will recover the great influence it had in Western Europe in the period 1945-1973, thus favouring again the majority of society; although this time not only favouring 'national' workers—which at times played against the interest of foreign poorer workers—but also the rest of workers all over the world (the global society). This will inevitably occur because social democracy is nowadays the sole available political doctrine for properly managing public goods, or for correcting externalities, and also for fighting against monopolies in some international markets of private goods.

Note that when in future this process towards global democracy has finally become a reality, extreme conservative doctrines on non-intervention in the economy will lose credibility, and political discussions in national parliaments and in the democratic UN will mainly range, according to circumstances, around the degree of the exerted intervention and control.

Watching again with acumen to what has happened in the formulation of national policies in the last century, we should admit that the margin for practising policies for defending exclusively either the individuals (liberal capitalism) or the collective (communism) has become progressively narrower in the last decades. One could observe that, since the beginning of the 20th century till the fall of the Berlin Wall, there were two very different ways of understanding Economics which were politically positioned as mortal enemies.

Errors of first communists in power in Russia and China made them socialise all production, although some produced goods were private, such as food, which at the end of the day resulted in deadly famines. This was a tremendous mistake, comparable to mistakes of traditional or neo-liberal capitalists, who declaredly preferred to produce all goods and services by private sector, and with minimal control, although it involved public goods, as f.i. security. But regrettably, total freedom of production initiatives by private sector, as desired by neo-liberal capitalists, has historically resulted either in frauds, catastrophic bank failures or in deep and long-lasting economic cycles, as happened in 1930s and is occurring again in the West.

After the bankruptcy of the Soviet Union in 1989, it became clear that the communist economic system had to be discarded and filed, as had been done in China a decade earlier. This meant that from 1990s onwards, politics could only oscillate from social democracy to neo-liberalism. However, the liberalisation of movements of capital, initiated in the 1990s, seemed to condemn social democracy to disappear, due to its apparent lack of margin for economically manoeuvring. This lack of margin 'forced' Western social democrats, when they took power, to concentrate their political action on marginal and at times pretended progressive-social policies, while in economic policy they more or less adjusted to the neo-classical economic approach.

Nevertheless, the economic crisis starting in 2007-08, forced political leadership (G-20) to put the focus on global governance and global economic regulation. In this regard, there is today an almost global consensus that global economic regulations cannot be provided by individual nations but only by the involved collective, the global society.

Consequently, we do believe that the space for political discussion has again become re-compressed, but this time re-centred. From the idea of the absolute supremacy of private sector, defended by traditional capitalism or by recent neo-liberalism (1973-2007), public sector and social economy of market has to regain importance. Of course communism will not return, as will not return extreme economic liberalism, because both extremes misuse a great part of the economic potential of nations. Possibly, in two or three decades, former dialectics on the duality of economic systems, or on the duality of two extreme versions of capitalism, only will be found in the books of the history of economic analysis.

So, the Marxist dream of the final arrival to a global communist society and the recent ideas of 'neo-cons' according to which from the collapse of the Soviet Union onwards, the history would have finished at the other extreme of the political spectrum seem to us wrong ideas. Evolution of demography and sustainability of the planet, existence of new global needs and externalities, globalisation of markets, and integration of various societies into a global one (the global society) will force global public intervention and control, giving again space for action to social democracy and mixed economy of market although this time to work at a global level. Consequently, current neo-liberalism will significantly lose space and will be in need of re-centring.

European Problems and Solutions:
Towards a Selective Federation

Despite the fact that citizens of the Eurozone countries and other EU-member states will continue enjoying comparatively high (but relatively declining) levels of per capita income, their GDP growth rates in the next decades will be weak, due to the already described reasons. Even more, Eurozone populations—with exceptions—have reached levels of stagnation, and their big multinational corporations (MNCs) have consolidated a manoeuvre for industrial investments outside the Eurozone that has generated more jobs abroad (Eastern Europe and Asia) and less in Europe.

Although not well known by citizens—and always veiled by Brussels—the economic performance of the EU or the Eurozone in the last three decades (1980-2010) has been seriously disappointing; underperformance that has resulted comparatively compounded in the last decade (2000-2010). In fact, while the GDP in the US evolved in the last two decades (1990-2010) at an average annual growth rate near 2.7 per cent, no European country of former EU-15—except the (proven non-sustainable) economies of Ireland and Spain—overcame or equated that annual rhythm of 2.7 per cent. In particular, Germany and France grew at average annual rates of around 1.3 per cent and 1.6 per cent respectively. Even more, Germany, currently seen as the engine of the Eurozone and the EU, grew annually only at a rate of 1 per cent in the period 2000-2010. Comparison of these low growth figures (and others referred to trade) with corresponding projections of emerging countries induces to think that the EU will *ceteris paribus* continue with its relative deterioration, not only in comparison to the US, but also—and much more sharply—in relation to Asia.

Note that mentioned modest and decelerating growth rates reached in Europe in the period 1980-2010 were harvested while the EU made important efforts for increasing horizontal cooperation with five enlargements—from that of 1981 (Greece) to the massive one realised in 2004-2007, and to the last one in 2012 (Croatia)—and for deepening in vertical integration with two main movements: the signing of the Single Act Treaty for constructing a unique market in Europe and the initiative in 1992 (the Maastricht Treaty) for setting up a Monetary Union (the Euro-system);

the latter being a Union whose architecture proved to be highly defective when a first serious economic obstacle appeared in its way, in 2008.

It is today well acknowledged and shared that, in the context of the Eurozone, the maintenance of fiscal fragmentation—with different rates in relevant taxes (income and corporate), and divers levels of deficit and public debt in GDP terms—the absence of a unique system for banking supervision (a Banking Union), and the massive enlargement of the period 2004-2007 which was mainly made for political reasons, were mistakes that have finally placed the Euro-system at the brink of failure.

In some countries of the Eurozone, the current problem of public debt has been created by the defficient behaviour of national governments in relation with their expenditures, at times exaggerated, or in relation to their revenues, often lower than necessary, and at times also induced by the lack of supervision of banks (by national central banks) that, with their bankruptcies, have increased, explicitly or implicitly, the public indebtedness of certain Euro-members. Consequently, at short term a united banking system for the Eurozone has to be set up, while a fiscal integration of the Eurozone will have to become a fact.

Now then, the construction at short term of a fiscal union and a banking union in the Eurozone—two indispensable initiatives for keeping the Euro-System afloat—faces a serious problem of 'inconsistency' induced by the conflicting governance of the EU-28 (the Commission of Brussels and the European Council) and the governance of the Eurozone. This 'inconsistency' makes that important countries belonging to the EU-28, but not to the Eurozone (mainly Britain), frequently exert their veto rights for arresting any initiative devised to reinforce the Eurosystem, or to advance towards deeper integration. The recent case of the opposition of Britain to the creation of the indispensable Banking Union—because this movement would put London under the control of the European supervisor and consequently degrade it as a superior financial centre—is just one example of what we are explaining. The same could be said in relation to taxation harmonisation, indispensable for the working of a fiscal union, which is strongly opposed by several members.

Particularly, at short term, a number of banks of the Eurozone—be these banks debtors of other banks and owners of 'non-performing credits,' mainly in Spain, or creditors of the latter (some German and French banks)—have had or may have new additional problems. To repair the banking system, some of these banks have been (or will have to be) orderly liquidated or re-floated with the support of public funds. This has implied (or will imply) a new re-driving of public financing to this activity while, to recover from past and exaggerated public deficit and indebtedness, it was (or will be) necessary to force a drastic reduction of certain public expenditures. Indeed, a difficult and dramatic operation to be realised in an economic context of almost nil or very weak real growth rates (which is the reality in the Eurozone today). This is a circumstance that probably will keep high unemployment rates in the Eurozone for a significant period, with independence of the problems induced by the industrial shift to Asia.

Certainly, mentioned pending operations for rescuing banks and simultaneous reduction of public deficit and indebtedness of several Eurozone countries could be realised with less 'macroeconomic' drama if Eurozone countries were authorised to reduce their public deficits more slowly, and the ECB was in parallel authorised to relax its monetary and debt policies for 3 years, thus enabling if necessary higher growth rates of prices (more inflation). This operation, in combination with more efficient public expenditure (administration reshuffling and rationalisation) and market reforms, would make possible, on the one hand, to pay with new money former excesses of public debt issued by over-indebted countries, and on the other, to overcome the problem of negative or weak real growth, which makes the burden of debt in which several Eurozone countries are trapped, insurmountable.

Nevertheless, we do believe that this authorisation for changing the economic policy of the ECB will not be easy reachable, due to the deep historical fears of Germany in relation to inflation, and the enmity of other northern Eurozone countries, including Germany, to apply any other economic model than the neo-classical one (aiming at zero public deficit and very low inflation rate).

On the other hand, if the Eurozone wanted to overcome current problems of the banking system, it is necessary: (1) to define the banks which will administrate the Eurozone Payments System (banks of deposits), thus separating the financial activities and control of the different entities (banks of deposits and the rest); (2) to submit a part of around 6,000 Eurozone banking entities—only those involved in the administration of the payments system—to a unique supervisor that could be the ECB, leaving the rest depending on other supervisors, not connected with the traditional protection of depositors; (3) to additionally increase the ratio of capital of the deposit entities in the Eurozone, thus additionally supporting the current rules of Basel III; (4) to set up a system of surveillance on the risks concentration in the banks of deposits, as for instance establishing a coefficient on the concentration of credits or financial investments in economic activities, public debt, etc.; and (5) to introduce special penalties in the penal code of every member country for certain behaviours of bankers (of deposits) related to their position as administrators of a public service.

Despite former suggestions on the possible economic alleviation of the Eurozone, we do believe that, regrettably, the daily problems of working of a banking union, as well as of the working of a fiscal common authority (a common Ministry of Finance) will be practically insurmountable due to the fact that the current 'rule of unanimity' will also be applicable to these two instututions as they deal with international issues of the Eurozone and the EU-28, thus tranfering to these two institutions the same inaction problems in decision making, as currently happens in the Eurozone and the EU-28.

Certainly, all European and Eurozone countries are small at a world scale, including the biggest one as Germany (with 82 million people, just slightly over 1 per cent of the population of the world). Besides, they are very uneven in population: only 5 have more than 45 million, while 12 of the 28 have less than 5 million (and 6 countries have even less than 2 million), and this while the EU rules for relevant decision making defines all member-states (regardless of their population size) as 'politically equal.'

As a result of their cultural and economic heterogeneity and diverse history, the members of the UE-28 have very different aspirations. Certainly, while some of them want to continue being 'global powers' (France and the UK)—which implies or could imply, high defence expenditures in proportion to their GDP—many others just want to economically benefit from their EU membership, with access to wider markets of goods and services, or to profit from the EU public and private financing (including offering unloyal financial transfers to own fiscal paradises), and this while they do not want to 'depend on the Union' in certain important issues such as costly international policies and/or armed interventions abroad.

Accordingly, as far as the project of Europe is one of a dynamic character—with five typified stages—many members seem today to prefer not to continue till the final stage: the political union. This is the reason why some of them—like the UK and others—will not go farther than the 3rd stage, the common market, while others, containing fiscal paradises, will first have to renounce the non-transparency of their banks.

Against this background, one should conclude that, the current EU-28 is destined to fall apart. However, against pessimistic opinions, our view is that mentioned 'natural trend towards its rupture' will finally induce a good result for all: while the most homogenous, transparent and pro-integration countries in the Eurozone will form a federation (finally reaching a political union), other Eurozone members may prefer going back (or will be sent back) to positions of common market with the pioneering countries. Rest of the current EU-28 could prefer not to continue progressing, thus remaining in their current status.

In brief, the unstable economic situation in Europe, the complicated global future that the Europeans will have to face in next 2-3 decades, and the constant wasting of time for decision making in the Eurozone (due to 'inconsistency of governance' with the EU-28), particularly in the past 6 years, will finally force several homogeneous countries of the Eurozone to form a voluntary federation. It seems to us reasonable and expectable that in some few years, a group of 8-12 Eurozone countries will start the federating process. Although many pessimists believe that this manoeuvre is not foreseen in the current treaties, the reality is that the current Union is just a treaty that can be 'substituted' by another. Indeed, nothing in politics— which produce negative results—may remain stationary forever.

Maintenance of fragmentation of internal EU markets, with partners that exert disloyal (although legal) competition on the others, in particular in relation to banking transparency, and above all, 'renouncing to the huge economies of integration' that could be obtained by means of the creation of a European Federation—up to 2 per cent of the joint GDP of federated countries—are issues that if not corrected, will induce the acceleration of the economic and political decline of the Eurozone countries.

Taking into account the current economic trends in the world and in Europe, only the formation of a European Federation could make possible that at the middle of the 21st century, Europe would be represented among the four more important powers of the world (China, US, EU Federation and India), thus giving Europe the opportunity to project at world level its historical experience in the fields of social democracy and human rights.

Global Problems and Appropriate Solutions: Democratisation of the UN

Till the last third of the 20th century, the existence of global public goods and global externalities had hardly been recognised by academicians and politicians. But it is today well accepted that without global peace and security, a healthy global environment, and optimal global economic regulations, the world may move towards economic and political stagnation or to something worse.

Historically, the provision of 'peace and security' was carried out either by regional traditional powers, or by current 'global' powers as it occurred in the military interventions of the North Atlantic Treaty Organization (NATO) in the last decade. Note that for reaching a certain peaceful and safer situation, as defined by them, and without the consent of targeted populations, these 'global' powers at times invaded and occupied strategic territories and subdued nations that 'did not behave' friendly to them.

However, the world has significantly changed in the last 65 years. Since the end of the Second World War, decolonisation and independence of many countries, and extension of democratic principles, have made that the small number of 50 countries that initially signed the Charter of the UN in 1945 have today changed into 193 UN member states, some of them (Brazil, Russia, India, China and South Africa; BRICS) involved today in rapid economic convergence. It is therefore totally illogical that, while the economic power of relevant countries of the world has strongly changed, the political organisation of the UN has practically remained the same as in 1945.

In this new context, former mentioned regional or 'global' powers will no longer be able of unilaterally defining and organising global peace and security mainly in their own interest. They will be forced to re-organise the UN on a democratic base. Consequently, future conflict interventions will have to be democratically voted in the UN by representatives of the whole global society, i.e., by the representatives of the 193 countries belonging to it.

Time has also arrived for the provision of a healthy and sustainable global environment, indispensable for the continuation of life on the planet. Indeed, a healthy global environment is a global public good that, as it happens with peace and security, cannot be provided or protected by a group of countries, but collectively by the global society; otherwise, free riding—as it occurs today—will avert reaching the target.

Reflecting on global environment, we have to recognise that the understanding of the problem is not complete and soaked in uncertainty. If climate change had been acknowleged as induced by mankind, there would be an historical debt of some countries, the industrialised ones, with respect to the others. Conversely, if the environmental change would not be recognised as provoked or accentuated by mankind, the historical debt would not be accepted by today industrialised countries. In this case, the latter would only agree to make efforts for offsetting or reducing current and future emissions, when proven.

Nevertheless, former considerations on uncertainty should not drive us to inaction. Similarly to the fact that most countries spend a figure around 2.6 per cent of their GDP in defence—although the probability of being attacked is almost inexistent in most cases—individual nations should also invest an important rate of their GDP to fight against climate change, just to avoid eventual highly catastrophic results. Consequently, it would be wise that the world starts spending a provisional budget for prevention and adaptation that, for example after 10 years phasing, could provisionally reach a level of 2 per cent of the global GDP.

Up to now, some investments or economic efforts have been realised by individual countries, in the framework of multilateral environmental agreements (MEAs). As known, these MEAs use to be on minima—for reaching wider consensus—and not on optima, while they are neither inclusive (many important countries do not sign) nor compulsive. Nevertheless, environment protection, as any other global public good, should also be collectively provided by a future UN agency to be developed by the new democratic UN: the World Environmental Organisation (WEO).

To conclude with the main global public goods, we will finally refer to the convenience of establishing a set of global economic regulations, for efficiently organising the main global markets (banking activities, capital movements, productions and prices of crude oil and strategic raw materials, etc.) and to dismantle the so-called fiscal paradises. In relation to fiscal paradises, it is our view that corresponding global regulation to be implemented by the Global Economic Regulations Agency (GERA)— also a new agency of the new democratic UN—should not only halt the development of new paradises, but also establish a not long phasing period for the total extinction of the existing ones. Sensitive global markets should also be supervised by GERA to avoid that private economic decisions made by MNC (including private banks), or individual or grouped countries [Organization of the Petroleum Exporting Countries (OPEC) or other cartels], result in abusive effects on production and prices of certain raw materials and staple food, or in the creation of global economic cycles.

Concerning global externalities and the application of public solutions to them, we have to say that there are circumstances that make global governmental interventions indispensable.

In relation to the distribution of charges or investments to be realised for reducing the emissions of as for example of CO_2, Western countries seem to support the principle of 'those who pollute must pay' (proportionally to exceeding emissions). But in our view, this principle should not be applicable to a problem affecting the whole global society, including rich and poor nations. Indeed, the absolute volume of non-sustainable (or exceeding) emissions—the sole target for political action as defended by Westerners— will have to give primacy to other variables as the 'per capita GDP' of every country, and to the 'non-sustainable per capita emissions.'

Note in this regard, that if the economic efforts were proportional with the 'non-sustainable' emissions of the different countries, then for solving the problem, corresponding agreement should just take into account proportionally both the per capita non-sustainable emissions and the number of inhabitants of every country, and not at all either the per capita GDP of every country—that would value the marginal economic effort of the individuals of the different countries—or the per capita non-sustainable emissions in a progressive way, as a preventive mechanism for continuing with the current polluting trend. As a consequence of this rationale, we defend that the economic efforts or contributions of the different countries for solving the problem of global pollution should be progressively related with their per capita GDP, and their per capita non-sustainable emissions.

Having said that, we will add that the absolute amount of the global or collective economic effort to be realised by the global society should be of a variable character: incremental if indicators of climate change continue deteriorating or decremental in the opposite case.

Continuing with necessary global public interventions for avoiding climate change, one may imagine what could occur in the planet if, in absence of a global authority, the future amount of international displaced people by climate change reached additional figures of around 200 million people as estimated by the International Organization for Migration (IOM) (around 2.8 per cent of the current global population). We do believe that in this case, the induced problem could be unbearable if such movements of people had to be realised in just two or three decades and if migrants should have to be resettled in already populated territories administrated by formal states, belonging to the current UN.

To continue with other necessary interventions of future democratic UN, we will refer more in detail to certain global economic regulations on global markets. In fact, the existence of 'non-competitive and inefficient international prices' in certain markets is calling for the reform of these markets. Indeed, non-intervened 'market prices' could be consistent with non-sustainable demands, while mentioned prices could be formed in non-competitive markets in which 'hoarding operations' are realised by certain MNC or by national superpowers.

The current markets of crude oil and other strategic resources (gold, platinum, red earth, diamonds, etc.) plus the international capital markets are cases for necessary global intervention. In this regard, we do believe that any abusive or defective administration of prices and flows of goods or capital should be averted in future by means of the intervention of a new agency of the new democratic UN (the already mentioned GERA), and not by a self-regulating organisation of producers-exporters (as OPEC), or non democratic international financial institutions (as current IMF).

The same could be said in relation to other markets in which agricultural products, cereal, sugar, etc., devoted directly or indirectly to the human consumption, are interchanged. The supplies of mentioned products have recently shrank at a world scale, due to the increase of the surface devoted to agricultural goods for the production of liquid fuels. In this regard, we do believe that the financial speculation on food realised or encouraged by subsidiary companies of big multinational banks should also be controlled by GERA.

This global entity, GERA, should also control the future exploitation of natural resources in the North and South Poles. We do believe that a fully democratic world cannot allow a new unequal and unfair distribution of the resources of the subsoil of the planet in remote and till now unknown and unexploited places. Particularly, in this historical time, these extraterritorial resources should be administered by a democratic UN in the representation and benefit of the global society, which should have absolute preference on individual nations in cases of *terra nullius*.

Finally, to end with the necessary interventions of the new democratic UN, we will refer to the role played by UN Institution for Development Cooperation (UNICO), the future agency suggested by us for increasing the financing of development cooperation. Note that the current UN Development Programme (UNDP) and World Bank would embody to UNICO.

In this regard, we have to underline that for decades, the Western countries, including the European ones, were neither capable of organising a convergent process through the markets, nor a decent financial plan to solve in a reasonable period of time (25 years or one generation) the main economic problems of food security, basic supply of energy, education and infrastructures and the building up of incipient social security systems in the poorer developing countries (LDC), mostly former exploited colonies.

We do believe that UNICO should in future take the reigns on the development cooperation that, as a minimum, should have a financial capacity equivalent to 1 per cent of the global GDP, a figure similar to that of 2 per cent of the GDP of donors, as in other times defended by Tinbergen, that would multiply almost by 4 the current squalid, fragmented, uncoordinated and inefficient Official Development Aid (ODA). In our view, UNICO could basically be financed with a complementary charge of around 20 per cent on the national inheritance tax all over the world (rich and poor countries), taking into consideration that economic legacies are always windfalls, and the taxes on them are non-recurrent and payable by heirs (not by defuncts).

From the moment in which the new democratic UN starts working, this organisation should intervene, at a global scale, directly administrating the global public goods, the global externalities, etc. The principle that every global public problem (be this a public good or a single externality) should exclusively be solved by one public administration should be accepted by all, because it enables to treat the corresponding problem in the most efficient way. A first derivative of this principle is that the provision of global peace and security—a clear global public good—should be carried out in the future only by the democratic UN, supported by a UN army/navy, and not individually by pretended hegemonic states.

A Democratic UN in Operations around 2040

The convenient reorganisation of the UN will occur in just 2 or 3 decades. We have deduced this relatively short period from econometric projections based on recent official economic figures published by the WB and IMF. Arrival to 50-50 per cent positions or shares in around two to three decades between developed and developing countries in sensitive economic magnitudes as global GDP, industrial production, and trade, plus arrival to 50-50 per cent equilibrium in defence expenditures in three decades are changes that will necessarily modify the multilateral political structures of the world.

Note that this short period of two to three decades is also consistent with the recent acceleration of history and political processes, initiated in the early 1980s and eased by the ICT revolution, and the current demographic disequilibrium which favours developing countries in a proportion 84-16 per cent.

Many Western commentators suggest—and they are right—that the UN cannot and will not democratise till the moment in which large populated countries like China have become democratic; otherwise, a non-democratic China, with almost 20 per cent of the population of the planet, would obtain a huge influence in issues of the global agenda. Notwithstanding that, we do believe that in 20-25 years, horizon 2035-2040, China will have a per capita GDP of around US$ 25,000-30,000 (constant US dollars of 2007) and an extended middle class, who with their political demands will force the appearance of a sustainable democracy in China.

For the creation of a new UN, we are almost sure that in a moment along the next two to three decades, the most important powers of the world will find it indispensable to meet in an intergovernmental conference in order to make a proposal to the global society for the complete reorganisation of the economic and political relations in the world, by means of reorganising the UN and introducing global democracy in it. Indeed, a long-overdue need felt by the global society, which will enable to finally reach a 'new and fairer economic and political order.'

Referring now to the main traits of the new democratic UN, we have to emphasise that the General Assembly will act as a sovereign World Parliament in relation to the issues of its limited but relevant agenda for global governance. Its decisions will be adopted by simple (50% plus 1) or reinforced (66%) majorities. Initially, the number of given votes to every country will be rather proportional to the size of their population, although corrected to give some representation to the smaller states. We do believe that time after, the global society will be directly involved in the selection of the representatives in the World Parliament.

The new Executive Council of the UN—substitute of the current Security Council—will be the delegated organ of the General Assembly for dealing with all issues. The UN will necessarily create an army-navy for its own service. These armed forces, besides being professional and neutral, will generate meaningful economies of scale, mounting around 1% of the total world GDP, and a great saving for the current police-states (as the US and main NATO members), which will finally be freed from their current direct implications and responsibilities.

Additional issues to be discussed when the Provisional Charter is elaborated will be the extension of the agenda of the new UN, and the enumeration and definition of the agencies to be developed for reaching the aims assigned to them. According to the Charter, a well-profiled UN agenda should establish the limits of action and intervention of the UN, actions and interventions that in no case would affect issues related to culture, language, religion, etc., except in cases of severe human rights violations or barbaric or irrational behaviour.

To shift the siege of the UN out of the US, for establishing it in a more central location around the Mediterranean Sea, would be by itself a good indication of the change of the UN. At the same time, the new siege could be less costly for most members and, therefore, more efficient for the collective.

Concerning the economic costs of the new democratic UN, we have to state that the new annual budget of the organisation—although not high in comparison to the value of the provided global needs—will nevertheless present a significant increase in its figures.

In brief, with the arrival of democracy to the UN, we do believe that the current UN budget could increase around 4-4.5 points in global GDP terms. Given the fact that, willy nilly, the upgrading of global human security, the sustaining of the environment of the planet, and also the bridging of the poverty gap will have to be finally accepted by mankind as indispensable, mentioned additional expenditures of 4-4.5 points in GDP will result in an advantageous transfer of funds from member states to the UN, that will significantly increase the efficiency (economies of scale) in the provision of global public goods and the correction of externalities and income gaps, with economic advantages for all.

The Disappearance of Hegemonic Powers and the New Global Political Scenario

In Chapter 6, we have described the four historical conditions for sustaining hegemonies, conditions which made it easy to abuse people or grabbing assets in subordinated nations. Today these four conditions either have already disappeared or are going to disappear in the next three decades.

One should add that keeping the position of hegemonic power, which is very costly in human and material terms, only can be justified facing own voters—democratic or not—if the exerted domination results in clear economic or political advantages.

Concerning the shift of power, we do believe that the concerns of the West in relation to the possibility that China becomes— following the US—

the next hegemonic power, are unjustified and present a biased view of what is politically coming.

Concluding, if the current economic trends in the world continue in the next two or three decades, moving in favour of developing countries to finally reach economic parity (in absolute GDP terms) with those developed, most important Western countries could progressively consider it convenient (and cheaper) to renounce their privileges and the extraordinary powers they hold in the current UN system (veto-rights), born at the end of the Second World War.

If the different main economies and the political power changed as expected, then at the brink of the second half of the 21st century (decade 2040-2050), the world will count with a different group of economic leading countries in charge (China, US, India, European Federation, Japan, Brazil and Russia). Note that this is a group of powerful countries rather different than those which led the world in 1945. The disappearance of Britain from the global political scenario will likely be the most surprising trait of the new family portrait; France and Germany, although not explicitly in the picture, will probably be the core of the selective European Federation.

Notwithstanding that, around 2040-2050, the most important economic countries quoted above will not be the political bosses of the world. In contrast with the world of 2013, the political power will be much more distributed, and mainly controlled by the parliament of the democratic UN, the General Assembly. A parliament that, counting with the support of an army-navy deployed in the five continents, will decide on the provision of peace and security. The General Assembly will also decide on global environment and climate change, on the necessary global economic regulations—including those referred to international monopolies and fiscal paradises—and on development financing.

If all that changed into reality, the world would have taken important steps towards a fairer global society: a society more equal and intertwined, much better administrated, and physically, economically and politically more sustainable, since the distribution of economic power will have moved in favour of the majority of the World.

Mistakes in the Past should not Induce Mistakes in the Future

We have to insist that the last steps of globalisation in relation to the liberalisation of capital movements, carried out in the early 1990s and done in an asymmetric way, very hasty in time, and combined with the immobility of labour, has induced adjustment problems in the West that in our view could have been foreseen in advance. Mentioned exaggeration on fast liberalisation of capital movements has finally, be it late, been recognised by the IMF in December 2012.

We do think that this operation of rushed liberalisation of capital movements was a failed bet of Western governments in favour of increasing Western GNI (vide Table 6.2), that necessary had to reduce the growth rates of the domestic GDP and employment in the West. Calculated or not, and similar to what occurred with the creation of the very imperfect Euro-system, the initiative taken in the early 1990s for fast liberalisation of movements of capital has resulted unfavourable for workers in the Eurozone and the West. However, letting aside pending problems in correcting distribution trends in most developing countries, the average results may have been very positive for workers in the middle- and low-income countries, as deducible from the catching up growth rates exhibited by all developing regions of the sub-continents of the world in the period 1990-2010 (Table 6.1).

Really, if the intention of the Western goverments had been to promote the catching up of the developing countries, they hardly could have done it better. But we believe that they did not do so on purpose: they just committed mistakes by negotiating fast access of western national entrepreneurs or MNC to low production costs markets in developing countries. But on doing so, they did not count with the important influx of cheap imports that years after would come from these countries, thus significantly degrading the industrial activity in the West. In this case, the invisible hand pushed economic contenders to shoot in their own feet by increasing competition for assumedly taking market share from others.

The results of the main economic policy developments, undertaken by Western governments in the last two decades—namely, liberalisation of capital movements and creation of a deceptive and unreliable Eurozone for a geographic area that moves near 20 per cent of the GDP of the planet—

have practically induced an economic deadlock. If the West moved back in the international division of labour—increasing protectionism in any of its different forms— the results would be bad. But if they do not, the recovering of moderate rhythms of growth may take many years.

Hence, the current attempt by the EU and the US to move towards a free trade zone (FTZ), mainly promoted as a defensive strategy for the protection of their joint internal markets, could in the long term result disappointing since, as the reader may know, the creation of internal trade in an EU-US FTZ could be partially compensated by similar or deeper movements among booming Asian countries. On the other hand, the citizens of this future EU-US FTZ could be prejudiced by the higher costs of production (diversion of trade) of some consumption goods in the EU-US zone. In conclusion, this EU-US initiative for building up a joint FTZ seems to have its roots more in politics than in pure economic rationale, the latter always favouring comparative advantage more than protected areas.

Certainly, all this sounds like an attempt of the West to reverse the current new trends in global trade and economic convergence (in per capita GDP terms) which are favouring the majority of the global society. Unfortunately, the attempted way of correction by Western leadership of past mistakes could again be a polical mistake from the perspective of the welfare of the global society.

More efficient would be if, in the current context of durable rough economic waters, Western governments fully restate their way of governance, renouncing to the past not well-conceived indefinite economic growth and overconsumption, and instead promoting a new far more moderate life-style taking into consideration the sustainability of the planet and the 'right to exist,' in fairer conditions, of the rest (84%) of the world population.

References

Abel, A. and B. Bernanke (2001). *Macroeconomics*. Pearson Education. p. 28.

Ahluwalia, M. (2002). "Economic Reforms in India since 1991: Has Gradualism Worked?", *Journal of Economic Perspectives* 16: 67-88.

Alvarez, R. and J.M. Andreu (1982). *Una Historia de la Banca Privada en España*. Situación, Banco de Bilbao.

Andreu, J.M. (1988). *Las Teorías del Ciclo Económico*. Madrid: UNED.

———. (1997). *Una Introducción a la Macroeconomía*. Madrid: Dyckinson.

———. (2010). *Measurement of Potential GDPs and Design of a Contracyclical Policy*. Spain: BICE, Ministry of Industry, Turism and Trade.

———. (2011). *Understanding the Economic Future of the West*. Spain: BICE, Ministry of Industry, Trade and Turism. March 15.

Andreu, J.M. and R.D. Rahman (2009a). *China, India y el Futuro en un Contexto Democrático Global*. Spain: Ramón Areces.

———. (2009b). *Global Democracy for Sustaining Global Capitalism: The Way to Solve Global Problems*. New Delhi: Academic Foundation.

———. (2010). *Towards the Democratization of the United Nations to Solve Current Global Problems*. Intervention in the UN. October 19.

Bernanke, B. and J. Rottemberg (eds.) (1995). "Capital Utilisation and Returns to Scale", *NBER Macroeconomics Annual*.

Boyce, J.K. (2002). *The Political Economy of the Environment*. UK: EE Publishing. p.135.

Chomsky, N. (2011). "American Decline: Causes and Consequences", *www.chomsky.info/articles*

Comunidades Europeas (2004). *Tratado por el que se establece una Constitución para Europa*. Belgium.

Darhendorf, R. (2002). *Die Krisen der Demokratie: Einsprach*. Summary published in Volkskrant.

De Grauwe, P. (1994). *The Econmomics of Monetary Integration*. 2nd ed. Oxford University Press.

Delors, J. (1992). Address to SIZ by the President of the Commission. Forward Studies Unit. May.

Eaglesman, J. (2006). "Blair Admits the West is Losing the War on Terror", *Financial Times*, August 2. p.4.

Elson, D. (1998). "The Trade Off between Equity and Efficiency", Comment to the Report *Gender and Economic Development*. Netherlands Economic Institute.

Ekelund, R. *et al.* (1988). *Economics*. Scott & Foresman Co.

Feyerabend, P. (1975). *Against the Method*. London: NLB.

Financial Times (n.d.). Financial. Several issues.

Friedman, M. (1953). *A Program for Monetary Stability and Banking Reform.* New York City: Fordham University Press.

Friedman, M. and A. Schwartz (1963). *A Monetary History of the US 1867-1960.* Princeton University Press.

Fukuyama, F. (1992). *"The End of History and the Last Man"", in The Great Disruption* (1998).

Goldman, Sachs (2003). *Dreaming with BRICS: The Path to 2050.*

Henry, S.J. (2012). "The Price of the Off-shore Revisited". Google.

Hirschleifer, J. (1993). "The Dark Side of the Strength". *www.eumed.net*

IMF (2007-2012). *World Economic Outlook.* Several issues.

Jaffee, D. (1989). *Money, Banking and the Credit.* Worth Publishers.

Kessler, F. (2005). *Le Monde.* Octobre 11.

Krugman, P. (2009). "To Prize the Bad Actors". August 09. *elpais.com (negocios).*

———. (2011). "The hole in Euro´s Bucket", *New York Times*, Oct. 23.

Krugman, P. and Obstfeld (2002). *International Economics: Theory and Policy*. 5th edition. Harlow: Addison-Wesley Longman.

Kuznets, S. (1955). "Economic Growth and Income Distribution", *American Economic Review* 45(1): 1-28.

Le Monde (2006). "La CNUCED denonce une croissance "sans employ" dans le pays le plus pauvres", *Le Monde*, Juillet 22.

———. (n.d.). *Le Monde*, several issues. Google

Lewis, A. (1955). *The Theory of Economic Growth.* Homewood, Illinois: Irwin.

Lipsey, R. and K. Lankaster (1956). "The Theory of the Second Best", *Review of Economic Studies* 24: 1.

Maddison, A. (1998). *Chinese Economic Performance in the Long Run.* Paris: OECD.

———. (2001). *The World Economy: A Millenium Perspective.* Paris: OECD.

Mankiw, N.G., D. Romer and D. Weil (1992). "A Contribution to Empirics in Economic Growth", *Quarterly Journal of Economics* 107: 407-37, May.

Markowitz, H.M. (1952). "Portfolio Selection", *Journal of Finance* 7(1): 77-91.

Muñoz, A. (2010, 2012). *Projections on the World Economy*. Non-published manuscript. Spain: UNED.

Musgrave, R. and P. Musgrave (1984). *Public Finance in Theory and Practice*. Mac Graw-Hill.

Nash, J.F. (1950). "The Bargainig Problem", *Econometrica* 18: 129-40.

Nehru, J. (1930). *Glimpses of World History*. Naini Jail, Allahabad, India.

Nordhouse, W. (1995). *"Locational Competition and Environment: Should Countries Harmonise their Environmental Policies?"*, from J.M. Andreu and R.D. Rahman (2009), *Global Democracy for Sustaining Global Capitalism: The Way to Solve Global Problems*. New Delhi: Academic Foundation.

Okun, A. (1975). *Equality and Efficiency: The Big Trade Off*. Brokings Institution.

Parker, R. (2006). *John Kenneth Galbraith*. Canada: Harper.

Perez Bustamante, R. (1997). *Historia de la Union Europea*.

Prodi, R. (2001). "Shaping Europe". Speech to the EU Parliament. February.

Rahman, R.D. and J.M. Andreu (2002). *A Federation with Enlargement for European Prosperity*. New Delhi, India: Rashtriya Printers.

———. (2004). *Responsible Global Governance: A Programme for World Stability and Institutional Reform*. New Delhi: Academic Foundation. p.81.

———. (2005). *Overcoming the EU Crisis*. Tunis: Ceres.

———. (2006). *China and India: Towards Global Economic Supremacy?* New Delhi: Academic Foundation.

Reddy, Y.V. (2000). *RBI Bulletin*. December. Mumbai: *Reserve Bank of India*.

Ricardo, D. (1817). *Principles of Political Economy and Taxation*. London: John Murray.

Riedel, J., J. Jin and J. Gao (2007). *How China Grows*. Princeton: Princeton University Press.

Romer, P. (1986). "Increasing Returns and Long Run Growth", *Journal of Political Economy* 94: 1002-37, October.

———. (1994). "The Origins of Endogenous Growth", *Journal of Economic Perspectives* 8: 3-22, Winter.

OECD (2004). "Summing Up", *OECD Economic Surveys*. Euro-area.

Saboul, A. (1972). *Precis Histoire de la Revolucion Francaise*. Paris. Editions Socials.

Samuelson, P. and W. Nordhaus (1999). *Economics*. Mac Graw-Hill.

Schumpeter, J. (1942). *Capitalism, Socialism and Democracy*. New York: Harper.

Sen, A. (2006). "Mondialisation et Justice Social", *Le Monde*. Samedi, Mai 20.

Smith, A. (1776). *The Wealth of Nations*.

Solow, R. (1957). "Technical Change and the Agregated Production Function", *Review of Economics and Statistics* 39(3): 312-20.

Srinivasan, T. and S. Tendulkar (2003). *Reintegrating India in the World Economy.* Washington, D.C.: Institute for International Economics.

Stern, N. (2006). "Report on the Economics of Climate Change." *The Economist,* November 4.

Stiglitz, J. (1998). *Economics of the Public Sector.* 2nd edition. New York: Norton.

————. (2000). *Economics of the Public Sector. 3rd edition. New York:* Norton.

————. (2001). *Globalisation and its Discontents.* New York: Norton.

————. (2005). "Reforms Take the Security of Social Security", *Financial Times.* March 21.

————. (2006). *Un autre monde. Contre le fanatism de marché.* Fayard.

————. (2012). *The Price of Inequality: How Today Divided Society Endangers Our Future.* New York: Norton.

Subramanyan, L. and D. Van Hoose (2012). "Bank Balancesheet Dynamics under a Regulatory LCRC", *Working Paper 1209.* Federal Reserve Bank of Cleveland.

The Economist (2005-2012). *The Economist,* several issues.

Todaro, M. (2003). *Economic Development.* 8th Edition. Pearson Education.

UNDP (2002). *Human Development Report.* New York.

Viner, J. (1952). *International Trade and Economic Development.* Oxford Clarendon Press

Willentz, S. (2005). *The Rise of the American Democracy.* New York: Norton.

Wilson, D. and R. Purushothaman (2003). "Dreaming with BRICs: The Path to 2050", *Global Economics Paper* No.99. *Goldman-Sachs Global Economic Website.* October.

World Bank (1992, 2010, 2012, 2013). *World Development Indicators.*

Index